Building Websites with Joomla! 1.5

The best-selling Joomla! tutorial guide updated for the final release

Hagen Graf

PUBLISHING

BIRMINGHAM - MUMBAI

Building Websites with Joomla! 1.5

First published: March 2008

Production Reference: 1240308

Published by Packt Publishing Ltd.
32 Lincoln Road
Olton
Birmingham, B27 6PA, UK.

ISBN 978-1-847195-30-2

www.packtpub.com

Cover Image by Vinayak Chittar (vinayak.chittar@gmail.com)

Credits

Author

Hagen Graf

Translator

Wolfgang Spegg

Senior Acquisition Editor

Louay Fatoohi

Technical Editor

Akshara Aware

Editorial Team Leader

Mithil Kulkarni

Project Manager

Abhijeet Deobhakta

Project Coordinator

Brinell Lewis

Indexer

Monica Ajmera

Proofreader

Chris Smith

Production Coordinators

Aparna Bhagat

Shantanu Zagade

Cover Work

Shantanu Zagade

About the Author

Hagen Graf was born in July 1964. Born and raised in Lower Saxony, Germany, his first contact with a computer was in the late seventies with a Radioshack TRS 80. As a salesperson, he organized his customers' data by programming suitable applications. This gave him a big advantage over other salesmen. With the intention of honing his skills, he joined evening courses in programming and became a programmer. Nowadays, he works in his wife's consulting company as a trainer, consultant, and programmer (`http://www.cocoate.com`). Hagen Graf has published other books in German, about the Apache web server, about security problems in Windows XP, about Mambo, and about Drupal. Since 2001, he has been engaged in a nonprofit e-learning community called "machmit. org e.V.", as well as in several national and international projects. All the projects are related to content management, community building, and harnessing the power of social software like wikis and weblogs. He chose Joomla! CMS because of its simplicity and easy-to-use administration. You can access and comment on his blog (`http://www.bloghouse.org/en/hagen`).

Table of Contents

Preface

Joomla! is life!

It is an open-source project that is in constant motion. It is unpredictable, sometimes indescribable, partially controversial, now and then slightly sleepy, and provincial. Despite this, or perhaps exactly because of this, it has been extremely successful for two years now and is popular with millions of users worldwide.

There is a stable, widely used, and popular version 1.0x. For the past two years, developers have hammered, tinkered, forged, modified, disagreed, deleted, expanded, and hammered again.

Two incredibly exciting years have passed since the foundation of Joomla! 2005.

The Joomla! team has organized and established itself in these years, it has enhanced Joomla! 1.0 up to version 1.0.13 and has now taken the biggest development step so far with version 1.5.

The users of the system have been equally ambitious. Many of them have converted their websites from Mambo to Joomla! And many users have come brand new to Joomla!, and there are still some people in this world that don't know the system.

Joomla! is the most widely used open-source Web Content Management System in the world.

One year after the foundation of the project, in the fall of 2006, the development team reported approximately 5,000,000 Joomla! installations on public web servers that were being used more or less continuously. There were 45,000 registered developers with 1,100 projects that expanded Joomla! with additional functionalities. There were 450,000 entries from 50,000 users in the forum at *joomla.org*.

Here are the numbers one year later, in November 2007:

- More than 20,000,000 installations
- 28 members in the development team and 16 members in the core team
- Over 2,000 projects that are preparing to expand Joomla!
- More than 1,000,000 (one million) entries and 100,000 users in Joomla!'s forum

That is an increase of more than 100 % in one year!

The scope of the websites rages from very simple homepages to complex business applications. In this book I will explain why Joomla! is so successful and how you can use it as well.

The word Joomla! is derived from "Jumla" from Swahili and means "all together".

Joomla! is the software result of a serious disagreement between the Mambo Foundation, which was founded in August 2005, and its development team. Joomla! is the continued development of the successful Mambo system and, like Mambo, is a piece of software that enables simple administration of websites from a web browser.

Joomla!, according to its own description, is a "Cutting Edge Content Management System and one of the most powerful Open Source Content Management systems in the world. It is used world-wide for anything from simple homepages to complicated corporate websites. It is easy to install, easy to manage, and very reliable."

What This Book Covers

First of all this book, naturally, is about Joomla! and how to use Joomla!. Joomla! is a tool with a myriad of options and depending on your imagination and needs you can use them in a variety of ways. In order for you to get comfortable with this tool, I have divided the book into the following chapters.

Chapter 1 covers the terms and conventions that will make it easier to work with Joomla!.

Chapter 2 describes how to install Joomla! in various environments.

Chapter 3 provides an overview by means of a tour of the structure of the example data that is available once Joomla! is installed.

Chapter 4 covers customizing Joomla! language and templates.

Chapter 5 covers the operation of the administration area, its configuration, and administration of content. It also discusses the elements in the Menu bar, Tool bar, and the Help menu.

Chapter 6 discusses how to customize the Site menu.

Chapter 7 discusses how to customize the Menus menu.

Chapter 8 discusses how to customize the Content menu.

Chapter 9 discusses how to customize the Components menu.

Chapter 10 discusses the Extensions menu.

Chapter 11 talks about the Tools menu containing administrator tools: a private messaging system, a mass mailing function, and the global checking in of content elements.

Chapter 12 presents examples of extension possibilities for Joomla!.

Chapter 13 deals with the design of your website and how to create your own templates.

Chapter 14 is written by Angie Radtke. Angie is the undisputed expert when it comes to Joomla! barrier-freedom and she is the mastermind behind the creation of the barrier-free Beez template with Robert Deutz.

Chapter 15 teaches you how to write your own extensions.

Chapter 16 helps create a practical application with Joomla! from concept to realization of the website.

Chapter 17 introduces two templates that you can use for your own website.

In the appendix you will find important details for updates, security, and other important subjects.

Conventions

In this book, you will find a number of styles of text that distinguish between different kinds of information. Here are some examples of these styles, and an explanation of their meaning.

There are three styles for code. Code words in text are shown as follows: "If you take a look in your database system, there are a whole bunch of components in the `[PathtoJoomla]/components` subdirectory and one of them is the `com_contact` component."

A block of code will be set as follows:

```
main .leading h2,#main2 .leading h2 {
background:#EFDEEA;
border-bottom:solid 0 #333;
color:#93246F;
font-family:trebuchet MS, sans-serif;
font-size:1.4em;
font-weight:normal;
```

Any command-line input and output is written as follows:

```
/etc/init.d/mysql start
```

New terms and **important words** are introduced in a bold-type font. Words that you see on the screen, in menus or dialog boxes for example, appear in our text like this: "clicking the **Next** button moves you to the next screen".

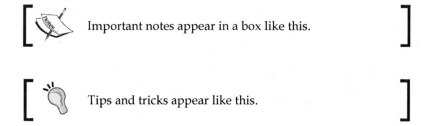

Important notes appear in a box like this.

Tips and tricks appear like this.

Reader Feedback

Feedback from our readers is always welcome. Let us know what you think about this book, what you liked or may have disliked. Reader feedback is important for us to develop titles that you really get the most out of.

To send us general feedback, simply drop an email to feedback@packtpub.com, making sure to mention the book title in the subject of your message.

If there is a book that you need and would like to see us publish, please send us a note in the **SUGGEST A TITLE** form on www.packtpub.com or email suggest@packtpub.com.

If there is a topic that you have expertise in and you are interested in either writing or contributing to a book, see our author guide on www.packtpub.com/authors.

Customer Support

Now that you are the proud owner of a Packt book, we have a number of things to help you to get the most from your purchase.

Downloading the Example Code for the Book

Visit `http://www.packtpub.com/files/code/5302_Code.zip`, to directly downlad the example code.

The downloadable files contain instructions on how to use them.

Errata

Although we have taken every care to ensure the accuracy of our contents, mistakes do happen. If you find a mistake in one of our books—maybe a mistake in text or code—we would be grateful if you would report this to us. By doing this you can save other readers from frustration, and help to improve subsequent versions of this book. If you find any errata, report them by visiting `http://www.packtpub.com/support`, selecting your book, clicking on the **Submit Errata** link, and entering the details of your errata. Once your errata are verified, your submission will be accepted and the errata added to the list of existing errata. The existing errata can be viewed by selecting your title from `http://www.packtpub.com/support`.

Questions

You can contact us at `questions@packtpub.com` if you are having a problem with some aspect of the book, and we will do our best to address it.

1
Terms, Concepts, and Deliberations

Before we dive into Joomla!, allow me to explain a few terms and concepts, and bring you up to date on some background material.

Content Management System (CMS)

Content Management System (CMS) contains the terms content and management, which imprecisely refer only to a system that manages content. Such a system could be a board and a piece of chalk (menu or school chalkboard), or some free online encyclopedia such as Wikipedia or an online auction house such as eBay. In all these examples contents are administered, in the last instance by numerous participants.

These participants play a major role in content management systems, on one hand as administrators and on the other as users and editors.

Apart from CMSs, there are terms such as **Enterprise Resource Planning** Systems (**ERP** systems—administration of corporate data), **Customer Relationship Management** Systems (**CRM** systems—maintenance of customer contacts), **Document Management Systems** (**DMS** systems—administration of documents), **Human Resource Management** Systems (**HRM** systems—administration of personnel), and many others.

It is difficult to define the term CMS because of its encompassing nature and variety of functions. Wikepedia's definition is my favorite:

A content management system, or CMS, is a computer software system used to enable and organize the joint process of creating and editing text and multimedia documents (content).

The abbreviation **ECMS** has established itself as the term for **Enterprise Content Management Systems**. The other abbreviations listed above are subsets of ECMS.

Joomla! belongs to the category of **Web Content Management Systems (WCMS)**, since its functionality is administered from a browser on the Web.

In general, the term content management is used in connection with web pages that can be maintained by a browser. This doesn't necessarily make the definition any easier.

A Quick Glance into History

While Sun Microsystems maintained in the nineties that "the network is the computer", Microsoft was not going to rest until a Windows computer sat on every desk. This prediction became a reality. Microsoft was able to rest and is actually looking for new markets and new products.

The computer that Microsoft was concerned with was a mixture of data files and binary executable files. Files with executable binary contents are called **programs**, and were bought and installed by customers to manipulate data. Microsoft Office was the winner in most of the offices around the world.

The computer that Sun was working with was a cheap, dumb terminal with a screen, a keyboard, a mouse, and access to the Internet. The programs and data were not stored on this computer, but somewhere on the net.

The *mine* philosophy governed Microsoft's practices whereas the *our* philosophy was adopted by Sun.

The motivation for these philosophies in both the companies was commercial interest. Microsoft primarily sold software for PCs to the consumer market; Sun, on the other hand, sold server hardware and programs to the enterprise market.

The Internet, invented in the sixties, underwent an explosive growth in the mid-nineties. Among other things, **Hyper Text Markup Language (HTML)**, the language used to write web pages, and the development of web servers and web clients (browsers) helped its expansion.

The Internet itself is merely a set of rules that various devices could understand and with which they could communicate with each other in such a clever way that it covered the entire planet in almost no time.

An individual without an email address could no longer be reached and a company without a website was not only old-fashioned, but didn't exist in the eyes of many customers. The whole world swarmed to the Internet within a short time to become a part of it. Movies like *The Matrix* became a huge hit and *1984*, a book by George Orwell, was successfully superseded.

Those who were used to buying programs bought HTML editors and created Internet pages with them. The others preferred to write their own HTML code with whatever text editor they had on hand. And the web agency, where one could order a web page, was born.

Both groups faced the problem that HTML pages were static. To change the content of the page, it had to be modified on a local PC and then copied to the server. This was not only awkward and expensive, but also made web presences like eBay or Amazon impossible.

Both the groups came up with fixes to more or less solve this problem.

The *mine* faction developed fast binary programs, with which one could produce HTML pages and load them via automated procedures onto the server. Interactive elements, such as visitor counters, among others, were built into such pages.

The *our* faction discovered Java applets and with them the capability of writing a program that resided centrally on a server and could be maintained from a browser. Entire business ideas, like online booking and flight reservation concepts, were based on this solution.

Both the groups tried to increase their market share in different ways. The result was quite a stable market for both, in which passionate battles over the correct operating system (Windows, Linux, or Mac OS X) constantly drove the version numbers higher and higher. Customers got used to the fact that nothing was easy.

There is always a third option in these situations. In our case, it was, among other things, the emergence of open-source scripting languages like PHP (http://www.php.net). Rasmus Lerdorf wanted to offer interactive elements on his homepage and with that a new programming language was born. From the outset, PHP was optimized in perfect cooperation with the MySQL database, which was also under the GNU/GPL license.

Fortunately, there was the Linux operating system and the Apache web server that offered the necessary infrastructure on the server. The display medium at the client side was the browser. **LAMP** (Linux, Apache, MySQL, and PHP) soon became synonymous with database-supported, interactive presence on the Internet.

The most diverse systems like forums, communities, online shops, voting pages, and similar things that made it possible to organize contents with the help of a browser were developed in an enthusiastic creative rush.

Soon after the 'difficult' things such as Linux and Apache had been created, the 'soft' products were developed.

The nineties were nearing their end; the Internet share bubble burst and all of a sudden the trend was to build unmitigated classical business models with unmitigated classical methods.

Whenever the economy isn't doing well, costs are scrutinized and the options for lowering costs are contemplated. There are now, as there were earlier, numerous options! PHP applications had distribution in the millions. We only need to look at the phpBB (`http://www.phpbb.com/`) and phpMyAdmin (`http://www.phpmyadmin.net/`) projects as examples. One developed to become the quasi-standard for forum software and the other, the standard for manipulating MySQL databases via web interfaces.

The source code of the PHP language and the applications became better and better quickly due to the enormous number of users and developers. The more open a project was, the more successful it became. Individual gurus were able to save enterprises immense amounts of money in next to no time.

Static HTML pages were considered old and expensive, and were overhauled. They had to be dynamic! Developers have been working in this environment for a decade now. Linux, Apache, MySQL, and PHP were readily accepted in the industry. The search for professionally usable PHP applications had begun.

With this search one looks for:

- A simple installation process
- Easy serviceability of the source code
- Security of the source code
- User-friendliness
- Easy expandability
- Simple development
- Simple job training for new developers
- Standardized interfaces to other programs
- Low costs
- Independence from the supplier

The special advantage of PHP applications is the independence from hardware and operating system. LAMP also exists as **WAMP** (**W**indows, **A**pache, MySQL, and PHP) for Windows, **MAMP** (Mac, Apache, MySQL, and PHP) for Apple, and for numerous other platforms. And now Joomla! finally enters the picture.

Joomla!—How was it Developed?

An Australian company, Miro (http://www.miro.com.au), developed a CMS called Mambo in the year 2001. It made this system available as open-source software to test it and to ensure wider distribution. In the year 2002, the company split its Mambo product into a commercial and an open-source version. The commercial variant was called Mambo CMS, the open-source version **Mambo Open Source** or **MOS** for short. By the end of 2004 all parties involved had agreed that MOS could officially be called **Mambo** and that a successful future for the fastest developing CMS of its time would be jointly secured.

The advantages of the commercial version were primarily the increased security for companies and the fact that they had Miro, which also supported further development, as guidance.

The open-source version offered the advantage that it was free and that an enormous community of users and developers alike provided continuous enhancements. In addition, it was possible for enterprises to take Mambo as a base and to build their own solutions on top of it.

In order to secure the existence and the continued development of Mambo, there were deliberations on all sides in the course of the year 2005 to establish a foundation for the open-source version of Mambo. In the fall of 2005 the establishment of the Mambo Foundation was announced on the Mambo project page. After positive reactions during the first few hours it quickly became obvious that Miro in Australia had established the foundation and that the developer team had not been included into the plans for the incorporation. Heated discussions erupted in the forums of the community and the developer team wrapped itself in silence for a few days.

A short time thereafter a position was finally taken by the developing team and published on opensourcematters.org, announcing that it would be advised by the neutral Software Freedom Law Center (http://softwarefreedom.org/) and that it was planning the continued development of Mambo under its own responsibility. The prospect of an improved Mambo based on new source code immediately made its way into the forums.

Quickly, a war of the roses developed between the Miro-dominated Mambo Foundation that was all of a sudden without a development team, and the development team itself, which, of course, needed a new name for the split entity, and an inflamed international community of hundreds of thousands of users. The parties sometimes called each other names in blogs, forums, and the respective project pages.

Meanwhile, development of both projects continued. The fork was called Joomla!

The development team put great value on democratic rules. The new project needed a logo and therefore a contest was announced to the 'new' community. By that time, about 8,000 users had registered with the new forum.

The Mambo Foundation soon thereafter introduced its new development team.

Version 1.0 of Joomla! was published on the 17th of September 2005.

Quickly many of the third-party developers, groups that had been developing Mambo components, switched the projects Simpleboard (today FireBoard), DOCman, and many others to Joomla! and therewith endorsed the trust in the new project. The prefix `mos` that had been used in so many variables and terms was quickly transformed to `jos`.

[A detailed summary of these events can be accessed on the Internet at: `http://www.devshed.com/c/a/BrainDump/Joomla-is-the-New-Mambo/`]

Two years after its foundation, Joomla! was one of the most popular open-source projects in the world. However, a lot of time was wasted in those two years on organizational trench warfare and intercultural misunderstandings due to the restructuring.

The Web 2.0 celebrated its victories. User-created content became more and more important. Second life and its virtual reality became world famous. The programming language Ruby and in particular Ruby on Rails was being used more and more to develop websites. Programming interfaces played an ever larger role.

Joomla 1.0x looked and looks a little old and gray in this company. It had not exhausted its developmental options, but users looked longingly at systems like Plone, Typo3, Drupal, and lot of others that did not have the problems that come with sheer size and reorganization and that were able to constantly incorporate new technologies into their projects.

For the past two years Joomla! version 1.0x has not really been expanded any further, but security updates with minor code changes have been released. A two-year waiting time for a new version is not good advertising for the project. Joomla! has often been declared dead and was frequently ridiculed during this time and derisive articles on the lines of *How to ruin an amazing software project!* appeared in the trade.

However, the project team has come through with Joomla! version 1.5. Now that everything has been discussed fully in forums, mailing lists, emails, and personal meetings, Joomla!'s future is now rosier than ever in my eyes.

On one hand, upgrading from version 1.0x to1.5x is going to take some effort, since there is no full downward compatibility due to the changed source code. However, on the other hand, this definitely launches Joomla! into the league of business-capable content management systems. The clever strategy of creating building blocks with Joomla! (Joomla! framework), with which developers can be part of the new developments, is going to pay dividends.

It is finally possible to choose various methods of authentication to create barrier-free websites in various languages, and to take part in the Web 2.0 mashups wave that is clearly spilling into enterprises. The road to developing components in environments such as Eclipse is now open.

With its existing community, developer, and installation density, Joomla! will simply blanket many sectors of this market. Many hosting providers are already offering Joomla! pre-installed to their clients so that there will be no serious problems when upgrading from simpler websites.

Structure of a Web Content Management System (WCMS)

Using Joomla! as an example, I will briefly explain the structure of a WCMS.

Front End and Back End

A WCMS consists of a front end and a back end. The front end is the website that the visitors and the logged-on users see.

The back end, on the other hand, contains the administration layer of the website for the administrators. Configuration, maintenance, cleaning, the generation of statistics, and new content creation are all done in the back end by authorized people. The back end is at a different URL than the website.

Access Rights

Whenever we talk of management, we talk of the clever administration of existing resources. In a WCMS, user names and group names are assigned to the people involved and each one of them is assigned different access rights. This ranges from a simple registered user through an 'author' and 'editor' up to the 'super-administrator', who has full control over the domain. Based on the rights, the website then displays different content; an option is available to edit content directly in the front end, or the user is given the right to work in the back end.

Content

Content can come in all kinds of forms; in the simplest case, it is text. However, content can also be a picture, a link, a piece of music, a snippet from an application like Google Maps or a combination of all of these. To keep an overview of the content, one embeds it in structures, for example, texts of different categories. The categories, of course, are also content that needs to be administered. Newsfeeds have become very popular, since Internet Explorer 7 now has the capability to read RSS feeds and more than 80% of computer users still use this browser. Newsfeeds give you the option of integrating information from other sources. Integration, categorization, rating, mashing, and updating of newsfeed content is becoming more and more important.

Extensions

Components, modules, templates, and plug-ins are all referred to as Extensions. They offer additional functions that are not contained in Joomla!'s core.

Components

Joomla! has to be expandable and should be able to grow with the requirements. Extensions that offer additional functionalities and that usually have their own area in Joomla!'s administration are called **components**. For example, typical components of recent years are an online shop, a picture gallery, and a newsletter or forum system. Today things like search engine optimization, user rights, multi-page forms, and variable content structures are becoming more and more important.

Components contain the business logic of their site and display content in the 'main body' of the website.

Templates

A template is a kind of visual editing pattern that is placed on the top of content. A template defines the colors, character fonts, font sizes, background images, spacing, and partitioning of the page, in other words, everything that has to do with the appearance of a page. A template is made up of at least one HTML file for the structure of the page and one CSS file for the design. It can also have a far more extensive structure in order to prepare Joomla! content for barrier freedom or for a completely different purpose.

Plug-Ins

A plug-in is a piece of programming code that is appended at certain places in the Joomla! framework to change its functionality. Such a plug-in can, for instance, be used inside content text to load the content of a module into the text. Plug-ins are also used in a comprehensive website search in order to integrate additional components. Sometimes plug-ins are used like a macro language in Joomla! Special modules pertaining to components are used to integrate content in the desired form into templates. The *Recent News* module, for example, delivers the headlines of the last five articles that were placed by the *Content component* to the template. Another module, for example, determines the number of users that are on-line at the moment and displays the result.

Workflow

By workflow one understands a sequence of operations. The bureaucratic set of three (mark, punch, and file) is an example of a workflow. A recipe for baking a cake is also a workflow. Since several people usually work with CMS content, well-organized workflows are a tremendous help.

In the past, one also referred to work inventories that a certain user has. For example, the editor sees a list of non-published pieces of news, which he or she has to examine for correctness. After examining them, the editor marks the pieces of news as correct and they appear in the work inventory of the publisher. The publisher then decides whether to publish each piece on the front page.

Configuration Settings

Settings that apply to the entire website are specified using the configuration settings. This includes the title text in the browser window, keywords for search engines, switches that permit or forbid logging on to the site or that switch the entire page offline or online, and many other functions.

API

Today an **Application Programming Interface (API)** has to be provided to be with the times. It has to be possible (and it is) to access Joomla! from other programs and to invoke it remotely to some extent. This opens up entirely new applications that were previously not feasible with Joomla! An API is the most important link between third-party extension developers and the Joomla! core.

Is Joomla! a Piece of Real Estate?

Joomla! is a kind of construction kit that, once installed on the server, enables you to create and maintain your website. Joomla! is like a house that you build on a property of your choice and that you can furnish gradually. Thus, to a certain extent, it is real estate.

Stop! I was talking about mobility all the time and now I'm asking you to build real estate? Have no fear, the real estate you build is physically at one place (your server), but is accessible from everywhere. To make a piece of real estate habitable, you need necessary services such as heating, electricity, and water supply. That is the reason your Joomla! is deposited at a server as as safe as possible, where hopefully, the electricity will never be cut. We are talking 24/7.

Just like with your house, you also have a certain room layout in Joomla!. You have a room to show off (content), for cooking and conversing (forum), for working (administration area), and a completely private one, one that you show only to good friends (member area). Perhaps you also have a large room that integrates all these areas.

It doesn't matter which room layout you decide on, you have to furnish your house, lay a beautiful floor, paper the walls, hang a few pictures on the walls (template), and of course, clean it regularly. This is because the numerous guests leave traces that are not always desirable.

A visitor needs an address (domain) to find your house. As many people as possible should be aware of this address. Since there is no residents' registration office on the Internet, you have to be the one that takes care of the topic, "How can I be found?"

Perhaps you also have a garden that surrounds your house and that has different entry gates. There is an official entrance portal, a back door, and perhaps another small, weathered garden gate for good friends.

And perhaps you don't like such types of houses and would rather use trailers, tents, mobile homes, hotels, or maybe you prefer community living and are glad to pay rent and don't want to think about all the details.

If you apply the last few sentences to your website, then you already see how important it is to know what you want, who you are, and how you want to look to your community. One cannot *not* communicate! One can, however, be quickly misunderstood. So plan your virtual house on the Internet properly. Put thought into the texts, into possible interactive elements like a calendar or a forum, and of course, an area that only registered users are allowed to see. Think about prompts that guide and don't patronize users and take a look at how others do it.

Talk with the people you want to address through your website. They will be honored to have been asked 'beforehand' and they will perhaps give you tips that were not obvious from your point of view. This is an economical and very effective option to gather ideas and to avoid the worst of mistakes. Invest your heart and soul into things that are absolutely crucial for the success of your website.

Joomla! Versions

As with all software, there are different development steps with Joomla!. The Joomla! team published a roadmap on the 1st of September 2005 that started with Joomla! version 1.0.

The first Joomla! version consequently received the number 1.0, so that there was no confusion with the existing Mambo versions. Version 1.0 is a revised version of the last Mambo version 4.5.2.3. The revisions relate to the new name, known errors, and security patches. Mambo, in the meantime, has released version 4.6.2

In the last two years, thirteen Joomla! 1.0.x versions, which have improved and corrected a lot of small details in the code, have been released. If you have followed the development, you have probably noticed that Joomla! has become more and more reliable from version to version.

Numbering System of Joomla! Versions

Joomla! versions abide by the three-step system.

- **Step 1 = major release number**: This is incremented whenever profound changes are made at the source-code level. The version with the higher number sometimes is not compatible with earlier versions.

- **Step 2 = minor release number**: This is incremented whenever significant changes to functionality are made. The higher version number is usually compatible (with minor customizing) with earlier versions.

- **Step 3 = maintenance release number**: This is incremented whenever errors are repaired and safety gaps are plugged. An increase of this number indicates only minor changes and very minor new features. These versions are fully compatibly with the versions of the same step 1 and 2 number.

- **Full release**: This is a change in the step 1 and 2 system. With these, alpha and beta test periods are given. The length of the test periods is not fixed and is at the discretion of the development team. Beta versions should be available for testing for at least three weeks in order to give component developers the time to customize their components.

- **Maintenance release**: This release can be used immediately.

Version 1.5.0 represents the first full release after two years. There were alpha and beta versions and release candidates. Third-party developers are customizing their components for the new version. The community tests the software for any incompatibilities with the prior version.

You can follow the reporting and fixing of bugs on Joomla!'s website and if you find a bug, you can report it there. You will also find the list of requested improvements (`http://joomlacode.org/gf/project/joomla/tracker/`) there.

The development process for Joomla! 1.5 has largely been unnoticed since the fall of 2005. The concepts for version 1.5 were already quite concrete at that time and in February 2006 the first alpha-version was released.

Road Map

This road map can, of course, change at any time, it does, however, represent a good framework for orientation. The following table shows the Joomla! roadmap (status as of November 2007).

Version	Date of Release	Comments
Mambo 4.5.2	17. Feb. 2005	Last stable version of Mambo
Joomla 1.0.x	From Sep. 2005	Transfer of Mambo version 4.5.2.3
		Corrections of bugs and security patches
		Last stable version of Joomla! 1.0.13
Joomla 1.5	Oct 2006	Internationalization (total support for UTF-8)
Beta 1		Administration interface capability for every language
		User plug-ins
		Database: Support for MySQL- and MySQLi-database servers
		FTP system, to sidestep the PHP safe mode with providers
		Fundamental changes and overhaul of the structure, the framework, of Joomla! itself and with it preparation for the possibility to create barrier-free websites with Joomla!
		Separation of programming logic and layout
		Improvement to search engine friendliness (SEF)
		Reworked caching mechanism

Version	Date of Release	Comments
Joomla 1.5 Beta 2	May 2007	Developer documentation (API, How-to's) API tuning
		Redeveloped caching
		Redeveloped support for search-engine friendly URLs
		Introduction of the MooTool Javascript Framework
		Barrier-free *Beez* template in the core
Joomla 1.5 RC1-4	July 2007 - December 2007	User documnetation
		Corrections
		Security and performance improvements
		Testing on various platforms and in various browsers
Joomla 1.5 stable	January 2008	The stable version
Future verions of Joomla	No dates given	New user access control system
		Version control for content
		Multi-site installations (many Joomla sites in one Joomla installation)
		Update mechanism
		Virtual file system
		Support for more databases

Changes In Detail

As can be seen from the table, the 1.5 version is the first true Joomla!. The Joomla! team spent the first year stabilizing the inheritance from Mambo under the Joomla! name and charting their own direction. The changes in Joomla! 1.5 clearly reveal future developments.

Internationalization

- Every piece of static text can now be translated into language files. This is in particular relevant for the administration area, which up to now was only available in English.

- Support of scripts that are written from right to left (i.e. RTL, Arabic, Hebrew, Farsi, and Urdu).

- Complete changeover to the UTF-8 character set for coding and displaying all characters in Unicode .

User Plug-Ins

Mambots are now called plug-ins and user plug-ins, authentification plug-ins, xmlrpc plug-ins, and system plug-ins now join content, editor, and search plug-ins.

Alternative login mechanisms from external programs, among others, can be used with the aid of these plug-ins.

XML Remote Procedure Call Support

XML Remote Procedure Call (XML-RPC) is a specification that allows software on different systems and in different environments to communicate. All the important programming languages are supported and there are libraries that change the code into XML-RPC (`http://en.wikipedia.org/wiki/XML-RPC`). Joomla! also offers such an interface. With it, for instance, it is possible to post an image from Flickr or write an article with OpenOffice and to subsequently publish it in Joomla! This opens up fascinating options for developers; for example they can now access Joomla! from a Java program.

Support of Several Databases

Joomla! 1.5 contains an abstraction layer that makes it possible to run Joomla! with various database versions. However, only one of these databases can be used for each particular Joomla! installation. At the moment MySQL 4.x, 5.x are supported. Additional databases will be supported in the future.

FTP System

An FTP layer has been added to avoid problems with file access rights. Therefore, installation of new components and other uploads can be handled via PHP upload and via FTP. The service providers' restrictive (but reasonable) approach in terms of the PHP language had made the installation of extensions and the downloading of files in general, more difficult.

Overhaul of the Joomla! Framework

There has been no such thing as a framework in terms of a packaged kit for Joomla! functionality so far. It did, however, become crystal clear after the fork that the old Mambo source code had to be improved just about everywhere. It became necessary to rewrite and code Joomla!'s functionality cleanly. A framework has to be flexible, scalable, separated from the output, and above all be comprehensible so that a third-party developer can write good components in a reasonable amount of time. A proprietary **API (Application Programming Interface)** is essential for that.

Barrier Freedom

Barrier freedom is an important topic and it has been a legal obligation in Germany for government websites to be barrier free since the first of January 2006. W3C has written standards for it. Joomla! 1.5 already has a complete barrier free template (Beez) and with it the option to comply with these standards.

Barrier freedom is achieved by compliance with these standards (valid HTML/ XHTML) and by the complete separation of content (text, images, etc.) from layout by the use of cascading style sheets (CSS). This statement applies 100% to the front end at the moment. The administration area is also scheduled to become completely barrier free in later versions. Currently it can be used by at least a person without vision.

Search Engine Friendliness

Support for search-engine friendly URLs has been removed from the Joomla! core and swapped into a plug-in. This makes it possible to add functionality with third-party components, which was very difficult before.

Google Summer of Code Projects

Since 2005 Google has been supporting talented students and their ideas in its Summer of Code Project (http://code.google.com/soc/2007/) with certain open-source projects to the tune of $ 4,500 each. Instead of taking whatever summer job is available to earn money, they can work on their hobby for the collective good and of course also to the benefit of Google. Every year the Summer of Code brings stunning amounts of PR, good ideas, and good programmers to Google. The open-source projects also benefit from the strategy of attracting new talent and of course from the results of the projects. In each case one member of the respective project community becomes mentor to one student.

The results of these projects will be and have been gradually integrated into Joomla!. Last year as well (2007), there were students programming for Joomla! and being paid by Google.

These projects included the following:

- *Extending the Nested Sets Model with 'Hardlinked Nested Sets'*–Enno Klasing, mentor Louis Benton Landry. (This has to do with the popular deep nesting of categories.)
- *Email interface for Publishing* – Nur Aini Rakhmawati, mentor Mateusz Krzeszowiec. (This has to do with the creation of Joomla! content by means of sending an email.)

- *Semantic Web Integration*–Mickael Maison, mentor Andrew Eddie. (This has to do with the integration of geographic standards such as KML and GeoRSS, in order to be able to manipulate these data in Joomla!, for example the home town of the user as a map-image.)

- *Eclipse Plugin for developing Joomla's Component/Module* – Muhammad Fuad Dwi Rizki, mentor Laurens Vandeput. (This has to do with the creation of a Joomla! plug-in for the popular developer environment Eclipse, in order to easily create Joomla! components.)

- *General content recommendation component for Joomla* – Faolan Cheslack-Postava, mentor Samuel Alexander Moffatt. (This has to do with automatic recommendation of content in a particular context at a particular time.)

Joomla! Features

The following is a listing of Joomla! features in point form:

- Free source code
- A large and eager community of users and developers
- Simple workflow system
- Publishing system for contents
- File manager for uploading and administering files
- Content summaries in RSS format
- Trash can for deleted content
- Search-engine-friendly URLs
- Banner management
- Multilingualism for website and administration interface
- Administration interface that is separated from the website
- Macro language for content (plug-ins)
- Caching mechanism to secure fast page creation with popular sites
- Simple installation of additional extensions
- Powerful template system (HTML, CSS, PHP)
- Hierarchical user groups
- Simple visitor statistics
- WYSIWYG editor for content
- Simple polling
- Rating system for content

There are numerous free and commercial extensions at `http://extensions.joomla.org/`, for instance:

- Forums
- Image galleries
- Document management systems
- Calendars
- And about 2000 more

Examples of Joomla! Pages

In order to get a feeling for what Joomla! pages look like and whether "the" Joomla! page even exists, have a look at a few:

Joomla.org

This is of course one of the largest Joomla! websites.

Travel Shop, Ireland

A tourist industry website with an interesting menu system from joomlart.com

Frank Lüdtke, Germany

A successful combination of Joomla! and Coppermine photo-gallery.

Hotel Schönruh, Austria

A simple website of a hotel in the Ziller valley.

Urth.tv, USA

A social platform for citizens of the world!

unric.org, Europe

The United Nations is also working with Joomla!. In this case thirteen languages have to be displayed on the website.

porsche.com.br, Brazil

Last but not least the Stuttgart SP Veículos Ltd from São Paulo. This company has taken part in the entire history of development from Mambo to Joomla! and has now upgraded to Joomla! 1.5.

 You can find a listing of Joomla! websites in the **Site Showcase** of the forum at:

`http://forum.joomla.org/index.php/board,58.0.html`

Summary

In this chapter we took a quick glance at the history of Joomla! and discussed the structure of WCMS. We familiarized ourselves with the Joomla! versions and features and saw a few Joomla!-powered pages.

2
Installation

The installation of Joomla! is a matter of five minutes. If you have installed it before, you can do it in three minutes. You will have the opportunity to test this claim in Chapter 16. In order to be able to even start the installation, your development environment must include a web server that supports PHP and a database that is supported by Joomla!.

The Joomla! files are copied into this system and are then installed with a web installer. This type of an environment is also called a **Client-Server System**.

Client-Server System

A Client-Server System is a network structure, in which an unlimited number of work stations (clients) can access services offered by a central server. The server is responsible for the delivery of the services. The client can communicate with the server and supplies the actual user interface. The client is an Internet browser. The servers, in our case, are called Apache and MySQL.

Accessing a Joomla! Website on the Internet

So you have a rough idea of what is going on behind the curtains, here is a simplified list of what has to happen in order for a computer to be able to access a Joomla! website:

- Establish an Internet connection via a provider.
- Call up the requested web address (URL) from the browser.
- The browser makes contact with the web server.
- The web server sends a query to the PHP-language interpreter that is installed on the server. The PHP language interpreter calls the Joomla! PHP files and interprets them.

- The PHP interpreter requests the necessary data from the database.
- The PHP interpreter creates either HTML or XHTML code, depending on the web server used.
- The web server delivers the 'page' or the generated code to the client browser.
- The browser 'detects' pointers to CSS and other files (images, flash elements, etc.) in the page just received and requests these from the web server separately.
- While loading all the necessary resources, the browser attempts to 'parse' and 'render' the page, in other words to take it apart and to display it.

You can see from this course of events that the system consists of a lot of components that have no specific relation to Joomla! at all.

Technical Requirements for Joomla!

Joomla! requires the following:

- An installed and functioning web server, for instance Apache version 1.13.19 or later or Microsoft IIS.
- PHP scripting language version 4.3 or later and support for MySQL and Zlib has to be compiled in PHP. **Zlib** is a library that enables PHP to read file packages that have been compressed with the ZIP procedure.
- The MySQL database system from version 3.23.x **on** or with Unicode character sets MySQL from 4.1.x on.

Necessary Elements for a Joomla! System Installation

You need all the components mentioned above to install a Joomla! system for yourself. PC, browser, and Internet connection are usually available. There are a number of options for web server, PHP interpreter, and database.

You can:

- Set the system up locally on your PC
- Set the system up on a server in a company's Intranet
- Rent a virtual server from a provider
- Rent or purchase a server from a provider (with root access)

You can also:

- Have the web server and database located on computers that are physically separated from each other

You can also, of course, use different:

- Brands of web servers
- Versions of PHP interpreters
- Versions of MySQL databases

And on top of that, you can install and operate all these components on various operating systems.

This freedom in choice of resources sometimes confuses the layperson, therefore we will discuss a few typical scenarios.

Local Test Environment

In the scenario where you are at home or in your office and want to set up a Joomla! website, then you can use any of the following operating systems.

Windows Operating System

For a Windows operating system you can use either of two web servers:

- Windows XP Professional and Windows Vista Ultimate both come with a web server, the Internet Information Server. You still have to install PHP and a database, and then you're ready.
- You take a preconfigured package (XAMPP), unpack it on your computer, and everything you need is there.

Linux Operating System

Here it depends on the distribution version you have. All the distributions allow simple installation (with a click of the mouse) of the Apache, PHP, and MySQL packages. At times, depending on distribution, they may already be preinstalled. So you can use:

- The programs contained in the distribution.
- A preconfigured package (XAMPP); extract it on your computer and everything you need is there.

Mac OS X Operating System

In Mac OS X operating system, you have a default web server (Apache) in your system that you have to activate, but unfortunately not PHP. There is no official version of PHP for Mac OS X, but there is a PHP Apache module that you can install (http://www.entropy.ch/software/macosx/php/). There are executable versions of MySQL for Mac OS X, which can be installed after the relevant download (http://dev.mysql.com/downloads/mysql/5.0.html).

So you can use:

- The installed Apache web server and install the missing software.
- The preconfigured XAMPP package for Mac OS X. Extract it on your computer and everything you need is there.
- Another complete package by the name of MAMP is also very popular with the Mac OS X environment (http://www.mamp.info).

Production Environment

You have several options here as well.

Rented Virtual Server

You rent a web-space package with database, PHP support, and often also your domain name from a provider. In this case you have a functional environment and you can install your Joomla! into it. Consult your provider as to the version choices (PHP, MySQL). Sometimes providers offer Joomla! preinstalled with various templates. If this is so, all you have to do is activate Joomla! with a click of the mouse and it is ready for you.

Your Own Server

You rent a server from a provider and install the operating system of your choice. You are the administrator of the system and you can work on it, just like on your PC at home.

Before you venture into the wilderness of the Internet, you should first practice on your local computer. This has the advantage that there are no connection fees, it is very fast, and you can practice at a leisurely pace.

You may even have a small local network at home where you can install Joomla! on one computer and access it from another.

Remember, that there are probably more current versions on the respective project sites on the Internet.

 If you install Joomla! in the wild, on a server on the Internet, you should always use the latest stable version. Never install a Beta version for a production site!

Setting Up the Local Server Environment

To install Joomla! locally you have to set up the appropriate server environment as described previously.

Windows

Windows is extremely user-friendly and immensely popular. Over 90 percent of all PCs work with Windows as their operating system. Windows XP and Windows Vista are the dominating versions. Unfortunately the Apache web server and the MySQL database, and PHP are not included with Windows.

You could install each of these programs separately, or grab a preconfigured package (this is very practical and it will save your nerves).

In Windows XP and Windows Vista, you log on to your system in administrator mode. If you don't know if you have administrator rights, check your account type: click **Start | Control Panel | User Accounts** and change your rights if necessary:

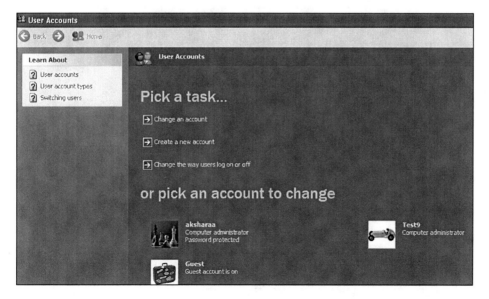

XAMPP for Windows

XAMPP is a project by Kai 'Oswald' Seidler and Kay Vogelgesang. For several years now, these two have been cooking up a complete development environment with the ingredients: Apache, MySQL, PHP, Perl, and various appropriate extensions. XAMPP can be downloaded from `http://www.apachefriends.org/` as a ZIP archive for various operating systems. This is immensely useful for people like you and me, who are primarily interested in Joomla! and not so much in how all of it works. The entire installation can also be removed from the computer with a single mouse-click without leaving a trace.

To download and install XAMPP:

1. Download the `xampplite-win32-1.6.5.exe` file from the website `http://www.apachefriends.org/en/xampp.html`.

2. Double-click on the file and the files are unpacked from the archive. You can unpack it to the drive of your choice.

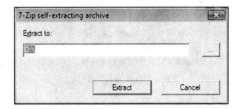

A directory, `xampplite`, is automatically created.

3. When you double-click on the `xampp-control.exe` file in the `xampplite` directory, Apache and MySQL start up. PHP is launched automatically as an Apache module. XAMPP makes no entries in the Windows Registry and sets no system variables.

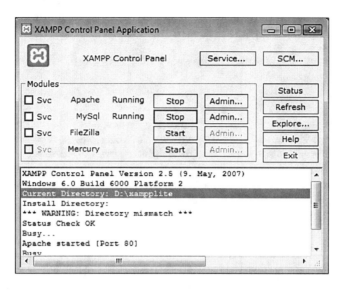

4. It is possible that Windows Firewall starts up and finds out indignantly that you have started two servers; it will ask you whether you really want to do this. Click on **Do Not Block Anymore**. After that you still have to explicitly click on **Continue** in Windows Vista.

5. Open your Internet browser and enter `http://127.0.0.1/` or `http://localhost/`. You should see the XAMMP start page now. Click on the **English** link and the following page will be displayed:

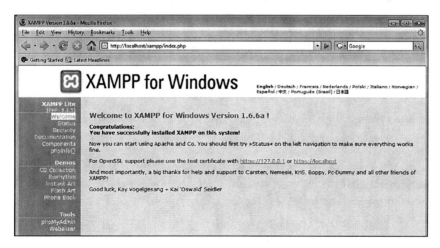

The document directory of your website is:

`[drive]:\xampplite\htdocs`

This directory contains all the pages that are accessible by a remote computer on the Internet. Carefully read the included `readme_en.txt` file for your own security. It also contains additional information about the necessary passwords.

To uninstall the package, stop all of the currently running servers and simply delete the `xampplite` directory.

> If the Apache web server does not start when you start `xampplite`, it could be that a different service already occupies port 80 of your computer. One very popular program that occupies port 80 with its older versions in its default setting and thereby prevents another program from using it, is Skype. You can either change the port number in Skype or start `xampplite` first and Skype after.

Linux

With Linux, everything is usually simpler. Various distributions with various standard configurations are available. Our dream team is usually pre-installed and just needs to be started. An XAMPP version can also be installed for Linux. My opinion, however, is that it makes more sense to grab the original programs. The installation is done by a package manager and is very simple.

openSUSE > 10.x

You can check whether Apache, MySQL, and PHP are already installed with the help of the YaST2 configuration program. If they are not, select the appropriate packages for installation and let YaST2 install them.

These are the packages in detail:

- `apache2`
- `apache2-devel`
- `apache2-mod_php5mysql`
- `php5-mysql`

You can find these packages via the YaST interface on the discs that come with your SUSE distribution or on special package pages on the Internet (`http://www.rpmseek.com/index.html`).

Start the Apache web server with the command:

```
/etc/init.d/apache2 start
```

Then start the MySQL database server with:

```
/etc/init.d/mysql start
```

You can stop both the servers with the `stop` command. By typing `help`, you get an overview of all of the parameters.

Debian/Ubuntu

With Debian and Ubuntu, the agent of choice is `apt`. You can install Apache, MySQL, and PHP with the program `apt`.

```
apt-get install [packagename]
```

The following are the packages in detail:

- `apache-common`: Support files for all Apache web servers
- `php5`: A server-side, HTML-embedded scripting language
- `mysql-common`: MySQL database common files (`/etc/mysql/my.cnf`)
- `mysql-server`: MySQL database server binaries

Then start Apache with the command `/etc/init.d/apache2 start` and MySQL with `/etc/init.d/mysql start`.

Your Own Server at a Provider (Root Server)

If you have rented a complete server from a provider, then you usually have shell access and free choice of the Linux distribution that you want to use. In addition, the system is preconfigured and contains all the necessary file packages and configurations. Usually special administration interfaces, such as SiteBuilder (`http://www.swsoft.com/en/products/sitebuilder/`) or Plesk (`http://www.swsoft.com/en/products/plesk/`), are used for configuring these servers. You can comfortably start, stop, and configure your server and the Apache and MySQL services from a browser interface with this tool.

Joomla! Installation on a Virtual Server on the Net

This topic is very complex, since there are an unmanageable number of providers and an even more unmanageable combination of installed Apache, PHP and MySQL versions and Webspace administration tools.

These are the sticking points during the installation:

- A PHP Safe Mode that can be activated if necessary
- Prohibited conversion of URLs with Apache because of the non-activation of the so-called Apache Rewrite Engine (mod_rewrite)
- Directory rights in Linux that are set differently than in Windows

In principle the simplest approach that for all intents and purposes always works is the following:

- Load the Joomla! 1.5.zip file onto your local PC and unpack it in a temporary directory.

- Load the just unpacked files with the FTP program onto your rented server. The files must be installed in the publicly accessible directory. These directories are usually named `htdocs`, `public_html`, or simply `html`. If other installations are already in this directory, you can specify a subdirectory within the directory into which you install your Joomla!. Many web hosts allow you to link your rented domain name to a directory. This name is necessary to call your website from a browser.

- You have to find out what your database is called. Usually one or several databases are included in your web hosting package. Sometimes the user name, database name, and password are fixed; sometimes you have to set them up. There is usually a browser-based configuration interface at your disposal. You can see an example of such an interface in the following figure. You will need these access data for Joomla!'s web installer.

You can get going after you have loaded these data onto your server and are in possession of the access data to your database.

Joomla! Installation

To install Joomla!, you need the source code. Download the `Joomla_1.5.zip` package and save it on your system.

Selecting a Directory for Installation

You have to decide whether Joomla! needs to be installed directly into a document directory or a subdirectory. This is important, since many users prefer a short URL to their homepage.

An Example

If Joomla! is unzipped directly in `/htdocs`, the web page starts when the domain name `http://www.myhomepage.com` is accessed from its local computer `http://localhost/` and/or from the server on the Internet. If you have created subdirectories under `/htdocs/`, for example, `/htdocs/Joomla150/` and you unpack the package there, you have to enter `http://localhost/Joomla150/` in the browser. This isn't a problem locally, but doesn't look good on a production Internet site.

However, some HTML files and subdirectories are already in `/htdocs` in the local XAMPP Lite environment under Windows, which, for example, displays the greeting page of XAMPP Lite. Depending on the distribution and the web server, a starting page is also displayed in your local Linux environment.

Directory

I recommend that you create a subdirectory named `Joomla150` under the document directory in Windows using Windows Explorer. (With Linux, use the Shell, KDE Konqueror or Midnight Commander.)

```
[home]/htdocs/Joomla150/
```

The directory tree in Windows Explorer should now look as follows:

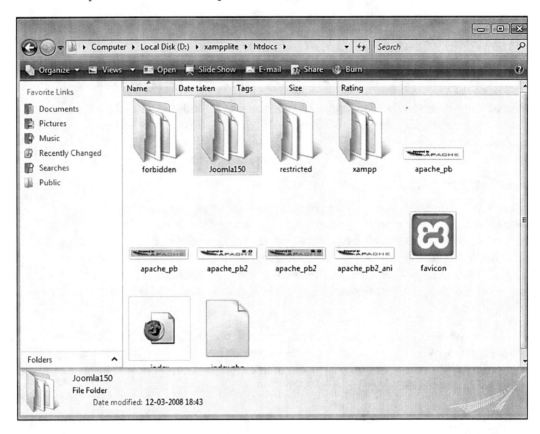

A page with an empty index appears in the XAMPP Lite version when you enter the URL `http://localhost/Joomla150` in your browser:

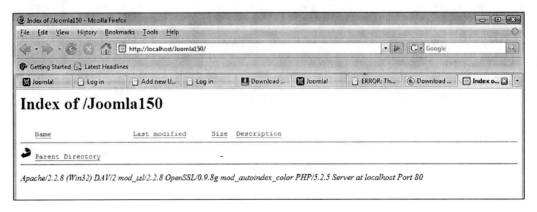

With Linux or another configuration you might get a message that you don't have access to this directory. This depends on the configuration of the web server. For security reasons, the automatic directory display is often deactivated in Apache's configuration. A potential hacker could draw many interesting conclusions about the directory structure and the files on your homepage and target your computer for an attack.

For security reasons, you are usually not allowed to access the appropriate configuration file of the Apache web server. Should you be able to, you should leave the content directories deactivated and/or only activated for those directories that contain files for downloading.

Unpacking

Now you can finally unpack the package file `Joomla-1.5.zip` into the designated directory. In Windows XP and Windows Vista you can unpack this package directly with the file explorer. In all other versions of Windows a separate unpacking program, like the free program, TUGZip, is required.

This structure is the same on all operating systems; only the presentation differs.

Joomla! Web Installer

From now on, everything is going to go lightning fast because the Joomla! web installer will be taking command. Go to `http://localhost/Joomla150/`.

Step 1: Language Selection

Choose Language is the first of a total of seven installation steps. Select the desired language and click on the **Next** button.

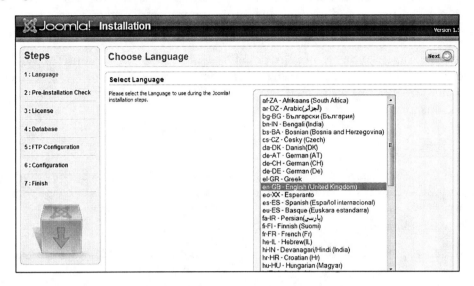

Step 2: Pre-Installation Check

Next, you will see the **Pre-Installation check**. This check should help you determine whether your server environment is suitable for a Joomla! installation.

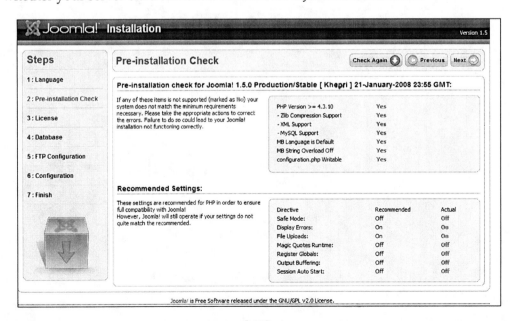

If you predominantly see green test results, it is a good sign. Depending on your configuration there can be discrepancies here. The Joomla! installer takes the configuration settings of the web server (in our case Apache), PHP, and the operating system into consideration. On Unix-based systems (Linux, Mac OS X) you have to pay attention to the write rights. This is in particular important for the `configuration.php` file. This file is created at the end of the installation with its customized values. If the installer does not have write rights in the folder, Joomla! cannot create this file and the installation will fail. If this happens, try to configure the rights appropriately and click on **Check Again**.

If you are working with the XAMPP Lite solution under Windows, your screen should like the previous screenshot. Click on **Next** and you are in the licensing step.

Step 3: Licence

Every piece of software is licensed under certain conditions. Joomla! uses the GNU/GPL licence, version 2.0.

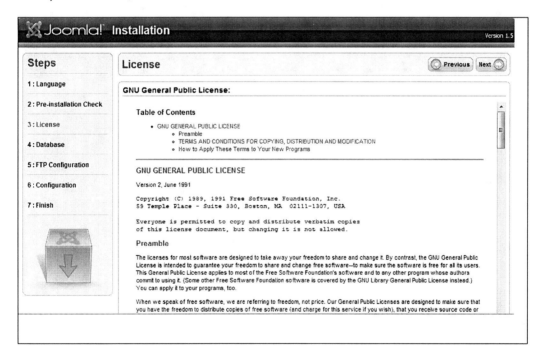

After you read this license click on **Next**.

Step 4: Database Configuration

In the fourth step, **Database Configuration**, your database parameters are queried.
You can set up as many databases as required in an XAMPP Lite server environment
and you have a MySQL user with the name `root` (without a password). The user
`root` is the MySQL administrator and can do everything in the MySQL system.
An installation without a password is a significant security risk. In the beginning,
locally, in order to get the system up and running as quickly as possible, this is not
a problem. But in the long term, you should absolutely provide your XAMPP Lite
installation with passwords in **security check** (`http://localhost/security/`).

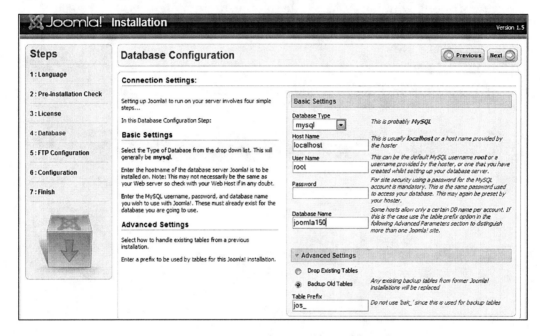

Enter the following parameters in a local XAMPP Lite installation:

- **Host Name: localhost**
- **User Name: root**
- **Password:** leave this empty — but be aware of the security risk!!

Now select a **Database Name**. An unlimited number of databases can be set up in a local XAMPP Lite environment since the user root has the right to do that. In an active environment with a provider, you presumably will have a set allocation of databases and the access data for the databases are usually preset.

Because of this, I can also enter a name of a database that does not exist yet in the installer. Here **joomla150** is the database name used.

By clicking the green triangle in front of **Advanced Settings**, you can activate additional options. You can select whether the tables of an existing Joomla! installation in this database should be deleted or saved and whether they should be provided with the prefix bak_.

The MySQL **Table Prefix** is very practical. The text that you enter into the respective field is written in front of every table created by the web installer. The web installer recommends jos_ as the default.

There is a simple reason for this. Sometimes you only get one MySQL database from an Internet provider. If you have to operate two Joomla! sites, there would be a problem in this case, since you cannot differentiate one table from the other. It is possible to distinguish between the tables of different Joomla! installations (jos_smith_ or jos_jones_) by means of the **Table Prefix**. In this case you should accept the default jos_. This prefix is also used to mark saved data (bak_).

Step 5: FTP Configuration

In order to stop problems with access rights and a possibly activated PHP Safe Mode in their track, you have the option of using PHP's FTP functions for uploading and handling of files starting with Joomla! 1.5. This is not necessary in the local XAMPP Lite installation. But if you install Joomla! on the virtual web server of a provider, enter here the FTP data that your provider has given to you. If your provider permits these functions, it is advisable from a security perspective to set up different FTP accounts for yourself as user and for Joomla! and to activate the Joomla! FTP account only for the respective Joomla! directory.

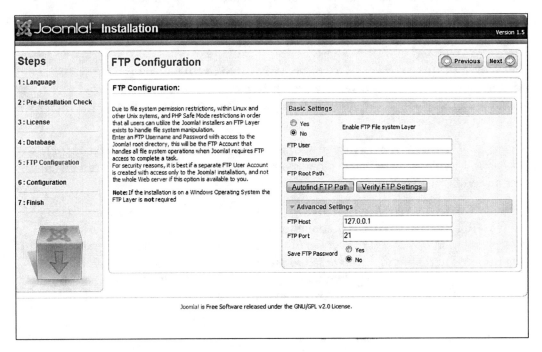

Step 6: Configuration

This main step of the configuration is divided into three parts.

The first part of the configuration has to do with the name of your website. This name appears in the header of the browser window when somebody accesses your website. This name is also used in other places, for example, with confirmation emails to registered users. I have chosen the name `Joomla! 1.5.0` for our example site.

In the second part, you are asked to enter the paths of the website, the administrator email address, and the administrator password. Write the password on a piece of paper (but don't stick it on the monitor or the keyboard!).

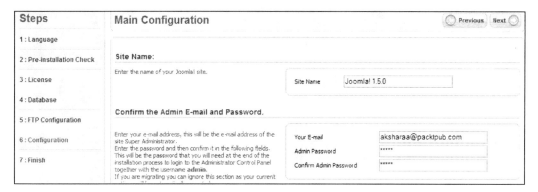

In the third part you define the type of data that your Joomla! installation is to contain.

- **Install Default Sample Data**: The data is the most important part of your installation. Joomla! allows you to, and explicitly recommends that you, install sample data so that you can experiment without any worries.

- **Load Local Joomla! 1.5 SQL Script**: You may already have created a local Joomla! website and now may want exactly this data in an online database. In this case you can specify the `.sql` file that holds your Joomla! data, which you have exported from the local version. Make sure that this file has the exact Joomla! 1.5 database design and is UTF-8 coded.

- **Load Migration Script**: This option ports a Joomla! 1.0.x installation into a Joomla! 1.5 version.

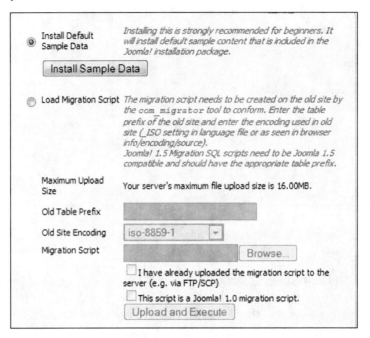

The **Install Default Sample Data** is selected as default. During the course of the book we will look at other options.

Click on the **Install Sample Data** button. The installer loads the data into your database and changes the display. The process is a little unimpressive but necessary for the installation of sample data. The button disappears and a small text window appears.

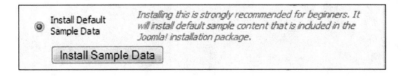

Now click on the **Next** button and your data are stored.

Step 7: Completion

The seventh and final step congratulates you on a successful installation. Let me congratulate you as well. There is a notice in bold text that prompts you to delete the `installation` directory. Take good heed of this notice, because your Joomla! website will not run without this step.

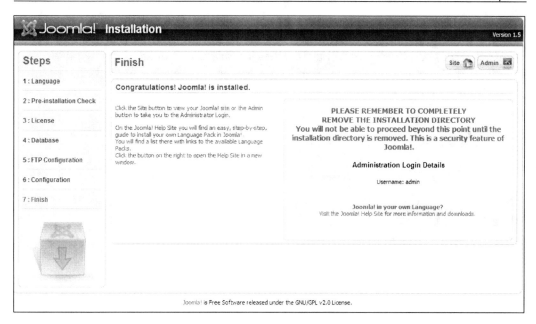

Readers who would like to follow a concrete example of how to build a website from scratch can go to Chapter 16.

A file with the name of configuration.php was created in your document directory. If you want to repeat the installation, you have to delete the configuration.php file before you delete the installation directory. After this, if you go to the URL that contains the Joomla! files from your browser the Joomla! installer starts again.

Your administration user name is always **admin**.

In case you have forgotten/lost your administrator password, there is a solution in the Appendix.

The installation is now complete and you have a choice between the buttons **Site** (to view your homepage) and **Admin** (administration interface). To take a look at your newly created homepage, click on **Site**. If you haven't deleted the installation directory as of yet, you will get a friendly reminder to delete it and to check out your page after you've done that.

Summary

The result already looks quite impressive. Take your time and look around, click on some options and try to orient yourself. Many of Joomla!'s functionalities are used in this homepage, which is loaded with sample data. We will look at these in later chapters.

3
A Tour of Your New Website

Now that you have installed your homepage and have carefully explored it, we can take a look at the result together. At first glance, these pages look a bit confusing. In principle, they are divided into a front end (your actual website) and a back end (the administration view of your website). Customers and web surfers see the front end; the back end is only accessible by co-workers and/or administrators.

Front End

You can see right away that the sample website illustrates a lot of the functions that Joomla! has to offer, giving you a good overview of Joomla!'s capability.

In order to get a better overview, I have marked and labeled the different areas in the figure overleaf.

The art of design now consists of recognizing the elements that are important for your website, omitting the unimportant ones, and presenting it to the user in a logical, easy-to-understand, and attractive format. The result is always a compromise between functionality and organization.

Space for a Logo

Newsflash

About Joomla!   Features   The Community

Top Menu

Search Field

Latest News

- Content Layouts
- The Joomla Community
- Welcome to Joomla!
- Newsflash 4
- Newsflash 5

Selected News

Popular

- Joomla! Overview
- Extensions
- Joomla! Features
- Joomla! Facts
- Content Layouts

Main Menu

- Home
- Joomla! Overview
- **Main Menu**
- Joomla! License
- More about Joomla!
- FAQ
- The News
- Web Links
- News Feeds

Key Concepts

- Extensions
- Content Layouts
- Example Pages

Resources

- Joomla! Home
- **Additional**
- Joomla! Help
- OSM **News**
- Administrator

Login Form

Username

User
Registration

Remember me

Login

Lost Password?
No account yet? Register

Welcome to Joomla!

Written by Administrator

Tuesday, 11 October 2006 11:54

`* Joomla! 1.5.0 Beta should NOT to be used for `live` or `production` sites. `* Joomla! is a free open source framework and content publishing system designed for quickly creating highly interactive multi-language Web sites, online communities, media portals, blogs and eCommerce applications.

Joomla! provides an easy-to-use graphical user interface that simplifies the management and publishing of large volumes of content including HTML, documents, and rich media. Joomla! is used by organisations of all sizes for Public Websites, Intranets and Extranets and is supported by a community of thousands of users.

Last Updated (Wednesday, 11 October 2006 16:37)

Read more... >>

First Page
Front Page
Start Page

Example News Item 1

Written by Administrator

Wednesday, 07 July 2004 11:54

Lorem ipsum dolor sit amet, consetetur sadipscing elitr, sed diam nonumy eirmod tempor invidunt ut labore et dolore magna aliquyam erat, sed diam voluptua. At vero eos et accusam et justo duo dolores et ea rebum. Stet clita kasd gubergren, no sea takimata sanctus est Lorem ipsum dolor sit amet. Lorem ipsum dolor sit amet, consetetur sadipscing elitr, sed diam nonumy eirmod tempor invidunt ut labore et dolore magna aliquyam erat, sed diam voluptua. At vero eos et accusam et justo duo dolores et ea rebum.

Last Updated (Wednesday, 07 July 2004 13:05)

Read more... >>

Example News Item 2

Written by Administrator

Wednesday, 07 July 2004 11:54

Lorem ipsum dolor sit amet, consetetur sadipscing elitr, sed diam nonumy eirmod tempor invidunt ut labore et dolore magna aliquyam erat, sed diam voluptua. At vero eos et accusam et justo duo dolores et ea rebum. Stet clita kasd gubergren, no sea takimata sanctus est Lorem ipsum dolor sit amet, consetetur sadipscing elitr, sed diam nonumy eirmod tempor invidunt ut labore et dolore magna aliquyam erat, sed diam voluptua.

Last Updated (Wednesday, 11 October 2006 12:08)

Read more... >>

Read more...

- How do I upgrade to Joomla! 1.5 ?

« Start Prev 1 2 Next End »

Page 1 of 2

Polls

Joomla! is used for?

- Community Sites
- Public Brand Sites
- **Poll** eCommerce
- Blogs
- Intranets
- Photo and Media Sites
- All of the Above!

Vote   Results

Who's Online

We have **Online?** and 1 member online

Advertisement

Featured Links:

Joomla!
Joomla! The most popular and widely used Open Source CMS Project in the world. **Space for**
Advertising
Joomla! Forge, development and distribution made easy.

Joomla! Extensions
Joomla! components, modules, plugins and languages by the bud at load.

Ads by Joomla!

Feed

Footer

Powered by Joomla!. Valid XHTML and CSS.

From the configuration, this structure reminds one of a daily newspaper like the New York Times or a portal like MSN or Yahoo!. On the left and right there are boxes with clearly defined content. In the center (main body) are the news items (categorized content).

A so-called template determines the layout of the page. Templates are exchangeable and modifiable, meaning that the same content can be displayed in different layouts. Every daily newspaper would envy you for this functionality.

Let's go over the example layout a bit more closely. There are five different categories of areas on the page.

- Menus
- Content
- Advertising
- Additional functions
- Decorative elements

Menus

Menus make navigation on the page as easy as possible for the user. There are different menus for different tasks. Joomla! has predefined six menus in the sample data. You can add as many additional menus as you want or, naturally, you can also disable them. Two of the menus, by the way, are not shown in our example. These are the so-called **User Menu** that the registered user sees after he or she has logged on, and the **Key Concepts** menu that is only shown when you click on the **Key Concepts** link.

Top Menu

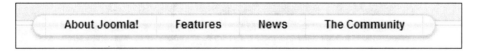

The top menu is as high up on the page as possible. It is designed to give the user quick access to the most important content. Such a menu often displays concepts, products, contacts, company address information, and language.

Main Menu/Breadcrumbs

The main menu is the central navigation area of the page. There should always be a link here to return the user to the first page. This menu should appear in exactly the same position on every page of the website.The main menu is an important point of reference for the user. The same is true for **Breadcrumbs**. This *breadcrumb navigation* should make it easier to navigate within the branches of a content tree. The name is based on the *Hansel and Gretel* fairy tale. The breadcrumbs are links to previously visited, superordinate or related content.

Other Menus

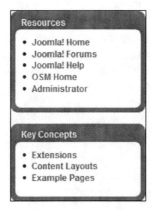

Other menus (other menu, key concepts) can pop up in all kinds of places (module positions). Depending on the content and context of the page it can make sense to offer additional menu options, such as a shop component or, here for instance, Joomla!'s core concepts.

Content

Finally we get to the content that we want to manage!

What is Content?

Content can be a message, an editorial article, or a static page with explanations. Content can also be a dynamic link directory (`http://www.google.com/`), a shop (`http://dell.com/`), or a flea market (`http://www.ebay.com/`).

Content can also be something completely dynamic and open to everybody. The free encyclopedia Wikipedia, for example, uses a content administration system that allows everyone to change the content. This special form of content administration is called a wiki. Everyone can change and even delete content. So far it is working amazingly well with Wikipedia, despite the frequent arguments about structure and content of articles.

The opposite of a wiki is static content, which once written, is valid for a long time. For example, this book. It will become outdated regarding the version numbers of the software discussed, although it has the advantage of explaining the topic comprehensively and cohesively. I produce content of a particular type and therefore operate a type of content management, not only in Joomla!, but also in OpenOffice.

Folders, flyers, stickers, business reports, and operating manuals are also usually of static nature. Created for a certain event, they become outdated or simply wrong after some time.

Many older web pages consist exclusively of static elements. On the Internet, however, the clock ticks a little faster. That which is complacently tolerated with books, folders, and other printed materials (after all, I can also read the book at the beach and in the subway), is regarded to be a serious shortcoming by visitors to your website. Nothing is worse for the image of your company than an old static website with a button announcing "Powered by...", which indicates hopelessly outdated software.

The presentational possibilities of content are inexhaustible. They depend on the available terminal, bandwidth, and many other things that are in turn dependent on the user and his or her creativity. The user of the message plays an increasingly important role. That reminds me: What is your actual target group?

There is a platitude that professes:

Content is King!

It depends on the content. Every web agency would now crack a smile and get on with the daily job of creating the next website. Millions of dollars in advertising budgets for products such as frozen spinach or beer are proof of the fact that successful communication also works without unique content.

The statement that content is crucial, is, however, fundamentally correct. If you have nothing to say or nothing to offer, nobody will listen to you of his or her own free will. Since you probably don't have a million-dollar advertising budget, you also can't seduce people to read your content. No matter how beautiful websites without content may look, or how many terminals may display them, nobody will voluntarily visit them.

First Page/Front Page

Content is announced on the first page of the website as shown in the following figure:

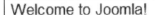 Welcome to Joomla!

Written by Administrator

Thursday, 12 October 2006 10:00

Joomla! is a free open source framework and content publishing system designed for quickly creating highly interactive multi-language Web sites, online communities, media portals, blogs and eCommerce applications.

Joomla! provides an easy-to-use graphical user interface that simplifies the management and publishing of large volumes of content including HTML, documents, and rich media. Joomla! is used by organisations of all sizes for Public Web sites, Intranets, and Extranets and is supported by a community of thousands of users.

Last Updated (Thursday, 08 November 2007 12:06)

Read more... >>

We are Volunteers

Written by Administrator

Wednesday, 07 July 2004 09:54

The Joomla! Core Team consists of volunteer developers, designers, administrators and managers who, together with a large range of Work Groups of dedicated community members have taken Joomla! to new heights in its relatively short life. This well-oiled machine is often copied but never surpassed. Joomla! has some wonderfully talented people taking Open Source concepts to the forefront of industry standards. Joomla! 1.5 is a major

Stick to the Code!

Written by Administrator

Wednesday, 07 July 2004 12:00

To ensure this code release, Wilco Jansen resorted to sending rum to joint lead-developer Johan Janssens. Johan, who's had a penchant for rum ever since the first "Pirate's of the Caribbean" movie screened, took the bait, mixed it with Cola, and here we are with our latest 1.5 release. It looks like pirate talk will figure quite a lot in future Joomla! development!

Last Updated (Sunday, 25 November 2007 22:37

Content has an author, in this case an administrator, a creation date, a heading, a teaser, and perhaps an image. The teaser is to make the visitor curious and to get him or her to click on a **Read more** link in order to read the entire message. As an option, links (icons) can be offered to read the content as a PDF, to print it, or to send it in an email to someone else.

The Newest Information/The Most Often Read Messages

The message can be displayed in different formats. People are usually interested in the *newest* and in what *others* are reading.

Because of that, our example layout has an appropriate area in which the last five articles are always displayed, and another area with the most often read articles. This second area is made possible by the fact that Joomla! logs every hit on an article in the database and tracks the number of times it has been accessed.

Latest News

- Content Layouts
- The Joomla! Community
- Welcome to Joomla!
- Newsflash 4
- Newsflash 5

Popular

- Joomla! Overview
- Extensions
- Joomla! License Guidelines
- Welcome to Joomla!
- What's New In 1.5?

Advertising

When your site becomes popular and if the content is right, you can sell advertising space. Advertising space usually means banner links. Banners are small graphics (in `.gif`, `.jpg`, `.png`, or `.swf` format) that induce the visitor to leave your website via a single click on the banner. If you really want that, look for a space in your layout and consider using it for advertising.

Banner Area

The banner area can administer text links and graphical banners. Here is an example of the prevalent banner size of 468 * 60 pixels.

Advertisement

Featured Links:

Joomla!
Joomla! The most popular and widely used Open Source CMS Project in the world.

JoomlaCode
JoomlaCode, development and distribution made easy.

Joomla! Extensions
Joomla! Components, Modules, Plugins and Languages by the bucket load.

Joomla! Shop
For all your Joomla! merchandise.

Ads by Joomla!

Functions

Functions are site elements that are necessary to make interactivity possible. In Joomla! these functions are built into modules.

Login Area

A login module is important if you want to split your website into a public and a protected area. The visitor then has to have a way of registering and logging on. Perhaps, he or she even occasionally forgets his or her password. The login module should be able to take all situations into consideration as shown in the following figure:

Polling

Since our content is designed for certain target groups, we should now and then ask the group that actually surfs our site for their opinion. This is the simplest way of getting usable opinions about your site.

Joomla! has an integrated polling component. You can see the display module on the sample page as shown in the following figure:

Who is Online?

This module is about communication and community. After the user has been able to see which articles are new and particularly popular, naturally he or she would like to know who is navigating the site right now. A distinction is made between guests and logged-in users as shown in the following figure:

Who's Online

We have 1 guest online

Deliberate carefully about whether you want to offer such features on your website. If you claim in your content that you are the largest ring-tone website in the U.S. and only one guest hangs out in your site, this will hurt your credibility. However, if you do indeed constantly have 10 – 20 visitors and logged -n users, this is a good way to demonstrate dynamics.

Feeds

News feeds are becoming more and more popular. These are standardized, machine readable collections of content, which can be processed further, to some extent the content of your site, without the encumbrance of the template and layout. The **Syndication** module offers the website's news feed. You will learn more about this technology later in the book.

Search Field

The functionality that underlies the search field contributes greatly to the user friendliness of a website. Many sites have search fields. Often, however, they only search through a portion of the website. With Joomla!, however, this is different, all pages are definitely scanned. If new extensions are added, their content is also searched.

You can type a search term and press *Enter* on the keyboard. The result is a hit list, with the desired term visually highlighted.

search...

Decorative Elements

After so many functions, modules, and content, the issue of design, corporate identity, and the *look* and *feel* of the website pops up.

A template represents the layout of the page and is laid on top of the content like a screen. Since it is hard to argue about taste or beauty, you have the option of providing various templates for the same content. For example, the look of your website could be different in winter than in summer, or it could have an Olympics look during the Olympic Games. (Chapter 13 covers the creation of your own templates.)

In principle, a template consists of a logo, a certain color combination, selected character fonts and sizes, and as clever an arrangement of the available content as possible. The example template of course has the Joomla! logo:

Outlook

I am sure that after this tour and from your own experience from exploring the sample data you can understand that the administration of content can be a very demanding task. Above all, it is important not to lose your overview.

Back end

The administration of the website takes place in the back end in the Joomla! Administration. You can get to the Joomla! administration under the URL

[Domain name]/administrator/

If you are also working with your local installation, the URL is

http://localhost/joomla150/administrator/

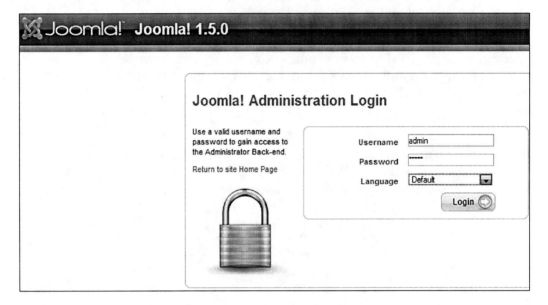

Log on with your ID, **admin**. You had specified the user data yourself in the web installer during installation.

You will see an interface with menus, icons, and tabs, identical to the graphic interface of your operating system.

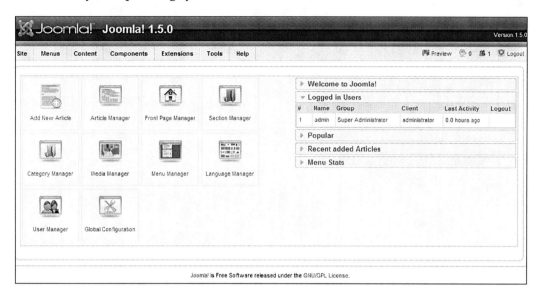

 For security purposes, you should protect the directory [pathtoJoomla]/administrator/

with an .htaccess file. Because of the popularity of Joomla!, hackers constantly attempt to get at the administration.

Summary

This chapter helped us get a feel of a Joomla! website. We are now familiar with the front end and back end of Joomla!. In the next chapter will learn about customizing Joomla! according to our requirements.

Customizing Joomla!— Language and Templates

In the last chapter I mentioned that you can customize your site, make changes, and fill it with content in the Joomla! administration area.

The first two things that the owners of a site typically want to perform are adjusting the language to their native language and changing the colors and layout.

So, we will first discuss these two things.

A Different Language for the Website and the Administrator

In case you want to reach a native target group with your site, you should understand the language of that target group and build the site in that language. If you want to address an international audience, you should use English as the default language.

Regardless of which language you choose, you need a customized language file.

Installation of a Different Language File

If you want to reach a German target group, for example, download the language files from the German translation team's website to your PC. There is a language file for the front end and a language file for the administration area. These language files were created by the German Translation Team of Nikolai Plath, Achim Raji, Antonio Cambule, David Jardin, Ulrich Eichenseer, and Joern Gerken.

To install the files, log on to your Joomla! Administration as described in Chapter 2, and click on **Extensions | Install/Uninstall**.

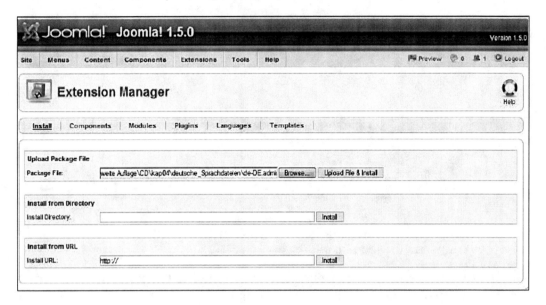

You now have three options for importing the German language files:

- By means of a file upload from your home PC
- From a directory in the document area of your web server
- From a URL that points to the appropriate language package

Let's choose the first option. Click on **Browse** next to the **Upload File & Install** field and first select the de-DE.site.joomla15RC3.zip file. Now click on **Upload File & Install**. If all rights are correctly set, you will receive the message:

Install language success

Repeat this procedure with the other file.

Now go to the language manager by clicking on **Extension | Language Manager**. You will see the available languages here, separated into the **Site** and **Administrator** tabs. Besides **English (United Kingdom)** now there is also **German formal — Sie** and information about the creator of the language file.

However, the green checkmark for the standard language is still next to English. Select the German option with the radio button and then click on the **Default** icon, which is on the top right. The icons that finalize actions and dialogs are always in this position in the administration interface.

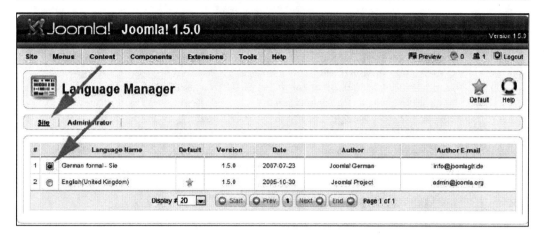

Don't forget to switch the administration interface to German as well. Your Joomla! will be speaking German with you in the back end and front end. Users have been waiting for this back-end functionality for years! Their wish has finally become a reality with Joomla! 1.5.

Translation of a Menu Entry

Your website now speaks German as well. Go to `http://localhost/joomla150/` and take a look. Look for a term with the **Browse** field.

This page displays a breathtaking mixture of both German and English languages. Everything that is programmed to function automatically, like the search procedure or the login procedure, is in German; but the rest of the content is not.

Why?

The answer is quite simple. Only the words and sentences that are known can be translated. A big part of the page, however, consists of user-entered content. This content appears in the language in which it was entered. In our case, the sample data was provided in English.

So what do you have to do to relabel, for example, the menu entry **Home** to **Startseite** or to rename the **Main Menu** to **Hauptmenü**?

In the case of **Home**, click on **Menus | Main Menu**. You are now in the **Menus** area.

> Joomla! version 1.0.x had an option to change the contents of the language packages by means of the language editor. This language editor is gone from the default version of Joomla! 1.5. It is, however, being offered as an installable add on (*translation manager*: http://extensions.joomla.org/component/option,com_mtree/task,viewlink/link_id,1776/Itemid,35/).

Don't pay any attention to the numerous configuration options being offered, simply replace the word **Home** with **Startseite** and click on **Apply**. **Startseite** will now appear in your **Main Menu** on the website!

> Joomla! differentiates between the **Apply, Save,** and **Exit** actions.
>
> **Apply** saves the changes and leaves you in edit mode.
>
> **Save** also saves the changes but closes the edit mode and returns to the list display.
>
> **Exit** doesn't save anything and exits the edit mode; it is, in other words, commensurate with **cancel**.

Modifying the Menu Name

In order to change the **Main Menu** to **Hauptmenü**, open the module manager by clicking **Extensions | Module Manager**. Click on the **Main Menu** link to get a form, just like with the menu entry.

Simply change the text, click on **Apply** and/or **Save** and **Main Menu** becomes **Hauptmenü**.

Changing the Template for Your Website

Now that everything looks a bit more familiar, you may want your site to have a completely different design. (You will learn more about templates in Chapter 13.)

At the moment, the default version of Joomla! 1.5.0 comes with the following templates: the previously introduced one by the name of Kepri, rhuk_milkyway, and a barrier-free one called Beez. To ensure barrier-freedom, the better part of Joomla! 1.0's source code essentially had to be rewritten. The Beez template was created by Angie Radtke and Robert Deutz and thereby evoked a month-long discussion about the meaning and the absurdity of barrier freedom. In the end, the template was included in the default version of Joomla! and in my opinion it will contribute to making Joomla! more popular in the German realm (more about Beez in Chapter 14).

There is a template competition at the moment at joomla.org. The winning template will be included as the third template with Joomla!'s default version.7

It is easy to switch to the Beez template. In order to have a wider choice and to see how easy it really is, simply install a new template.

Go to the Joomla! installer from the **Extensions | Install/Uninstall** menu. Click on the **Browse** button and upload the tmpl_bertrand.zip file. Click on the **Upload & Install** file button. The new template will be installed and the installer will report the result.

Use **Extensions | Templates Manager** to get to the template area. The template that is currently active is marked with a yellow star. If you slide your mouse cursor over the link with the name of the template, a small thumbnail view appears.

To assign this template to your site, select the radio button in front of the name of the desired template and click the **Default** icon in the menu bar. The yellow star is now beside the selected template. Switch to your website and click the **Update** button in the browser. Now you already have a different layout and a completely new appearance. You can see the Beez template in the following figure. Creating your own templates is covered in Chapter 13 and Mr. Bertrand's website is created in Chapter 16.

Changing Colors in the Template

The default template rhuk_milkyway has another few surprises up its sleeve. You can choose a different color scheme by means of the parameter settings.

Select the standard template again and go the the edit mask by activating the radio button in front of the template and clicking on the **Edit** icon. This takes you to the configuration of the template. There are various parameters with which you can change the colors and width of the template, and even asign special menu points.

Play with the options and keep going back to the website to check the impacts the changes make.

Joomla! allows you to work with tabs in the browser window. Internet Explorer from version 7 on also supports register navigation (tabbed browsing). With this technology you can keep the website and the administration area open in a browser window and switch between these views with a click on the tab. Other browsers, such as Firefox, Opera, Safari, and Konqueror have had these features for years, but are still not as popular as Internet Explorer.

Summary

In this chapter we saw how to customize our website in terms of language and templates.

5
Configuration of Joomla! Administration

Joomla! tries to offer the same user friendliness as any program with a graphical user interface, such as Windows, KDE, Gnome, or Aqua (Mac OS X). This is unusual for websites and is made possible by the generous use of JavaScript and the integration of AJAX elements. JavaScript is executed locally on your computer and can also be deactivated in the browser at any time. If you deactivate it, you can no longer work in Joomla! administration.

Browsers, however, have been able to deal with JavaScript quite well for several years now and there aren't any more serious security concerns. Therefore, you should enable JavaScript. In this context, I would highly recommend the two open-source Internet browsers Mozilla or Firefox to Windows users. Both are more secure and easier to use than Internet Explorer. Both are significantly more secure, faster and more user friendly than Internet Explorer. The main difference, however, is that, in contrast to Internet Explorer, these browsers implement the W3C Internet standard.

Screen Layout

Menu Bar

Joomla! administration, just like your site, consists of different elements. The menus are in the top menu bar as shown in the following figure:

There are four elements on the right-hand side:

- A link to the website (**Preview**)
- A note on whether you have received any messages and how many
- Another note on how many users are logged on to your site at the moment
- The **Logout** button

Tool Bar

Underneath the menu bar is the tool bar. Here is an example of menu entries in the **mainmenu**:

In the left area, the name of the current edit area and its corresponding icon are displayed (tool bar). To the right of it, depending on the manager, there are various disabled icons. If you slide your mouse cursor over one of these icons, a frame appears and you can click the left mouse button and implement the appropriate function. The following are the most popular icons and their relevance.

Toolbar Element	Relevance
Cancel	The editing is canceled without saving.
Enable	The selected element is enabled and thus published.
Apply	The changes are saved, the dialogue remains open.
Edit	The selected element is loaded into the edit module.
Disable	The selected element is disabled (hidden).
Appy	Content is enabled and thus published.
Upload	The chosen file is uploaded to the server.
Help	Joomla!'s online help.
Copy	The selected element is copied to another section or category.
Delete	The selected element is deleted.
Trash	The selected element is put in the trash container.
Save	The selected element is saved and the dialog is closed.
Block	Content is disabled (hidden).
Default	The selected element becomes the default.
Move	The selected element is moved to another section or category.
Preview	The chosen element is shown in its own preview window.
Restore	The selected element is retrieved from the trash container.

Submenus

Underneath the toolbar there are often additional menus depending on the current manager. The following figure displays the submenus of the **Banner Manager**.

You will find the tabs **Banners**, **Clients**, and **Categories** there. These are also called submenus or subcategories. Depending on the context, system messages can also appear here.

Filter Elements

Underneath the submenus are filter elements. These can filter the information by different criteria depending on the displayed list. You can search with a search string or, for example, you can display only the modules at particular positions, only particular module types or, as is done here, you can display only the enabled modules here in this overview of modules.

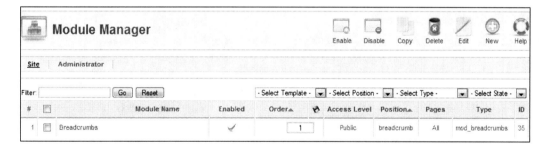

Content Area

Underneath the filter elements is a large area where the actual content is displayed. There are essentially three types.

Lists

A list of elements that can be edited after you check the appropriate checkbox and/or click on its name. If you click on the top checkbox, all elements are selected for collective editing. Also you will often find a sort function in this list as well as the option to enable and/or disable an element with a single click. Underneath the list of elements is the navigation. You can change the number of displayed list elements here and browse through the pages. Here is an example from the key concepts menu.

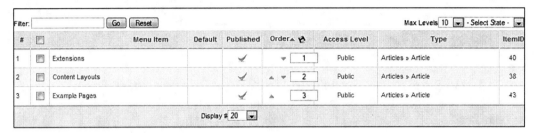

Dialogs

Depending on the dialog, the main content is usually displayed in the left area and the parameters for this element in the right area. A semantic separation of properties and parameters of an element is at times not very easy; therefore, there are some other framed areas that have configuration options on the left side.

Miscellaneous

With this I mean information, for example, the **Control Panel**, which is the first thing you see when you log on to the administration area. The most common menu commands are on the left side in the form of icons. Information about your website (admin module) is on the right side. Sometimes the Joomla! content does not fit into the list/dialog scheme; therefore you will find other areas now and then that are structured differently. This display problem sometimes occurs with more complex additional components.

Menu	# Items
ExamplePages	4
keyconcepts	3
mainmenu	9
othermenu	5
topmenu	4
usermenu	4

Help

Help is important and for that reason Joomla! tries to offer it at as many places as possible.

Help Icon

In most lists and dialogs there is an icon by the name of **Help** in the icon bar on the right border. If you click on this icon, and you are connected to the Internet, the appropriate help page from the joomla.org help server pops up in a browser window. The idea behind this is that there are help servers in various languages that have localized help texts and that therefore you are assured of current help.

Help with Speech Balloons

Speech balloons are a handy solution. These help texts are entered into the language files and are also displayed on a local basis without an Internet connection.

Help Menu

The **Help** menu that is at the very end provides you with concentrated information for Joomla! and its environment. It contains two menu entries—**Joomla! Help** and **System Info**.

Joomla! Help

The work area is separated into three parts. There is a search field and a bar with links in the top part.

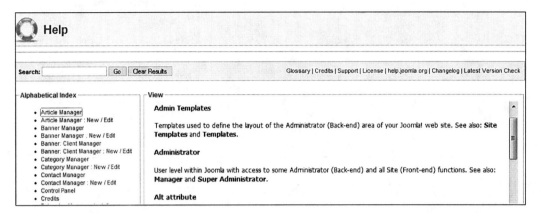

Below that on the left, there is an index of the available online help texts and on the right the respective display area. By default, you will see the new features of the Joomla! version that you are using. The links that are associated with the help texts point to the `http://help.joomla.org/` server. You can configure this help server for your language (see Chapter 6). The search also accesses this server and, of course, to use it you have to be connected to the Internet. This is necessary anyway unless you are just running a local version without Internet connection.

The other links refer to the text of the GNU/Public License, and the change log that documents the modifications of the individual developers.

System Info

You can find the system information in the **Help | System info** menu item. This information is divided into five tabs.

- **System Info**
- **PHP Settings**
- **Configuration File**
- **Directory Permissions**
- **PHP Information**

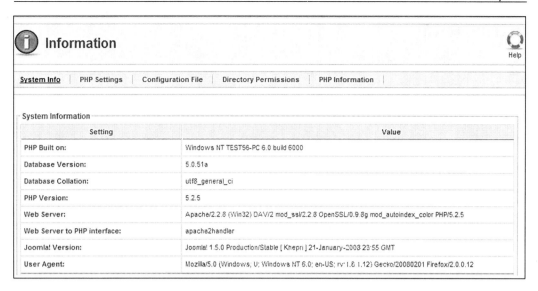

The **System Info** tab, for instance, displays a summary of the relevant data of the operating system and the server environment that is most important to Joomla!. Right now I am working locally with Windows and the XAMPP Lite environment (for the installation procedure, refer to Chapter 2) and am therefore running very up-to-date software versions (Apache 2.2.6 and PHP 5.2.6) compared with servers rented on the Internet.

The **PHP Settings** tab displays all of the important information from the php.ini file. This file, for example, determines whether the PHP safe mode is enabled or disabled. With most rented servers you cannot make any changes to the php.ini file.

The **Configuration File** tab displays the values of the variables in the configuration.php file. This file is created during the installation. For security reasons, the database data are displayed masked.

The **Directory Permissions** tab displays the rights of your subdirectories. In order for Joomla! to run error-free, all directories must be writable (not write-protected). You can change the directory rights in your FTP program with the chmod command.

The **PHP Information** tab displays the results of the PHP function phpinfo(). This has to do with the complete configuration of the PHP interpreter. Depending on the provider, it is possible that you may have a say in the configuration of this file, for example to increase the available storage space.

Summary

This chapter covered the operation of the administration area, its configuration and administration of content. We learned about the elements and their relevance in the menu bar, tool bar, etc. We also took a look at the help menu.

6
Site Menu

There are global settings that apply to all individual pages and to your server. All of these settings are summarized in the **Site** menu.

Five menu items apply to this (refer to the following figure):

- Control Panel
- User Manager
- Media Manager
- Configuration
- Logout

Control Panel

The first menu item, **Control Panel**, takes you back to the start page of the administration section. You can use the **Control Panel** to switch to various areas of administration either by selecting a menu item or by clicking on the displayed icons. Once you have some experience with administration, the fast-access icons are the way to go.

User Manager

Users have a special role on your Joomla! site. You can set up as many users as you want and, depending on their rights, they can create their own content and/or view content that has been created for particular users.

At the moment, you are the only user that the Joomla! administration recognizes. Your name is **admin**. You can work on everything in your Joomla! installation. If you allow user registration on your site (see the *Configuration* section), presumably there will be a lot more users very shortly.

In the user work area (refer to the following figure), you can edit and delete users, assign different rights to them, and you can, of course, also set up new user accounts.

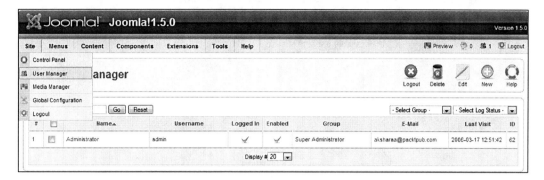

In the overview list you can see the most important information about the user—The real **Name** of the user (**Administrator**), the **User name** (**admin**), if the user is **Logged In** at the moment (marked by a check mark), if the user is activated, the user's **Group** assignments (**Super Administrator**), his or her **E-Mail** address, and the date of his or her **Last Visit** to your site. This refers to logins to the front end and back end. You can also check the **ID** number that this user has in the database (**62**).

You can filter the display by user groups and login status in the filter area. The search field on the left allows you to search for user accounts by entering partial names.

From the tool bar in the user area you can select from the dialogs **Logout**, **Delete**, **Edit**, **New**, and **Help**. Some actions can be applied to several users at once, for instance **Delete**. You just have to check the boxes on the left or the checkbox on the very top to select all users in this list. Then click on the **Delete** icon.

Logout Users Icon

This function is useful if you want to eject a logged-in user. This can act as a great emergency brake.

Delete Users Icon

With this function you can delete one or several user accounts by marking the checkboxes.

Edit Users Icon

This allows you to edit an individual user. Let's take the administrator account as an example. Click on the **Administrator** link or mark the checkbox and click on the **Edit** icon.

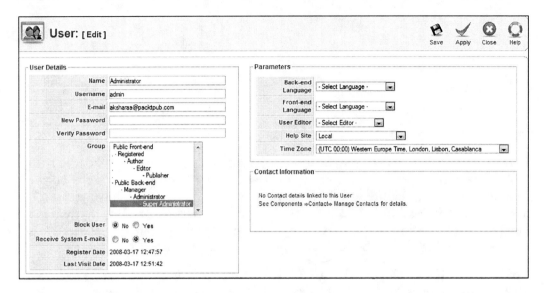

From this screenshot you can see that there are three fields:

- **User Details**
- **Parameters**
- **Contact Information**

User Details has the following fields:

Name: The real name of the user (here **Administrator**).

Username: Usernames are for identification during the login process and are independent of the real name. A user name should be short and easy to remember. For instance, `hgraf` could be used as username for `Hagen Graf`. Joomla! allows spaces, special characters, and all the valid Unicode characters in usernames. However, keep in mind that under certain conditions you might be sitting at a keyboard that doesn't support these special characters. How are you going to log in then?

Email: The user's valid email address.

New Password and Verify Password: The user password has to be entered twice for verification. If you leave this blank, your old password is maintained. The password has to be at least six characters long.

Group: Every user is assigned to a group with certain rights. The group assignment is divided into two large areas. Users that are only allowed to visit your website (**Public Front-end**) and users that can log on to the Joomla! administration (**Public Back-end**). All content in Joomla! can be assigned to these groups. The following table shows the front-end user group:

Group	Rights
Registered	A registered user can log in and see parts of the site that the visitor cannot see.
Author	The author can do everything that a registered user can. An author can also write information and modify his or her own information. There is generally a link in the user menu for this.
Editor	The editor can do everything that an author can. An editor can also write and edit all information that appears in the front end.
Publisher	The publisher can do everything that an editor can. A publisher can also write information and edit every piece of information that appears in the front end. In addition, a publisher can decide whether information is published or not.

The following table shows the back-end user group:

Group	Rights
Manager	A manager can create content and can see various pieces information about the system. He or she is not allowed to: Administer users Install modules and components Upgrade a user to super administrator or modify a super administrator Work on the menu item **Site | Global Configuration** Send a mass mailing to all users Change and/or install templates and language files
Administrator	An administrator is *not* allowed to: Upgrade a user to super administrator or modify a super administrator Work on the menu item **Site | Global Configuration** Send a mass mailing to all users Change and/or install templates and language files
Super Administrator	A super administrator can execute all functions in Joomla! administration. Only a super administrator can set up another super administrator.

In the **User Details** area you can furthermore determine whether the user should receive system emails or not.

You can see the date the user registered and the date of his or her last successful login procedure.

> **Special Users**: During the course of this book we will come across issuing rights to Special Users. A special user is any user that has more rights than a manager. At the moment it is not possible to create your own user groups in Joomla!. The special users group is therefore helpful in limiting content elements to this group. That can be very helpful if, for example, one wants to offer links to internal help files only to these special users. Modification and expansion of these groups was originally earmarked for Joomla! version 1.5.0, but is now on the roadmap for the next version and a Google Summer of Code Project team is working on it. This feature may be implemented by the time you read this book.

The **Parameters** field contains switches for the user's language. You can also select the editor that is enabled for this user, and the help server in the requested language.

Since it is possible to operate the front end and back end in Joomla! 1.5 in different languages, it is possible that you could have mixed-language administrator accounts. In the **Back-end Language** and **Front-end Language** fields, you can select the valid languages for this user account from the available languages.

You can do the same with the **User Editor**. So that you can edit texts in a user-friendly fashion, Joomla! 1.5 includes the TinyMCE WYSIWYG Editor:

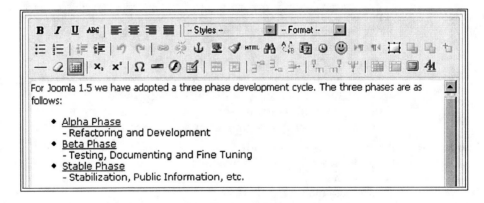

You can purchase file and image-management software from the TinyMCE website (`http://tinymce.moxiecode.com/`). There are numerous other editors such as the JCE (`http://www.cellardoor.za.net/`) and the FCKeditor (`http://www.fckeditor.net/`) that can be used in Joomla!. For clean XHTML code you can use the XStandard-lite freeware editor (`http://www.xstandard.com/`). This is a very capable WYSIWYG-Editor that outputs valid XHTML code and offers extensive options for integration. The actual editor, however, is not bundled with Joomla!, but has to be downloaded from the company's website. There is a free lite version and a Pro version that you can purchase. Firefox will notice the conversion and if necessary will reinstall the editor as a plug-in. After the installation of the editor and the selection of the user account, it is then shown in the appropriate edit fields.

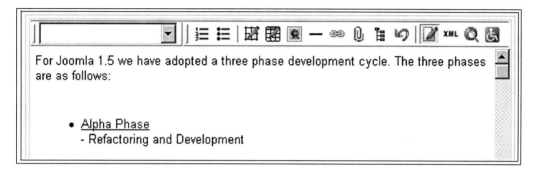

You can also select an individual **Help Site** from a list in the parameter area. Because of Joomla!'s great popularity, there are now numerous local help servers.

The **Contact Information** section finally also provides information about available contact forms that are linked with this user. Joomla! contains a component that lets you create individual contact forms (see the *Contact* section in Chapter 9 or go to **Components | Contacts | Contacts**).

You can save your changes and exit the dialog by clicking on the **Save** icon. Clicking on the **Apply** icon saves your changes and leaves you in the edit template.

New User Icon

Now that you have made a few initial changes, set up a user account with your own name. Assign the user to the group of registered users and set up whatever parameters you want. My user is called `Hagen Graf`, his user name is `hgraf`, he is not logged in at the moment (but already activated), is in the user group called **Registered** and has the **ID 63**. There is an error message due to the fact that the greeting email could not be sent. Since we are working locally and since we have not configured a mail server, the PHP interpreter cannot send emails.

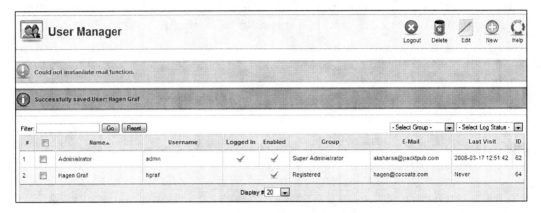

The new user can now log on to the front end by using his or her username and password. As administrator you have the choice of setting the user up the first time or allowing the user to register himself or herself. We will come back to this topic in the *Configuration* section.

Media Manager

You can envision the **Media Manager** work area like a file explorer or like an FTP program in your operating system. You can upload files with `bmp, csv, doc, epg, gif, ico, jpg, odg, odp, ods, odt, pdf, png, ppt, swf, txt, xcf, xls, BMP, CSV, DOC, EPG, GIF, ICO, JPG, ODG, ODP, ODS, ODT, PDF, PNG, PPT, SWF, TXT, XCF,` and `XLS` suffixes and administer them in various directories. This manager is especially useful if you don't have FTP access even though you have administration rights.

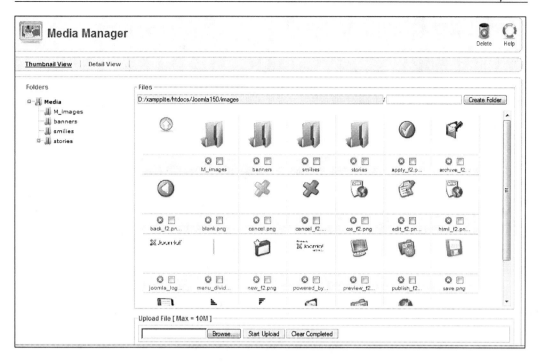

There are two tabs in the media area: **Thumbnail View,** which displays preview icons of the files, and the **Detail View,** which displays the name and size of the files in a list.

There is also a separate area for folders and files. If you click on a folder on the left, you will see the files contained in that folder on the right.

All of the media that Joomla! normally accesses are administered by the media manager. This in particular applies to the smilies and graphics in the M_images folder.

The following functions are available in the media section:

- Creating and deleting directories (you can only delete from **Detail View**)
- Uploading and deleting one or several files (you can only delete from **Detail View**)

Creating Directories

In the **Files** section you can see the path to your current directory. It has an input box and a **Create Folder** button. Enter your choice for directory name in the input box (here it is **france**) and click on the button. The directory is created and displayed with the directory icon:

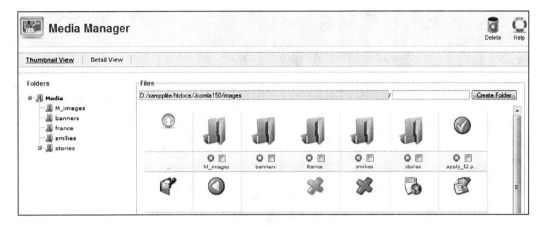

Uploading a File

There is a **Browse files** button in the lower part of the media window. You can call up your operating system's file selection dialog and then select as many files as you want for uploading.

After you click on the **Upload File** button, the files will be saved to your new directory and displayed in the overview. Later we will insert them into various pieces of content.

When you click on a thumbnail, the image is displayed in its original size on a darkened background.

 Keep in mind that it is not a good idea to display 5 MB images from a digital camera on your website in that resolution. Images should at most be 50 to 150 KB. There are people who do not have high-speed access to the Internet!

Keep the ground rule download duration for a 100 KB file (about the size of a portal's web page with pictures) displayed in the following table in mind. Even if you have one picture that is 300 KB on that page, you will lose all vistors that have ISDN and normal telephone line access.

Type of connection	Download of 100 kilobytes of data
DSL	Depending on the DSL provider, less than one second!
ISDN	about 15 seconds
Modem (56 k)	about 25 seconds

Global Configuration

In the **Global Configuration** section you can define all the settings that are valid for the entire website. The values of the variables are saved in the configuration.php file. Vital information like access data for the database server for instance, and 'lesser' parameters such as the predetermined length of displayed lists are stored in this file. The work area is divided into three tabs:

- **Site Settings**
- **System Settings**
- **Server Settings**

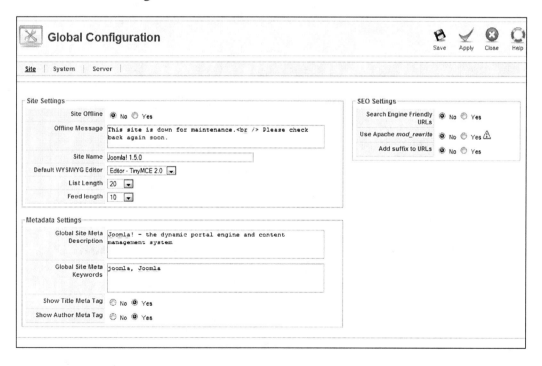

Site Section

The site section in turn is divided into three visual areas: **Site** settings, **Metadata** settings, and **SEO** settings.

Site Settings

We will discuss each of these settings in detail.

Site Offline: If you want to make changes to your website and inform your visitors of this, then you can click on the **Yes** radio button in this area.

Offline Message: The text that you enter here is displayed in the top area of your website when it is "offline". Try it: Set **Site Offline** to **Yes**, click the **Apply** icon and go to your website. The website can no longer be accessed. Users that have rights to the administration area (**Rights | Manager**) can still log on.

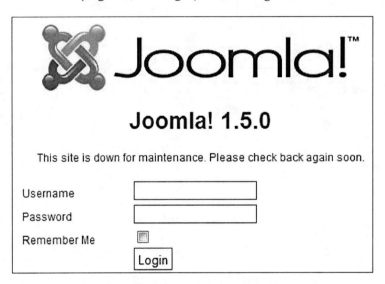

Site Name: The name of the site that you entered during the installation. It shows up, for instance, in the header of the browser, as the sender of system emails, on the newsfeed, and in various other places that have to do with easy recognition of your website.

Default WYSIWYG Editor: WYSIWYG is the acronym for **What you see is what you get** or (which some say is much closer to reality, *This is what you wanted, now you have it!*). This term comes from the early days of graphical user interfaces when it first became possible to see text on the screen the way it would look when it was printed. Today it is less about the printing, and more about how it will look on your website.

On the Internet, you will normally fill out forms without any formatting options. The formatting is done via HTML tags or program-specific mnemonics. A WYSIWYG-editor is more user-friendly since you just have to click on the appropriate icons, similar to editing text. The editor is automatically enabled in the text fields that need formatting. It works with all popular current browsers. Joomla! also offers the option to install other HTML editors, such as XStandard lite. By default, Joomla! currently uses the TinyMCE editor.

List Lenght: Lists such as news and links will surface all over the place on your website. With this you set the default number of items a list should have.

Metadata Settings

You will find the settings for Metadata in this section.

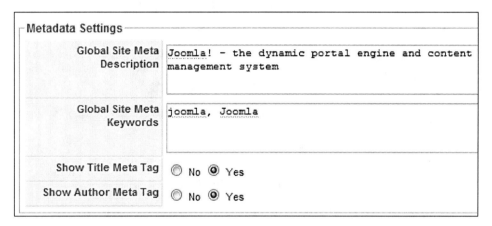

Metadata are data about data, for instance a description of your website. Metadata are important with search engines and are written in XHTML. Exactly how important metadata are in the rating by search engines is debatable. However, metadata represent a good way to describe your website in short and precise words. If you check out the HTML source code of a Joomla! site, you will see the following meta tags in the top area.

```
<head>
  <meta http-equiv="Content-Type" content="text/html;
                 charset=utf-8" />
  <meta name="robots" content="index, follow" />
  <meta name="keywords" content="joomla, Joomla" />
  <meta name="description" content="Joomla! - the dynamic portal
                 engine and content management system" />
  <meta name="generator" content="Joomla! 1.5 - Open Source
                 Content Management" />
```

Global Site Meta Description: This description of site content is often displayed as the result by search engines. You should pay special attention to this tag, since the user who has entered a search term often uses this information to make a decision on whether to visit a site or not. You can add further information to the global description with additional descriptions on each individual page.

Global Site Meta Keywords: Keywords are the pivotal relevant information of a document. You should list the most important terms of your website with them. Some search engines particularly index keywords. The individual words are separated by commas; several words can be entered between two commas with normal spaces in between. The keywords should be limited to a maximum of 1,000 characters; more than that will not be read by the search engines. Note that the use of fewer key words can help each individual word get a higher validity in the search engine. Deliberate carefully about which are the most often used keywords and which are likely to be searched the most. You can enter additional keywords to add to the global keywords on each individual page of your website.

Show Title Meta Tag: The content title for individual content pages is shown as a meta tag, for instance:

```
<meta name="title" content="Welcome to Joomla!" />
```

Show Author Meta Tag: The author's name for individual content pages is displayed as a meta tag, for instance:

```
<meta name="author" content="Administrator" />
```

SEO (Search Engine Optimization) Settings

This option is about search engine-friendly URLs. Normally a Joomla! URL looks like this:

```
http://www.example.com/Joomla150/index.php?option=com_contact&Itemid=3
```

This type of URL is not normally stored by search engines, since the search engine assumes that the content is constructed dynamically and will probably change soon.

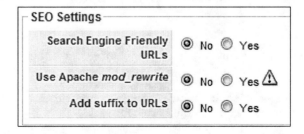

Search Engine Friendly URLs: With this switch you can transform a dynamic URL into a search engine-friendly URL. If you set this switch to **Yes**, the link will look something like this:

```
http://localhost/joomla150/contact
```

Use Apache *mod_rewrite*: This switch activates the mod_rewrite module. The principle is based on a function of the Apache web server, which can manipulate URLs at will with its *rewrite engine*. Besides activating the switch, you also have to rename the `htaccess.txt` file in the Joomla! directory to `.htaccess`. In Windows, such a renaming is only possible with particular programs, for example, with the Ultraedit editor (`http://www.ultraedit.com/`) or in the command line with the following command:

```
rename htaccess.txt .htaccess
```

Under Linux, the renaming works without any problem; the file, however, subsequently is no longer displayed in its FTP client (depending on the server configuration). In addition, the provider may not permit `.htaccess` files, since they represent a security risk for the web server.

In order for your Windows/XAMPP site to also be transformed into a search-engine friendly URL, you have to edit the following file:

```
[drive]:\xampplite\apache\conf\httpd.conf
```

Open this file under Windows with a programming editor or with WordPad and look for the following line:

```
#LoadModule rewrite_module modules/mod_rewrite.so
```

Remove the # sign from the above line, so it reads:

```
LoadModule rewrite_module modules/mod_rewrite.so
```

and save the file. Then start the Apache web server again from the XAMMP lite control panel. The search-engine friendly links should now work.

Add a suffix to URLs: This appends a `.html` to the URL after the file name extension so that the site looks like an HTML site. The effect that this has on search engines, however, is debatable.

System Section

System Settings

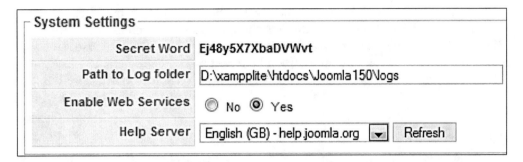

Secret Word: When you install Joomla!, a random sequence of characters that is a kind of seal is created. This secret word is used in connection with the XML/RPC-interface. This is to ensure that in the future only registered and/or authorized remote systems can use this interface to get access.

Path to the Log folder: If you want to use Joomla!'s log function, you naturally have to enter a path. The path is predefined by default and can be changed here. This path should be outside the publically accessible path, in other words outside your htdocs document directory.

Activate Web Services: Joomla! is equipped with an xmprpc interface. This interface makes services available that can be activated or deactivated. Outbound XML-RPC connections are not affected by this, only inbound ones!

Help Server: Here you define the default help server. You can configure a separate help server for every user account.

It is also possible to access a local help server. The help texts have to be loaded in the appropriate language (in our case German de-DE) into the C:\xampplite\htdocs\Joomla150\administrator\help\de-DE directory. Automatic installation for these help texts is not available at the moment. The German texts are created by the German tanslation team.

Users Settings

In this area you will find the global settings for user accounts.

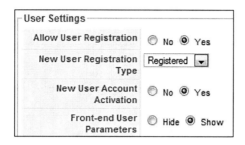

Allow User Registration: Here you can select whether you want to permit users to do their own registration or not. If you operate a company site, you could set up user accounts for your coworkers, but prevent them from creating their own account. With a community site, on the other hand, it is desirable for users to register themselves.

New User Registration Type: Here you can define to which user group the newly registered user will be assigned.

New User Account Activation: In order to protect yourself from automated programs that could automatically create 20,000 user accounts on your site, you can ask for separate activation. After registration, the user gets a one-time automatic email sent to the address entered by him or her. This email contains a link that activates the account. After activation he or she can log on normally.

Front-end User Parameters: With this you define whether the users can set up their own language and time-zone parameters:

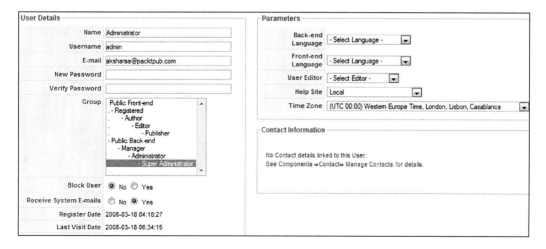

Media Settings

This is where you configure the parameters for the media area. You can define the extensions for files that are acceptable to be uploaded and paths into which these files are to be saved:

Media Settings	
Legal Extensions (File Types)	bmp,csv,doc,epg,gif,ico,jpg,odg,odp,ods,odt,pdf,png,ppt,
Maximum Size (in bytes)	10000000
Path to File Folder	images
Path to Image Folder	images/stories
Restrict Uploads	○ No ◉ Yes
Check MIME Types	○ No ◉ Yes
Legal Image Extensions (File Types)	bmp,gif,jpg,png
Ignored Extensions	
Legal MIME Types	image/jpeg,image/gif,image/png,image/bmp,application/
Illegal MIME Types	text/html

Besides the file extensions, you can also define MIME types (http://en.wikipedia.org/wiki/MIME). This helps to have the content of files checked for security. If the necessary modules for this are not enabled in your Apache web server, you can make sure that front-end users can only upload images with the **Restrict Uploads** switch.

You can also define the maximum size up to the predetermined PHP maximum size (see the following note).

 The maximum file upload size is ultimately determined by the PHP configuration of your provider's server. Here it is 16 MB. Larger files have to be uploaded with FTP or the upload value in the php.ini configuration file has to be changed.

Debug Settings

Programmers talk about debugging when they are looking for errors. This term has evolved over the years. A bug is a beetle, and 50 years ago it was indeed beetles that got comfortable next to the warm vaccuum tubes of a computer and thereby caused shorts every now and then. Debugging (removing the beetles) was to be taken literally in those days. Today these bugs are errors in software, for instance database queries that don't work.

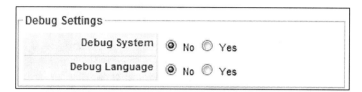

Debug System: After activating this function, the database queries are displayed below the website. Sixteen database queries are required in order to generate a single Joomla! page:

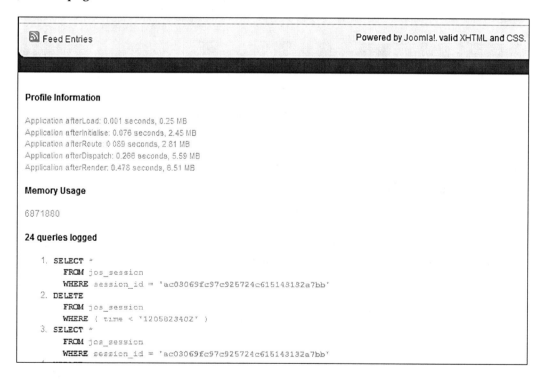

Debug Language: The debug messages, in this case, refer to language strings. The accessed language files are displayed.

Thick black marks are positioned before and after all of the identifiers so that you won't forget that you are in debug mode:

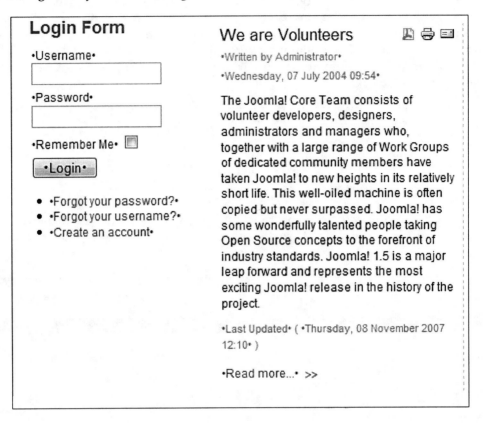

Cache Settings

A **cache** is a temporary storage facility. Your browser, for example, has a picture cache, which makes pictures that have already been downloaded once available faster from then on. Joomla! uses a similar mechanism on the server to cache pages generated by PHP. This option can drastically reduce response time with frequently visited pages.

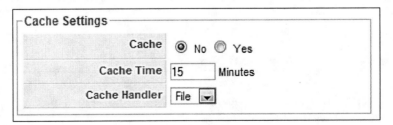

Cache: This is where you enable and disable the cache.

Time: You define the time that has to pass before content in the cache has to be renewed.

Cache Handler: You define here whether the cache is to be file-based or database-based (at the moment only file caching has been implemented).

Session Settings

Session Lifetime: Whenever you log on as a user, you create a so-called session. If you don't log out, the session will be terminated after the duration entered here.

Session Handler: Here you define whether it should be a file-based or database-based session. In high-traffic websites the database-based method is substantially faster than the file-based method.

Server Section

In this tab you configure the technical information of your server environment.

Server Settings

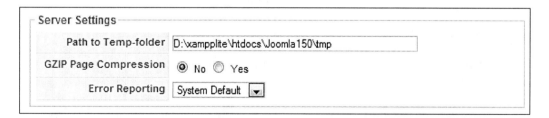

Path To The Temp-folder: Joomla! creates temporary files, for example during an upload. These have to be stored somewhere in the interim and this is where you can decide where that is.

GZIP Page Compression: You can enable compression of the pages with this. If both the browser and the web server support this function, the pages are sent in ZIP format and extracted at the client browser. This can significantly increase the speed of a page download, in particular with slow Internet connections. If your server handles a heavy load, you should only use this option if the respective GZIP libraries are directly installed at the server level. Depending on server configuration, it is possible that the server runs faster without this option!

Error Reporting: PHP's own error reporting mechanism is activated with these switches. Error logs are not sent to a file for future evaluation, but messages are displayed directly in the browser! The following table shows the error report categories:

Option	Description
System Default	This adopts the settings from the `php.ini` confi guration file.
None	Errors are not logged. This setting is recommended for working sites in order that an attacker is not shown possible points of attack.
Simple	Errors and warning messages are logged. This setting is equivalent to the parameter: `error_reporting (E_ERROR|E_WARNING|E_PARSE)`.
Maximum	Errors, warning messages and instructions are logged. This setting is equivalent to the parameter: `error_reporting (E_ALL)`.

Locale Settings

Time Zone: This setting can be used to display the time zone your server operates under; for example, if the server that Joomla! runs on is located in the USA, but the site is meant for visitors in Germany. The base for the calculation of the time is UTC (`http://en.wikipedia.org/wiki/Coordinated_Universal_Time`).

FTP Settings

File Transfer Protocol (FTP) is used to circumvent problems with security settings at providers. If it is not permitted to upload files with PHP, the FTP method is used instead. Enter the access data for your provider's FTP server here. The **FTP Root** field deserves a special mention. Depending on your provider, you are linked to a particular directory after your FTP logon. At this point, you have to report the path of your Joomla! installation relative to the access point of the FTP connection, for example `/htdocs/Joomla150`.

```
┌─FTP Settings────────────────────────────────────────────┐
│              Enable FTP   ● No  ○ Yes                     │
│              FTP Host    127.0.0.1                        │
│              FTP Port    21                               │
│           FTP Username   [                ]               │
│           FTP Password   [                ]               │
│              FTP Root    [                        ]       │
└──────────────────────────────────────────────────────────┘
```

Database Settings

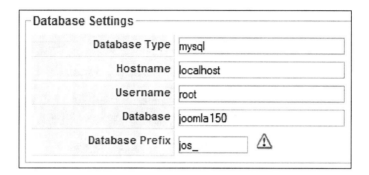

You can change the parameters of your database here. Please keep in mind that you can corrupt Joomla! if you make a typing error here. That means that you will no longer be able to access the back end.

If something like that happens, you can edit the configuration.php file with a text editor. All the settings that you make in the **Site | Global Configuration** menu are stored in variables in the configuration.php file.

```php
<?php
class JConfig {
        var $dbtype = 'mysql';
        var $host = 'localhost';
        var $user = 'root';
        var $password = '';
        var $db = 'Joomla150';
        var $dbprefix = 'jos_';
        // …
        // many other variables
        // ---
}
?>
```

Mail Settings

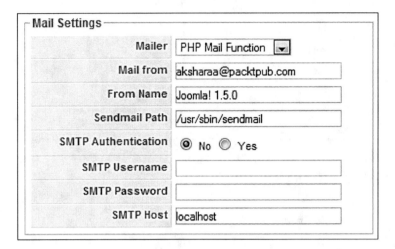

In this tab you can make all the decisions about sending emails from Joomla!

Mailer: Here you decide whether you want to use the built-in PHP mail function, the Sendmail program or another e-mail account such as Yahoo!, Google, or GMX.

Mail from: This email address is automatically entered as sender of Joomla!-generated mail.

From Name: This name is also automatically entered as sender of Joomla!-generated mail.

Sendmail Path: If you want to use the Sendmail program that presumably can be used on all Linux servers instead of the PHP mail function, you have to enter the path to the program here.

SMTP Authentication: Select if you want to use an external mail server (Yahoo!, GMX, your own server).

SMTP Username: Your username with this email provider.

SMTP Password: Your password with this email provider.

SMTP Host: The SMPT server of this email provider.

Logout

By clicking on this menu item you are logged out from the back end and are automatically redirected into the front end.

Summary

In this chapter we saw how to customize the Site menu. In the next chapter we will learn about the Menus menu.

7
The Menus Menu

There are numerous menus in the front end. They are often displayed as standalone boxes. The menu items are generally arranged one below the other.

Menus can also be integrated into the design horizontally so that at first sight they aren't even recognizable as cohesive menus.

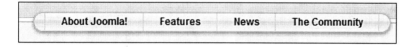

CSS menus, which can even be transparent, are very cool. Here is an example from joomlart.com:

These menus and the menu links are dynamically administered in Joomla! from database content in the **Menus** work area. Joomla! has six different menus in the sample data (main menu, top menu, other menu, user menu, example pages, and key concepts). The **Top Menu** is a horizontal menu; the other menus are vertical. Each menu is coupled with a so-called module, which is administered in the module manager.

Menus

By clicking on this menu item, you get an overview of the available menus. You can also access the content of these menus by means of the menu bar—**Menus | Main Menu, Top Menu**, ... or by clicking the respective menu link in the overview.

This **Menu Manager** serves as an overview and shows you the number of **Published** and **Unpublished** menu items, the number of menu items that are in the **Trash** can and the respective menu **ID**. In this section you can, for instance, copy a menu or create a new one.

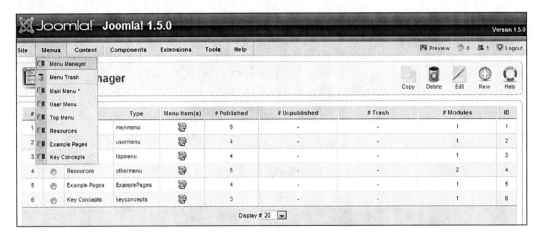

Customizing an Existing Menu

Experiment a little with the menus to get a feel for things. The following edit steps are the same for all menus. Go to the menu item **Menus | Main Menu**. You will see a listing of the menu items that turn up in the **mainmenu**.

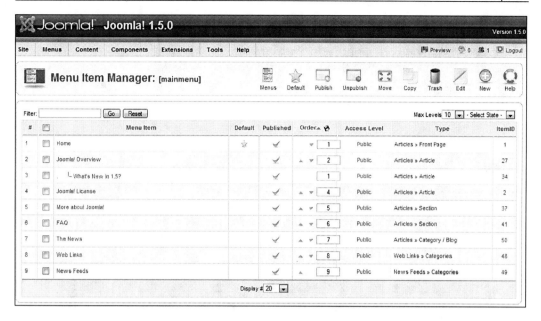

Several functions can be executed in the table with a simple mouse click. By clicking on the checkmark, you can enable or disable a menu link. You can change the order of the items by clicking on the triangles or by typing numbers into the fields under **Order**. If you use the numbers method, you have to click on the disk symbol in the header in order to effect the change.

In the **Access Level** column, via mouse click you can decide whether the menu is available to all users (**Public**), only to registered users (**Registered**), or only to a particular circle of users (**Special**). The menu items are then displayed or hidden, independent of the user's rights.

Menus Icon

If you click on this icon, you are taken to the menu overview screen.

Default Icon

The menu item that is marked as default here with a star is displayed as the start page when someone calls up the URL of your website. At the moment this is the menu item **Home**, but you can designate any element that you want as the start page. Just mark the checkbox and click on the **Default** icon.

Publish/Unpublish Icon

The status of a content element can either be published (activated) or unpublished (deactivated). You can toggle this status individually by clicking the green checkmark and/or the red cross, or marking the checkbox and subsequently clicking on the appropriate icon. If you follow the later method, you can toggle several menu items at the same time.

Move Icon

This entails the moving of menu entries. Let's move the text **More about Joomla!** into the top menu. Select the respective menu elements or even several menu elements and click the **Move** icon. This opens a form, listing the available menus. On the right you will see the elements that you want to move:

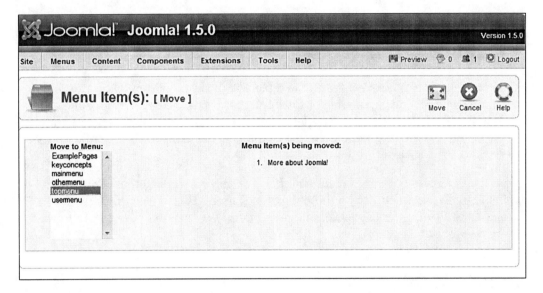

Select the menu into which you would like to move the marked menu items. Here, we have moved **More about Joomla!** from **Main Menu** into the **Top Menu**. You can admire the results in the front end.

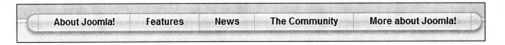

Copy Icon

You can also copy menu items. To do that, select one or more menu items and click on the **Copy** icon. Just as with moving, a form with the available menus opens. Select the menu into which you want to copy the marked menu entries.

Trash Icon

In order to protect you from inadvertently deleting items, when editing them you cannot delete them immediately; you can only throw them in the trash.

To throw them into trash can, select one or several menu elements and click on the **Trash** icon. The marked menu items are then dumped into the trash can. You can display the content of the trash can by clicking on **Menus | Menu Trash**.

Edit Icon (Edit Menu Items)

Here you can modify an existing menu, for instance the **Web Links**. After clicking on the name **Web Links** you will see the edit form for menu elements:

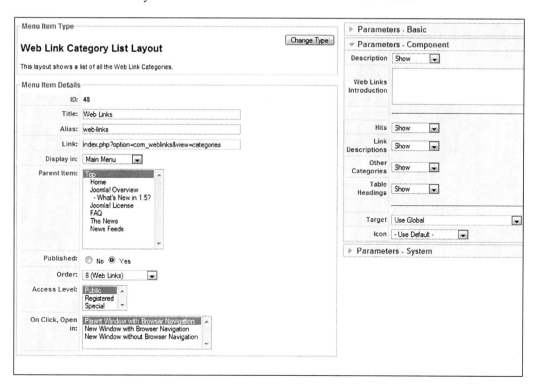

The form is divided into three parts.

- **Menu Item Type**
- **Menu Item Details**
- **Parameters**

Menu Item Type

Every menu item is of a particular type. We will get into greater details when we create new menus. For instance, a menu item can refer to an installed Joomla! component, a content element, a link to an external website, or many other things. You can see what the type of the link is in this section; in our case it is a link to the Joomla! weblinks component, and you can also see a button with the label **Change Type**. If you click on that button, you get the following screen:

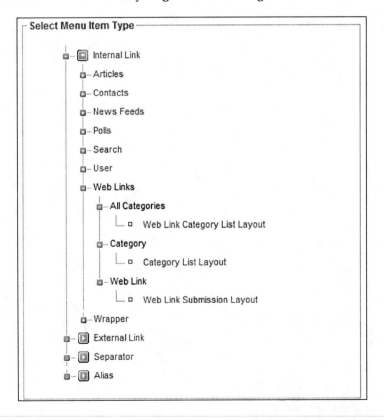

This manager is new in Joomla! version 1.5 and really handy. In version 1.0.x there was no option to change the type of a menu item. You had to delete the old menu item and create a new one. Now you can change the display to a single category or to a link-suggestion menu item, with which you invite other users to suggest links.

Now close this; we will get back to it when we create a new menu.

Menu Item Details

It contains the following options:

ID: Everything in an administration requires an ID number and so does our menu item. In this case the menu item has the ID number **48**. Joomla! assigns this number for internal administration purposes at the time the item is created. This number cannot be changed.

Title: This is the name of the menu and it will be displayed that way on your website.

Alias: This is the name of the search-engine friendly URL after the domain name. When this is enabled, the URL for this menu will look as follows:

```
http://localhost/joomla150/web-links
```

Link: This is the request for a component, in other words also the part of the URL after the domain name with which you call up your website. In this case it is `index.php?option=com_weblinks&view=categories`.

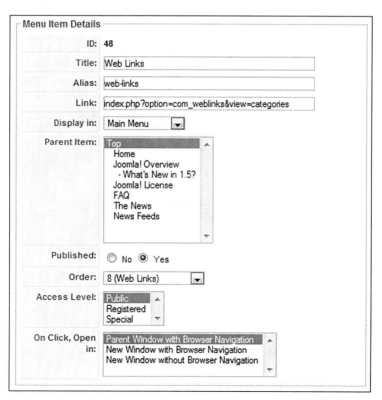

Display in: With this you can change the place where the item is displayed; in other words you can move it to another menu. The options field presents you with a list of the available menus.

Parent Item: Of course menus can also contain nested, tree-like items. **Top** means that the item is at the uppermost level. The rest of the items represent existing menu items. If, for instance, you classify and save **Web Links** under **The News**, the display on the item list and the display on your website are changed. The following figures show the change. The menu item **Web Links** has now moved into **The News** on your website. So you have to first click on **The News** in order to see the **Web Links** item. Your website can easily and effectively be structured like a database tree in this manner.

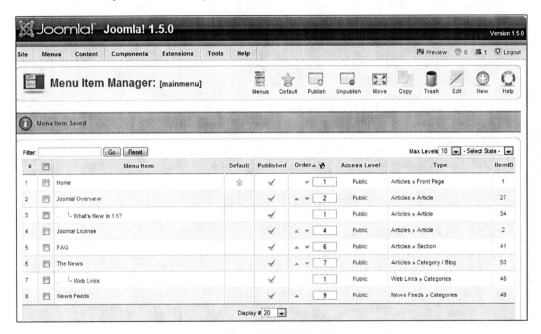

Published: With this you can publish a menu item.

Order: From the options list, you can select after which link you want to position this link.

Access Level: You can restrict users that can see this list.

On Click, Open in: A very handy option that influences the behavior of the link. The page is either opened in the existing window or in a new browser window after clicking. You can also define whether the new window will be displayed with or without browser navigation.

Parameters

The possible parameters of a menu item depend on the type of the item. A simple link, of course, has fewer parameters than a configurable list or for example the front page link.

In this case we have a link to the categories (these components will be described in detail in Chapter 9). The number and type of parameters depend on the type of the menu item. You can open and collapse the parameter fields by clicking on the header. If the parameter fields are open, the arrow next to header points down.

Parameters–Basic

The basic parameters are the same for all menu links.

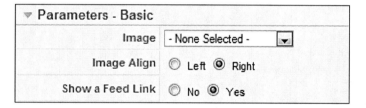

Image: Here you can specify an image that must be in the root directory of the media manager (`/images/stories/`). Depending on the template, this picture is displayed on the left, next to the menu item.

Image Align: You can decide if the image should be on the left or right.

Show a Feed Link: It is possible to create an RSS feed for every list display in Joomla! 1.5. This could be desirable or undesirable depending on the content of the list. In this case, with list displays, RSS feed links that contain the list items are enabled in the browser.

Parameter—Component

This section of parameters deals explicitly with the component addressed in the link, in this case the **Web Links** component. It consists of several levels. When we first click it, the available categories and a default text are displayed in our configuration.

Weblinks

We are regularly out on the Web. When we find a great site we list it.

- Joomla! Specific Links   (6)

If you click on **Joomla! Specific Links,** you will see a table with the respective links:

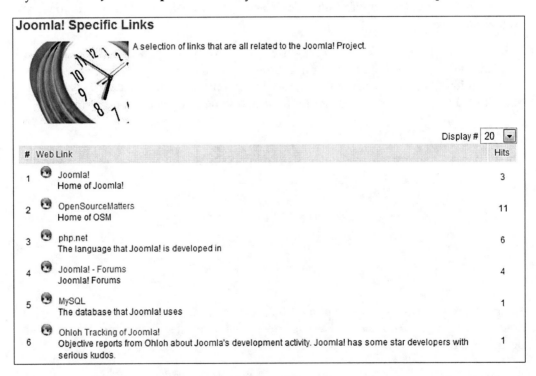

Joomla! Specific Links

A selection of links that are all related to the Joomla! Project.

Display # 20 ▾

#	Web Link	Hits
1	Joomla! Home of Joomla!	3
2	OpenSourceMatters Home of OSM	11
3	php.net The language that Joomla! is developed in	6
4	Joomla! - Forums Joomla! Forums	4
5	MySQL The database that Joomla! uses	1
6	Ohloh Tracking of Joomla! Objective reports from Ohloh about Joomla's development activity. Joomla! has some star developers with serious kudos.	1

You can change this construct in the component-specific parameters:

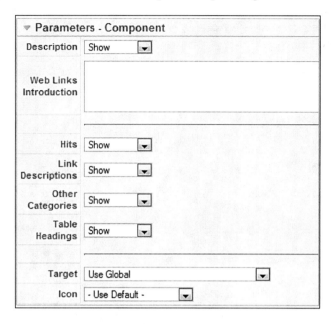

Description: The header above the categories can be displayed or hidden with this.

Web Links Introduction: You can assign an individual header with this:

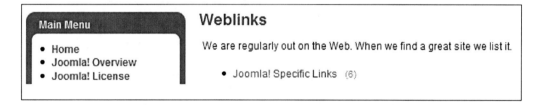

Hits: The visitors' hits on the respective links of your pages are tracked in the hits column. You can display or hide this hits column.

Link Descriptions: With this you can display or hide the description that is below a link in the link list.

Other Categories: When you are in the links table display, you will either see the default text or the texts that you have set up in the parameters. Below that, there is a list of usable categories and sections (if there are other categories). This list can be displayed or hidden.

Table Headings: With this option you can display or hide table headers above the links.

Parameters—System

You will find additional parameters here that influence the appearance of the link.

Page Title: Here you can enter text for the page title; this will be displayed in the top bar on the website and in the browser.

Show the Page Title: This is where you decide to display or to hide the page title.

Page Class Suffix: You can enter a text string here, for example my_menuitems. This description is then appended to the class name in the HTML code. You have to set up a corresponding class in the CSS file so that the block will appear with a different design.

SSL Enabled: Here you can select whether the created link supports the secure HTTPS protocol. This selection requires a functional SSL environment on your server. The SSL encryption works without any problems on your local XAMMP Lite environment.

New Icon

This icon is used to create new menus. We will learn about this in the section *Creating a New Menu*.

Menu Trash

The trash can collects your deleted menu items:

If you select the deleted elements and click the **Restore** icon, you can retrieve them all from the garbage can:

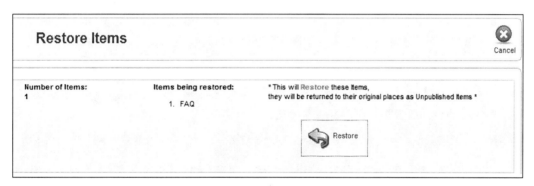

If you click on the **Delete** icon, they are all irretrievably deleted.

Creating a New Menu

In this section, we will create a new menu named **Joomla! 1.5 Book** with a link to `http://www.joomla.org/`, which is to be displayed in a new window. We want it positioned on the left side below the main menu.

Go to **Menus | Menu Manager | New** and enter the internal name of the menu in the **Menu Type** field. Make sure that you pick a meaningful name without spaces. Type the name that you want to be displayed later on your website into the **Title** field. The menu consists of the internal, actual menu into which you can add menu links and a corresponding module, which can be positioned later.

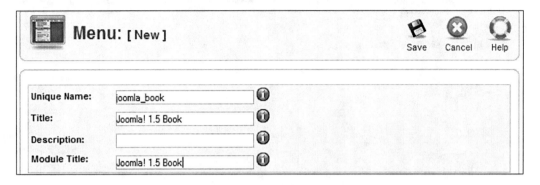

Unique Name: This is the name that Joomla! uses in the code. You are not allowed to use any spaces. Here we are using `joomla_book`. This name will not be shown on the website; it strictly exists to create a link between the menu and the module.

Title: The name of the menu. Here it is `Joomla! 1.5 Book` (with the spaces).

Description: A description of the menu. This description is only displayed internally, in the back end, for instance in the display of lists.

Module Title: The name of the module—`Joomla! 1.5 Book` here as well.

After you click on **Save,** Joomla! creates a new module with the specified parameters. You are redirected into the menu overview and you will see a new menu there that is still empty of items.

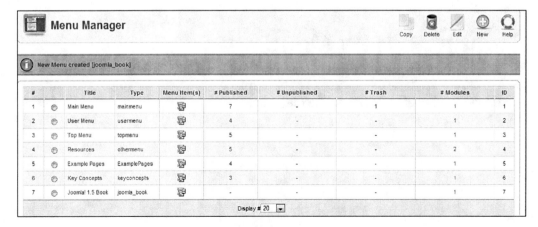

If you click on the pencil icon on the right, next to the Joomla! 1.5 Book link, you will end up in the overview screen for the content of the Joomla! 1.5 Book menu.

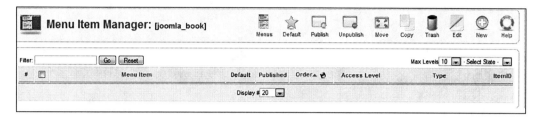

Since there isn't any content yet, click on the **New** icon. You can now select the menu item type from different areas on the selection screen, which appears now. Since we are still in infancy with our Joomla! knowledge, let's just insert a simple external link to an external website.

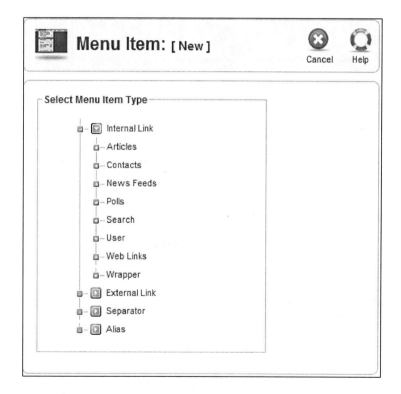

To do that, click on the **External Link** button. You can now define the details and the parameters of the link.

Title: The name of the link that appears in the menu (Joomla! Project Website)

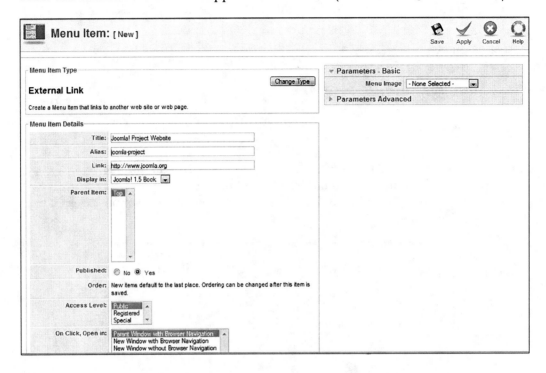

Parent Item: Since this is the first item, there are no parent elements yet.

Alias: Name of the short URL (joomla-project).

Link: The link to the page (http://www.joomla.org).

Display in: Of course in our new **Joomla! 1.5 Book** menu.

Published: Click on **Yes** for the menu to be published.

Order: Since this is the first item, there is no order yet. New items are put at the end by default. The order can be changed after the first save.

Access Level: Should this menu item be visible to our **Public** (visitors), **Registered**, or **Special** groups?

On Click, Open in: What should happen when someone clicks on the link? Should the target be displayed in the same browser window, a new browser window with navigation, or a new browser window without navigation?

When you click on **Apply**, your information is saved. If you click on **Save**, your information is saved and the dialog is closed.

You have just created a menu and provided it with a link. But before it can be displayed in the front end, you will have to publish the newly created module. In the menu, click on **Extensions | Module Manager** and there on the red cross in the **Activated** column. You can position the new menu below the main menu by using the triangles.

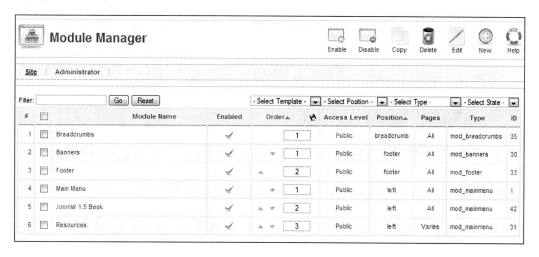

If you call up your website now, your new menu Joomla! 1.5 Book menu should appear.

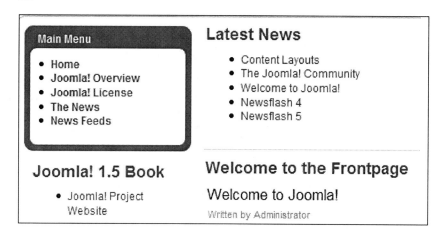

Unfortunately your menu looks different than the main menu above it. The blue border is missing. That attribute is defined in the CSS file of the template and can, of course, be modified. For that, the module has to invoke a particular CSS class. In our case, the class with which our menu is displayed is called `module`. You can check that by taking a look at the HTML source code of the website:

```
<div class="module"><div><div><div>
<h3>Joomla! 1.5 Book</h3>
<ul class="menu">
<li class="item54">
<a href="http://www.joomla.org" target="_blank">
<span>Joomla! Project Website</span>
</a>
</li></ul></div></div></div></div>
```

The main menu, on the other hand, invokes the class `module_menu`. Source code for the main menu:

```
<div class="module_menu"><div><div><div>
<h3>main menu</h3>
<ul class="menu">
<li id="current" class="active item1">
<a href="http://localhost/joomla150/">
<span>start page</span>
</a>
</li>
... additional links ...
</ul>
</div></div></div></div> </ul>
</div>
```

During the editing of the module, you can ensure that the new menu also invokes that class. Click on **Extensions | Module Manager | Joomla! 1.5 Book**. Simply enter the missing text, `_menu`, into the **Module Class Suffix** field.

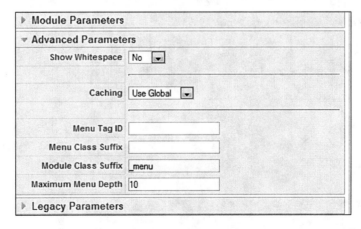

After this modification, your menu will be displayed the way you wanted. If you click on the **Joomla! 1.5 Book** link now, a browser window with navigation should open and the website of the project should appear.

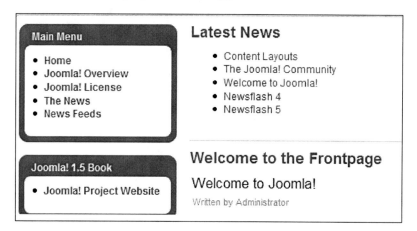

Summary

In this chapter we saw how to customize the Menus menu. In the next chapter we will learn about the Content menu.

8
Content Menu

The **Content** menu contains everything that is associated with content. Content in terms of text formatted with HTML is called an *article* in Joomla!. Joomla! articles are organized according to the following structure:

```
Content -+- Section1 -+- Category1 -+- Content1
         |            |             +- Content2
         |            |             +- Content3
         |            +- Category2  +- Content1
         |                          +- Content2
         +- Section2 -+- Category1 -+- Content1
         |            |             +- Content2
         |            |             +- Content3
         |            +- Category2  +- Content1
         |                          +- Content2
         +- Static Content -+- Content1
                            +- Content2
                            +- Content3
```

This structure can be compared to the file tree on the hard disk. You can create as many sections and categories as you want. You can use this structure with an article but you don't have to. You have the option of archiving elements. In that case, the structure is carried over into the archive.

This structure has advantages and disadvantages. The biggest advantage is that, since there is a structure, the administrator must abide by a certain hierarchy. This enhances the overview to begin with and serves to keep the website manageable.

The disadvantage is that this two-stage structure cannot be changed at the moment and therefore some administrators feel limited in their ability to individualize their website. But this is mostly subjective. By using a clever combination of menus and content, every imaginable navigational structure can be produced.

The biggest issue usually is: *What do I want to present and in what context?*

The **Content** menu offers several workspaces for working on content and structures:

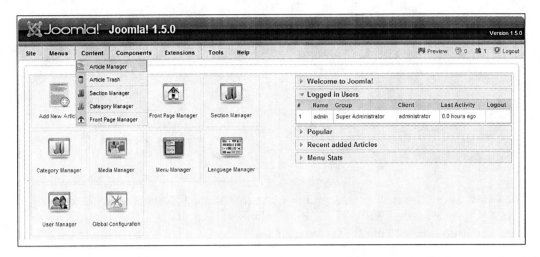

Article Manager

The menu item **Content Articles** menu takes you to the overview screen for your articles. This is the central control for the organization of the articles on your website.

You can filter the displayed content according to **Section**, **Category**, **Author**, and **State** in your options lists in the information area. There is also a search field, which you can use to search through the titles.

There is a navigation bar in the lower space that you can use to leaf through the content. One of the options lists lets you define how many items you want to see in the list. The setting that you entered previously is the default.

The list is sorted by **Section, Category, Author,** and **Title**. You can change this sorting order by clicking on the respective column view.

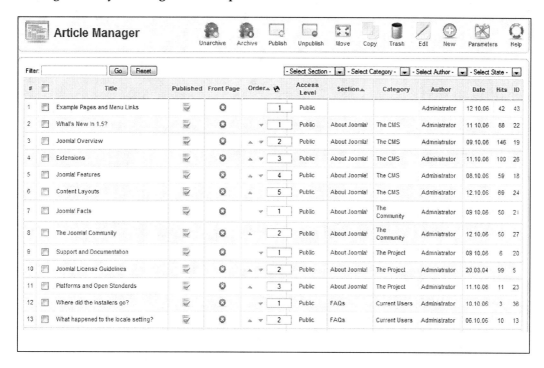

Description of the Articles List

There is a checkbox in front of the title that you can use to select the items that you want to edit. If you select the checkbox in the header, all the items in the list are selected.

The **Title** is the link for the edit mode of the article:

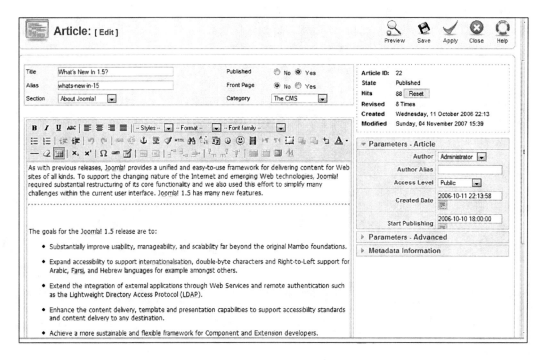

Published displays whether the article is published (green checkmark) or not (red cross). Besides these two symbols there is also the possibility that the article has past its expiry date and that the element is already in the archive. There is a legend for the icons in the footer of the page. The symbols for pending (in wait mode) and expired are also explained there.

Front Page displays whether the article is published on the start page (green checkmark) or not (red cross).

In the **Order** column, you can move the items by clicking on the arrows for each article. You can also sort the items by entering a number and subsequently clicking on the disc icon in the header.

Under **Access Level**, you can see green **Public** links. You can change the access rights between the three groups of **Public, Registered**, and **Special** by clicking on one of these links.

Section is the section that the article is assigned to. If you click on the link, you are taken to the **Section: [Edit]**. Uncategorized corresponds to static content from Joomla! 1.0.

Category is the structure underneath the sections to which this item has been assigned. Clicking on the link takes you to the **Category: [Edit]**.

Author is the author of the article. Clicking on this link will take you to the **User: [Edit]**.

Date is the creation date of the article.

ID is the number of the dataset inside the database table. This **ID** will show up again in the **URL** for this article.

There were two text fields in Joomla! 1.0.x. One was for the teaser and the other for the rest of the text. This separation has been discontinued in Joomla! 1.5, but the functionality remains. You can now insert the appropriate separators (**continue reading, page break**) with a mouse click in a single window. The separation of static and dynamic content elements has also been discontinued. Static articles are simply **uncategorized** articles and these can also be published on the front page.

Editing Icons for an Article

To edit one or more articles in one go, you have several functions available:

Archive, Unarchive

The idea behind an archive is that you don't delete older content, but rather preserve it for later use. You can archive the articles in **Article Manager** by clicking on the **Archive** icon. The article is then displayed in gray color in the overview:

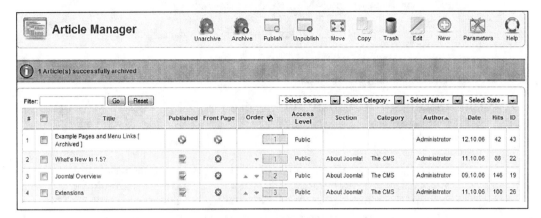

If you select **Archived** in the **State** filter, you can limit the display to archived articles. The archived articles can be shown in various positions on the website.

Approve, Block

Here you can approve articles for publishing or block them.

Move, Copy

You can move or copy one or several articles into other categories and sections here.

Trash Basket

Here you can toss one or several articles into the Trash basket.

Parameters

In the article parameters area, you can define defaults for all articles. These settings initially apply to every article. If you want to give an individual layout to an article, you can do so in the article management parameters.

 In Joomla! 1.0 many of the presets could be found in **Global Configuration**. With Joomla! 1.5, those presets were removed and put into the individual components. So now you will find the presets for articles in the central article management section and presets for logging of search strings, for example, in the search component.

Creating a New Article

Let us use the example of a piece of *News* that you want to display on the front page to go through the creation of an article. Click on **New**. An input template appears with a large editor text field as shown in the following figure.

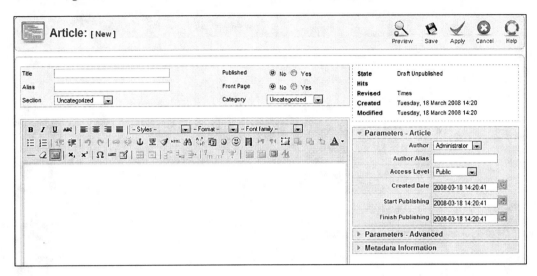

Enter a **Title** and some text. Select:

- **Section: Uncategorized**
- **Category: Uncategorized**
- **Published**: Yes
- **Frontpage**: Yes

Click on the **Save** icon and take a look at your website. Your piece of news is indeed on the front page.

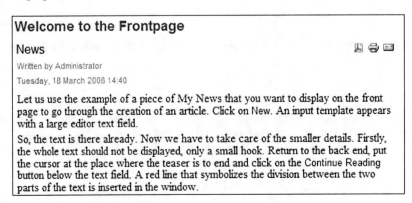

So, the text is there already. Now we have to take care of the smaller details. Firstly, the whole text should not be displayed, only a small hook. Return to the back end, put the cursor at the place where the teaser is to end and click on the **Read more** button below the text field. A red line that symbolizes the division between the two parts of the text is inserted in the window:

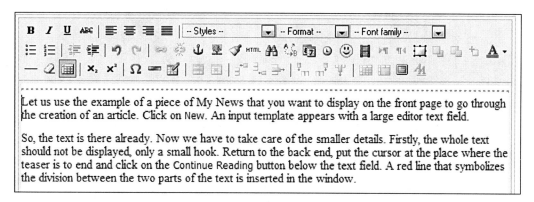

You can also use the editor tools to format the text. After you click on **Save**, your front page will look like the following:

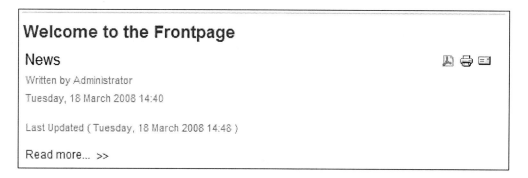

Parameters

There are various parameter blocks here as well, just like in the creation of menus. You can see general information about the article above the parameter blocks.

Article ID: The dataset number of the article.

State: Current status (currently published).

Hits: How often this article has been accessed. If you click the **Reset** button, the hits are reset to **0**.

Revised: In the beginning, the article has version number 1. Every time it is saved, the version number increases by 1. (This provides a foundation for the planned version administration).

Created: Date of creation.

Modified: Date of editing.

Parameters—Article

The first block represents the base parameters:

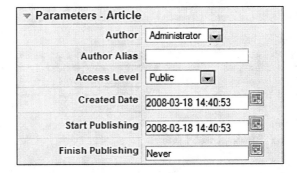

Author: You can select the writer of the piece of news from a list. All existing users are displayed in this list.

Author Alias: You can enter an author pseudonym that will then be displayed on the website.

Access Level: This option is used for providing access to the three user groups.

Created Date: At this point you can change the creation date of the article. If you click on the calendar icon, a graphic calendar will appear to help you with the input.

Start Publishing: This lets you set a start date for publication. By default, content is published immediately. If you click on the calendar icon, a graphic calendar will appear to help you with the input.

End Publishing: Here you can enter an expiration date for the content. By default, content *never* expires. If you click on the calendar icon, a graphic calendar will appear again.

Parameters-Advanced

In the **Parameters-Advanced** section you can overwrite the parameters that were defined for this content. These settings are only valid for request of the complete article in **Site | Global Configuration**. These settings are only valid for the call up of the complete article, in our case after clicking on the **Read more** link.

Show Title: Should the page title be displayed or hidden?

Title Linkable: Overwriting of the global settings.

Intro Text: Should the teaser text be displayed or hidden?

Section Name: Should the section name be displayed or hidden?

Section Title Linkable: Should the section name be displayed as a link to all articles in this section?

Category Title: Should the category name be displayed or hidden?

Category Title Linkable: Should the category name be displayed as a link to all categories in this section?

These seven parameters overwrite the global settings for this individual article:

Content language: The language of the article can be defined with this. This new feature offers interesting options with language control in conjunction with Alex Kempens' Joomfish (`http://www.joomfish.net/`). Depending on the content, the website could be displayed in one or another language.

Key Reference: References for export into the DocBook (`http://en.wikipedia.org/wiki/DocBook`) format can be defined here. At the moment this is only relevant for developers in connection with the help system.

Alternative Read more: An alternative text can be entered here for the **Read more** link. This is relevant when creating a barrier-free website.

Metadata Information

In this tab you can enter a specific description and keywords for every page section as metadata. The texts entered here are then inserted with the message in the meta tags into the HTML source code of the website in addition to the metadata specified in the **Global Configuration**:

In the **Robots** section, search words for robots can be entered. The respective meta tag is then enabled.

```
<meta name="robots" content="word1 word2" />
```

In the **Author** field you can also enter a special author name for the meta tags.

Images

How do images get into the content? The images issue is a recurrent theme in the CMS world. The image has to be created (camera), transmitted (cable, WLAN), edited (image enhancement), loaded onto the server (FTP, PHP-Upload), and linked to the article.

Joomla! by default allows you to link images that are in the Media Manager into your article by means of a selection dialog.

Position the cursor at the place within the text where you would like the image to be displayed. Then click on the **Image** button below the text window. The following screen should be observed:

You can link whichever image you want from the media section into any piece of content. If the image isn't in the media section yet, you can upload it by clicking the **Upload** icon while you are editing the content.

Select a subdirectory and click on the image that you want to insert. Click on the **Insert** button. Now you can add a title for the image and align it. Your image now appears in the text window as seen in the following screenshot:

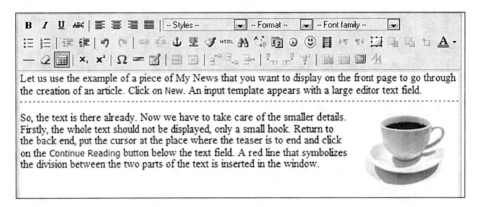

The parameters of the image can, of course, be edited with the TinyMCE editor. Mark the image by left-clicking on it. Then click on the icon with the tree above the text window. The image dialog box of the TinyMCE editor opens. You can now define additional parameters like links, pop-up windows, attitude, and some other parameters. Here a 15-pixel space has been defined around the image.

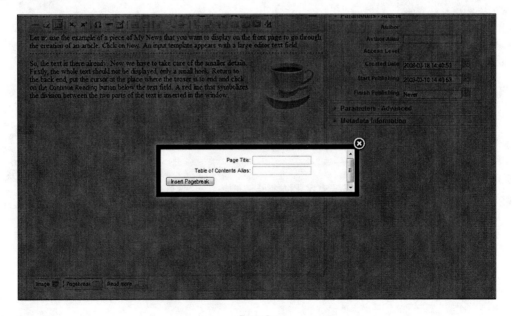

After you have clicked on the **Apply** icon, check the result either on your website or by clicking the **Preview** icon. You can insert page breaks as easily as the **Read more** link or the images. Position the cursor where you want the page break to be and click on the **Pagebreak** button below the text field. The following screen should be observed:

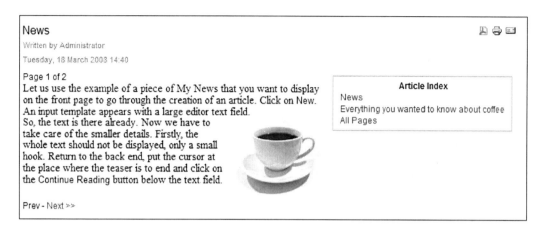

You can enter a **Page Title** for the next page with this. In addition you can enter an Table of Contents Alias for the table of content that Joomla! automatically produces. For example, here the title of the article is *My News* and in the content directory there is now a heading by the name of *Everything you ever wanted to know about coffee*. Now click on **Insert Pagebreak**. The page break is displayed as a gray line in the text window.

Above the article text you can now see Page *x of y*, there is a *Article Index* top right with the text that you entered and below the text of the article are the links **Prev** and **Next** to navigate between the pages. You can integrate as many images and page breaks as you want into a text.

Article Trash

Just as with the menu items, you cannot delete articles directly. By clicking the **Trash** icon in article management, the articles are dispatched into the trash basket. Clicking the **Restore** icon in the trash basket will restore the deleted articles, clicking the **Delete** icon will irretrievably delete them:

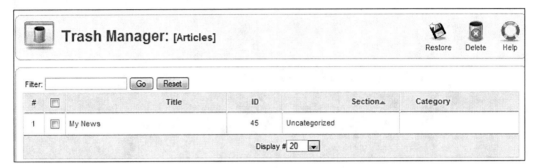

Section Manager

The overview table of the section manager lists the information in the structured format that you have already seen in other lists. In this case, it includes the categories that are contained in a section as well as a count of how many are active and how many are in the trash basket:

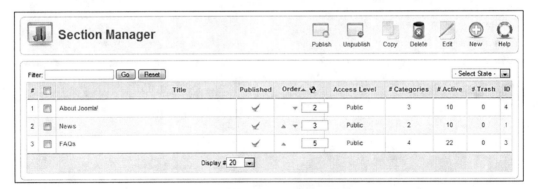

You can publish, copy, delete, and edit the existing sections and create new ones here.

Editing Sections

As an example, let us modify the already existing section **News** and link it to our **Joomla! 1.5 Book** menu. Put a check on the checkbox in front of **News** in the section list and click on the **Edit** icon:

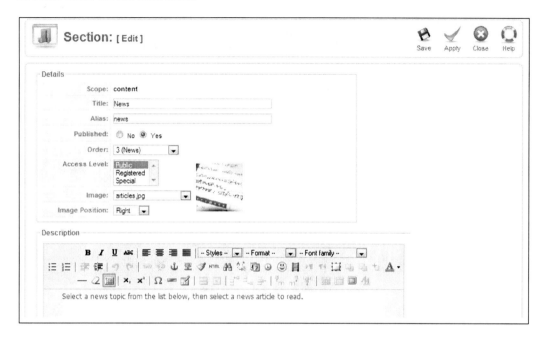

Title: Title of the section (also appears in the browser's title line).

Alias: The name in Joomla!'s internal register.

Published: Whether the section should be published immediately or not.

Order: The sorting of the sections is defined here.

Access Level: Who has access to this element?

Image: With this you can select an image that will be displayed on the website when the category is requested. This image has to be in the root directory of the Media Manager—here it is `articles.jpg`.

Image Position: You can define the alignment of the image here.

Description Window: This is the description of the section. If you have selected a WYSIWYG editor in **Site | Global Configuration**, you will be offered a basic text editor here.

The only thing missing now is a link to the Joomla! 1.5 Book.

You can link this section using Menus | Main Menu. Here you can specify Joomla! 1.5 Book in the Display in option.

Go to **Menus | Main Menu** and click on the **New** icon. Then click on the **Articles** menu item type.

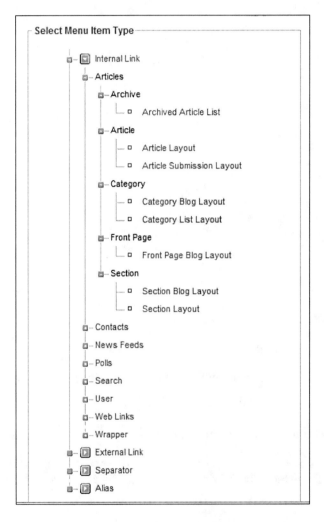

You have a lot of options for the type of display format. What we want to do is display the News section, and we have a choice between the following two layouts:

- **Section Blog Layout**
- **Default Section Layout**

You can link articles as lists or as so-called blog displays (just like that on the current front page).

The display format list shows all the categories that are assigned to this section. The header comes from the section that we have just changed. In our case, this includes only the two categories, **Latest News** and **Newsflash**. These wound up in the table display of the content by simply clicking on the category link.

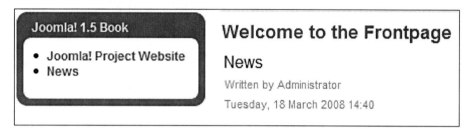

The blog display with Joomla! is a list of items with their intro texts (hooks, teasers) and depending on the article, a **Read more** link. In both cases, there is an orange-colored button in your browser, behind which you can find a news feed for the respective items. The **Archive Blog** display format is exactly like the blog view, but the content in this case comes from the archive (you can archive articles in article management).

It is best to try both versions. After you click on your choice of display type, you land in the edit screen for that link. You have dozens of what are hopefully self-explanatory parameters that you can change and try out.

Category Manager

You can edit categories the same way as sections. You can see the information structure in the overview table that you are already familiar with from the section display, but this time it is expanded by the assigned section, the number of articles it contains that are active, and those that are in the trash basket:

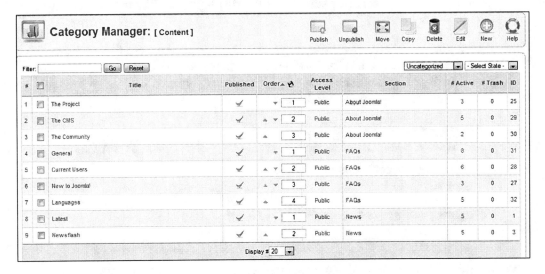

When you assign your newly created articles by means of the menu item **Content | Article Manager | Edit** to the **Latest News** category and the **News** (or **Newsflash**) section, they automatically appear in the newly created section lists.

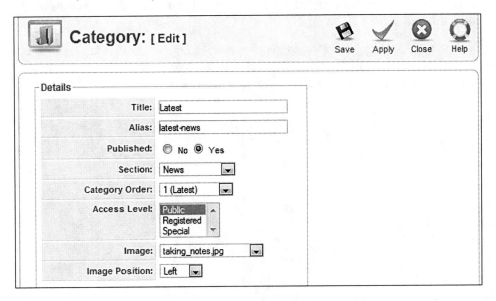

Front Page Manager

The **Frontpage** has a special mission. The front page is the title page of your website. Joomla! suggests that it should contain the articles that you would like to have there.

Sometimes, such as with a simple website, you may not want that type of a start page. A single article may be enough under certain circumstances. This brings us to the question: 'What should my website look like later?'

If you will want a start page with several articles later, then the selected content should be in a blog display format. When you are editing the individual articles, you can activate the **Front Page** switch. The article is then shown in the Frontpage Manage . The construction of the list is similar to that of the articles list. You can sort the articles within the front page here. You can see the title, section, category, and author of the article. uncategorized articles are called **Static Content** here. You can limit the list with the filter options. If you have more articles than will fit on the front page, navigation links are activated on the website below the front page articles.

You can change the layout of the start page in the link menu
(**Menu | Main Menu | Home | Edit**).

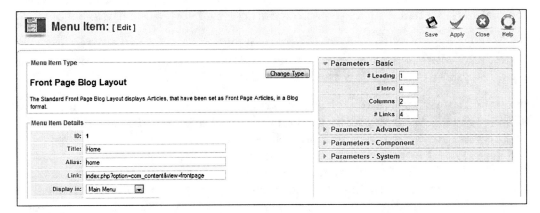

Editing Content from the Front End

If you log on with a user name, you should use the user `admin` the first time; that
user has rights to change content. You will see a pencil symbol next to the articles.

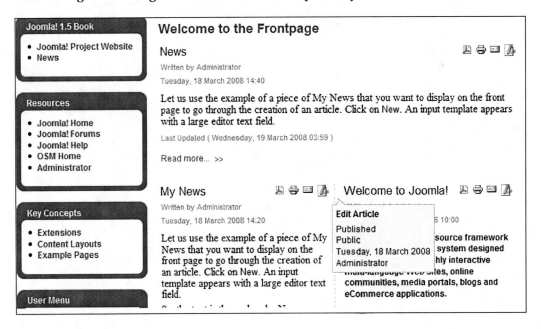

If you click on this pencil symbol, you can edit the content in a fashion similar to how you did it in the back end.

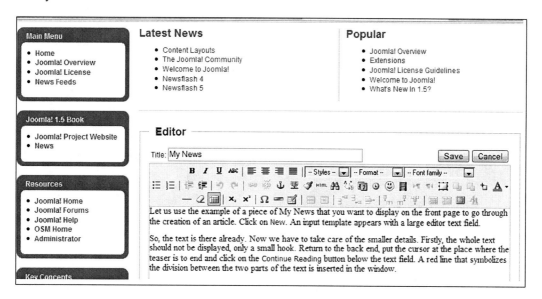

The edit screen contains selected additional parameters from the editor and also permits image uploads and image selection just like that in the administration interface.

Summary

In this chapter we learned about customizing the Content menu. In the next chapter we will learn about the Component menu.

9

Components Menu

In software development, a component is usually a program or a piece of programming code that contains business logic, that can be accessed over defined interfaces, and that may possibly also have a user interface.

Simply think of a component as a *black box*. You put something in the front and something comes out of the back: you don't have to know what happens inside; what matters is that you can use the black box for various completely different purposes.

Components can be designed in a generic way and bundled into handy packages. The idea of a software component is similar in Joomla!. Business logic, such as banner administration or a forum, is written in a generic way and then works in Joomla! in concert with all of the templates and with the Joomla! administration. A module often assumes the display of a website and a plug-in adds additional functionality to existing text (similar to a scripting language). By now there are over 2,000 supplemental components for Joomla! 1.0, and bit by bit more and more are being readied for Joomla! 1.5. But first take a look at the components that are shipped with Joomla! 1.5.

Banner

Banner consists of Banners, Clients, and Categories.

Banners

The banner component makes the display of advertising banners on your site possible. Banner switching with Joomla! is accounted for on the basis of purchased banner impressions. A banner can consist of graphics or text. Just like the wildly successful Google model, Joomla! websites can also sell advertising links. Every time that your site is accessed, a different banner is displayed from your banner administration. Every display counts as an impression. The text link is clickable and links to the site of the customer. In addition to text links, graphic banners can also be placed.

The banner component offers customer, category, and banner administration. With graphics banners, often so-called full banners are switched. A full banner is 468 x 60 pixels and should not exceed 20 KB in file size. The format is `.gif`, `.jpg`, or `.png`.

Let's walk through one of the two versions of banner switches. Create or copy a banner with the dimensions of 468 x 60 pixels:

Test Banner ;-) Click me now!

Clients

Before you can switch a banner, you need a customer. Click on **Components | Banners | Clients | New**, open a new customer account, and save it by clicking on the **Save** icon:

The **Banner Client** Manager, where you wind up after saving, now displays your new customer as well as the number of active banners for this customer.

Manage Banners

Now you have to enter the banner and/or the text link of this client. Click on **Components | Banners | Banners**. You can see the overview of the existing banners:

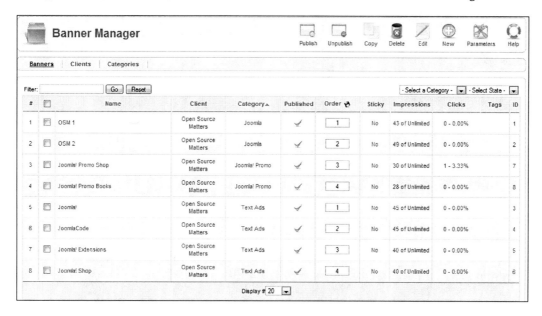

You will see the following categories:

Name: Name of the banner

Client: Client of the banner

Category: Category assigned to the banner

Published: Banner published or not

Order: Defines the order in which the banners are switched

Sticky: Sticky banners are preferred or not

Impressions: The number of successful impressions and the number of remaining impressions

Clicks: Clicks on the banner in numbers and as a percentage of impressions

Tags: Tags (categories) for the banner can be assigned with this. The display of the banners can be controlled with these tags.

ID: Dataset key

Graphic Banners

To switch a new full banner, first upload the file from the media area (**Site | Media Manager**) into the /images/banner/ directory. If you want to delete a banner file, switch to Detail View in the media section and click on the red cross:

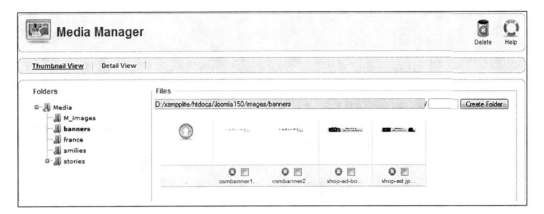

After you have uploaded the banner, click on the **New** icon in the banner section (**Components | Banners | Banners menu**) and fill out the form:

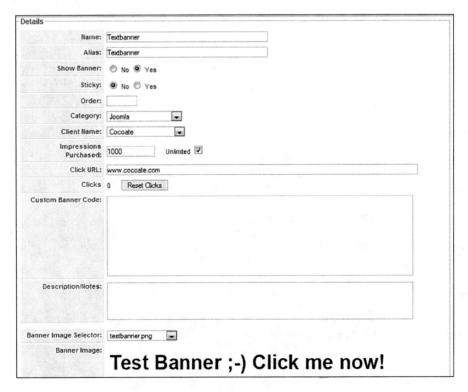

You will need to give the following details:

Banner Name: Give the banner a meaningful name so that you can recognize it in the banner manager.

Alias: This file has no other use yet in Joomla!. I assume that it will be used for the URLs of the banners in the future.

Show Banner: You can take a banner out of rotation by un-setting this.

Sticky: Banners that are marked **Sticky** are displayed first.

Order: Here you define the order in which the banners are to be displayed.

Category: You can assign categories and then display banners from particular categories on the website. Every banner has to have a category assigned to it and then you can administer it with **Components | Banners | Categories**.

Client Name: Select the client from the option list of existing clients.

Impressions Purchased: Enter the number of impressions purchased or check the **Unlimited** checkbox.

Click URL: Enter the URL of the website that the banner should be pointing to.

Customized Banner Code: Here you enter special banner codes from the Affiliate-Partner program.

Since this template is also designed to edit banners, you will also find a display of successful clicks and a **Reset Clicks** button that sets the clicks back to 0.

Description/Notes: Internal information for this banner.

Banner Image Selector: This is where you select the image for the banner. It will be displayed below this field after you select it.

Tags: Define tags for this banner.

After a click on the **Save** icon, your banner should now be in rotation and be displayed on your website.

Text Links

To integrate a text link, simply enter the link in HTML format into the **Customized Banner Code** field. To be able to differentiate between different banner types, you should predefine the appropriate categories (for example **Text Ads**).

The banners are displayed on the website by means of modules. You will learn more about banner modules in the *Modules* section in Chapter 10.

Contacts

It is often difficult for a customer surfing your site to contact you. Many employees normally work in different departments in companies and often only one email address (for example, info@company.com) is shown on the homepage or on a form and the customer has no idea who receives it.

To avoid this, Joomla! makes it possible to define contact categories. You could, for example, enter the various departments of the company into these categories, and then you can enter the contact persons for your company in those categories. Depending on the configuration, Joomla! then displays a table of employees and/or a contact form for every staff member on the site.

Contact Manager

This is where the individual employee contact forms are administered. You will find an employee by the name of **Name** in the sample data, who is assigned to the group **Contacts**. To follow this functionality, simply set up a new staff member. Click on **Components | Contacts | Contacts**. You will now see the **Contact** section and the previously mentioned contact from the sample data:

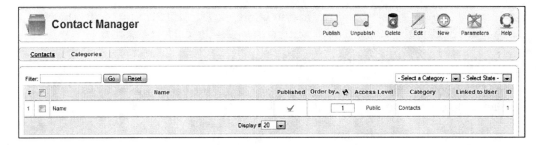

Click on the **New** icon and set up a new contact. The template that pops up now is divided into three parts and is very comprehensive:

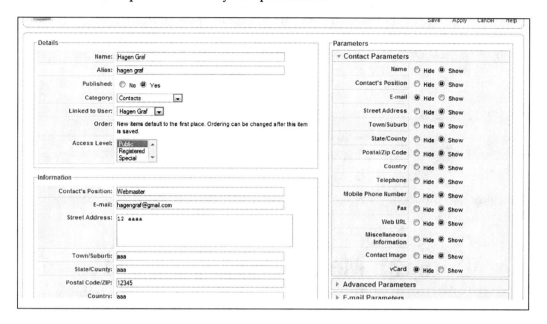

Details

This section has the following options:

Name: Name of the contact

Alias: Short URL

Published: Yes or no

Category: Select the contact category. At the moment we only have the sample category **Contacts**.

Linked to User: This option allows you to link a contact with a user account.

Access Level: Which user group can access this contact?

ID: Dataset number of the contact

Information

Here are the information fields for this contact. Fields that don't have any values in them are automatically hidden. The **Miscellaneous Information** field can be used for individual descriptions. You can display a picture of the contact from the /images/stories/ subdirectory in the **Image** field. You can upload the image in the **Site | Media** menu.

Parameters

Here you can decide which fields you want to display and which you want to hide. A vCard is a file format that can automatically be entered into numerous address directories.

Save the new contact by clicking on the **Save** icon. The new contact will now be displayed in the list.

Creation of a Menu Link for the Website

To build the link to this contact into the top menu of the website, click on **Menus Top | Menu | New**, and then on **Contacts** under menu item type. You can now choose between a contact category that displays a list of all contacts in that category (**Contact Category Layout**) or a single contact (**Standard Contact Layout**). Select **Standard Contact Layout**.

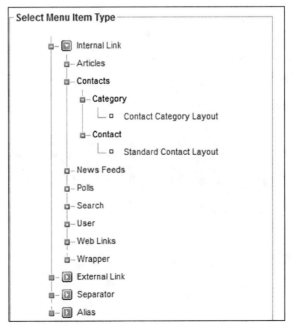

In the **Categories** section you can set up new categories and edit existing ones. This section can be accessed via the **Components|Contacts| Categories** menu.

You still have to enter a name and an alias for the menu link and the correct contact in the parameters in the edit template that now appears. You can also set up new parameters here.

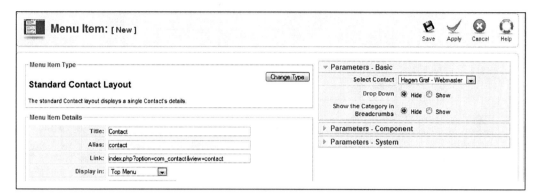

Now take a look at the website and click on the **Contact** link in the top menu. You will see the contact data and an automatically generated form for establishing contact. The email address that the information is sent to remains invisible in this construct and therefore avoids presenting an invitation to spammers.

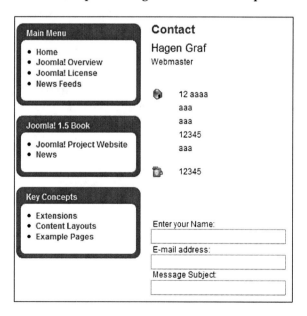

Another choice was a list of contacts. This list looks a little tattered around the telephone number and I don't really want the cell phone number and the fax number to be public knowledge.

To fix these two things, you have to edit the menu link. Click on **Menus | Top Menu** and bring the **Contact** item into the editing state. You can now configure the table by means of the parameter column to your heart's content.

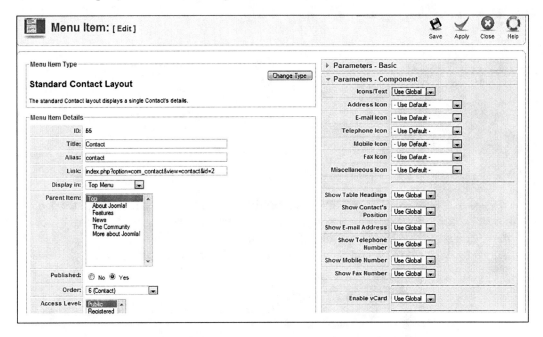

You can also exclude certain email addresses and words in the **Parameters-Component** section. Once your table is completely edited, you can click on the name of your contact. This will display the desired information and a contact form.

Categories

In the **Categories** section you can define new categories and modify existing ones. You get there from the **Components | Contacts | Categories** menu and via the **Categories** tab in the Contact Manager.

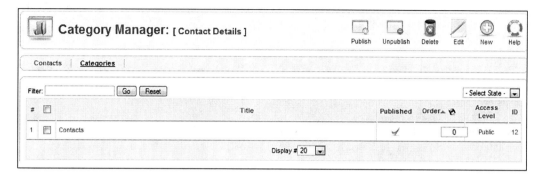

The edit form is displayed after you click on the **Edit** icon or on the category name. You can integrate an image and edit the description with the WYSIWYG editor.

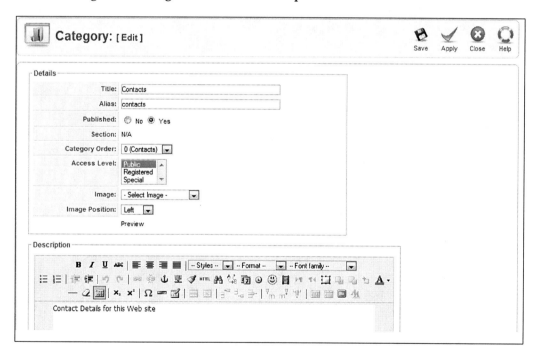

News Feeds

News feeds are absolutely terrific. The ever-growing information abundance on the Internet makes it necessary to try effective organizational methods. It takes too much time to regularly visit even just twenty web pages to check what's new. With fifty or a hundred it is absolutely hopeless to try to keep an overview. News feeds are an attempt to solve this problem.

With the news feed component you can merge feeds from other sites into your site. To accomplish that, a Category Manager and a Content Manager are at your disposal. The sample data already contains several categories and numerous news feeds.

To integrate your own news feed, you can use a search engine for this purpose or look for the small orange RSS button on the sites that you visit.

Feeds

In order to show you an example, we will enter the feed from my own blog `http://www.bloghouse.org/blog/7/feed`. Click on **Components | News feeds | Feeds | New**:

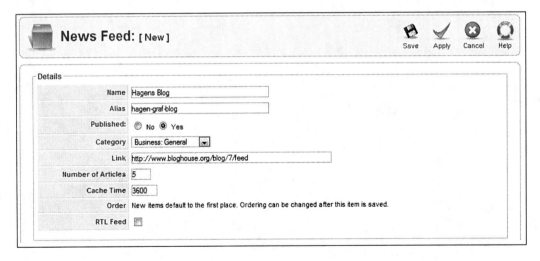

These are some of the options:

Name: This is the name of the news feed that appears on your page.

Alias: The short URL.

Published: For it to be published immediately—**Yes**.

Category: Select a suitable category from the existing ones.

Link: This is the link to the news feed, the blog link given above.

Number Of Articles: This refers to the number of articles that are to be integrated.

Cache Time (in seconds): How long should the break between updates be (in seconds)?

Order: By default, the news feeds are at the beginning. This order can be changed after it has been saved.

Assuming that you have Internet access, your new news feed is now displayed on your website.

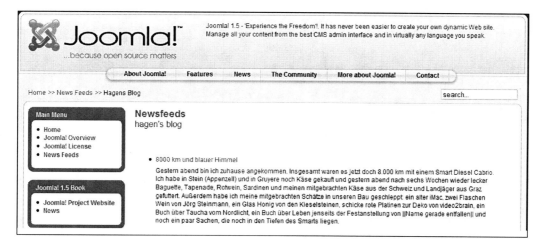

Categories

This is where you administer the news feed categories. This manager works the same as the **Category Manager** in **Contacts**.

Polls

The integrated poll module makes it possible for you to publish polls on your site. One poll is already included with the sample data.

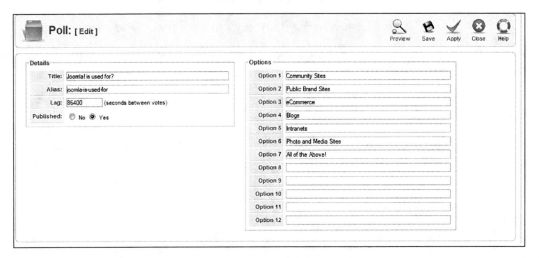

Title: This is the title of your poll.

Lag: This determines the time in seconds that has to elapse before another selection can be made. This lag offers some kind of protection against falsification of poll data.

Options: Here you can enter up to twelve answer options.

Click the **Preview** icon to get a preview of your poll. To actually display it on your site, make sure that the poll module is located at the desired position. The module is positioned on the right side by default.

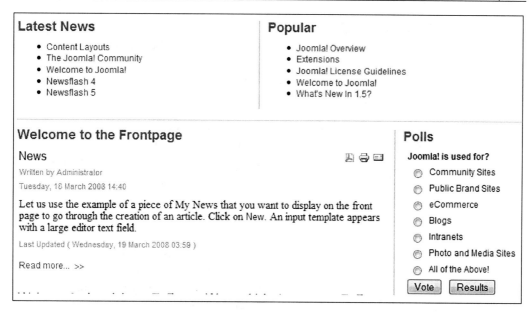

If you try the poll out and select an answer, a report template appears. The poll itself is no longer displayed, since by default it was assigned only to the front page.

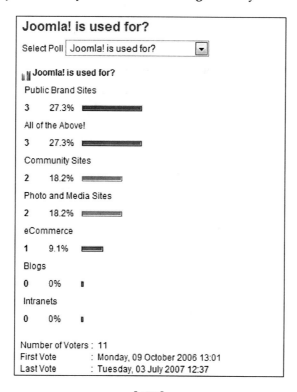

Search Statistics

Joomla! 1.0 had numerous options for collecting statistics about your users' access to your website. The logging of access data sometimes required a significant amount of storage space on the server and because of this, the Joomla! core team decided to purge the statistics part (in the age of Google analytics an understandable decision).

Probably the most important piece of information for the operator of a website is: "What are users searching for on my website?" With Joomla! 1.5, you can find the search terms and their frequency in the search statistics. In order for this to work, you have to explicitly enable capture of search words in the presets.

Web Links

With this you can construct a link list or a download section that you can integrate into your website. Joomla! provides the categories again and counts the hits on the links. In the user menu, you can have your registered visitors suggest links to be added to the list. These links will then appear in the list that can be requested from the **Components | Web Links | Links** menu. These links, depending on user rights, may still have to be published.

Links

You can see all the links that have been entered so far with their assigned categories, as well as the hits up to now in the links overview template:

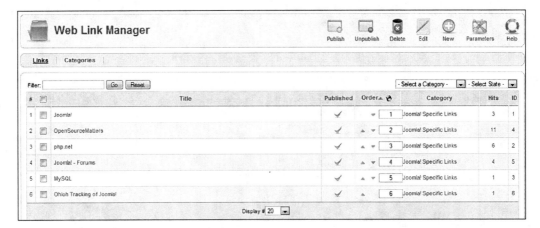

The parameters that are valid for all links can be edited in the presets. You can enter individual links from scratch, and decide about publishing them and edit them:

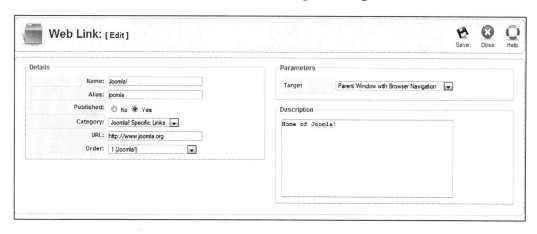

The details include:

Name: The name of the link that appears on your website

Alias: Short URL

Published: Should the link be published immediately?

Category: Selection of an existing link category

URL: The URL of the link

Order: Sorting of the links

Parameters: Here you can select whether the link should be displayed in a new window (with or without navigation) or in the same window.

Description: You can enter a comprehensive description of the link.

Categories

The link categories, which can be accessed in the respective **Category Section**, are administered in the **Components | Web Links | Categories** menu:

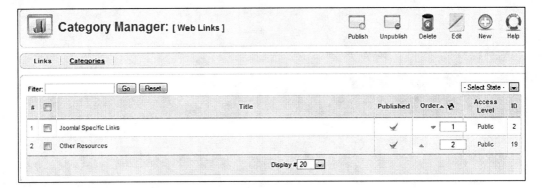

Summary

In this chapter we learned about the component menu.

10
Extensions Menu

Other than the components, all the extension options that are available are listed in the **Extensions** menu. These are modules, plug-ins, templates, and languages. There is also a central installer here that makes it possible to install and uninstall Joomla! extensions with just a few mouse clicks.

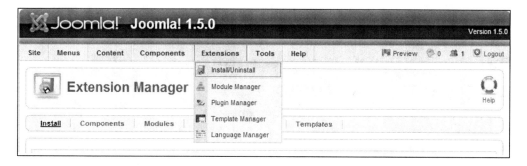

Install/Uninstall

In principle, anyone can write a Joomla! extension, pack it according to set rules, and integrate it into the website. You will find an overview of the installed extensions in this section. When you call up the **Extensions | Install/Uninstall** menu item, a template appears that gives you three options for installing extensions:

- Uploading of a file package
- Installation from a directory
- Installation by entering a URL

The **Install, Components, Modules, Plugins, Templates** and **Languages** tabs each contain listings of the installed extensions. We will cover the installation of additional components in Chapter 12.

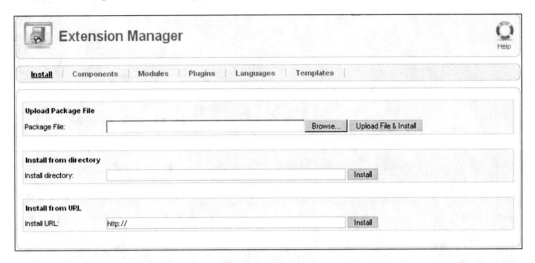

Install, Components, Modules, Plug-ins, Languages, and Templates

Each of the tabs, for instance under **Components**, displays a list of the components that have been installed by default. You will see the version information of the component, the date of creation, and the author's information. To uninstall a component, select it and click on the **Uninstall** icon in the toolbar.

Careful!

After uninstallation, the component is really gone, and sometimes with it all of the stored data! There is no such thing as a component trash basket!

This is absolutely intentional. It is up to the component developer to decide on a strategy. Sometimes not deleting the tables makes sense, for example when you do an update. However, sometimes irreversibly deleting all the tables that were created makes sense. You will learn more about these techniques in Chapter 15. It is imperative that you read all of the documentation of the respective component so that you are familiar with its characteristics.

Module Manager

The structure of a module is a lot simpler than that of a component. It is a code fragment that is integrated and interpreted by another part of the program. Due to the scripting language PHP's capabilities, modules can collect data from all kinds of sources. The sources could be on your own website (the last five articles) or a weather, stock quotation, Amazon, or eBay web service.

A module contains business logic and a user interface. It does not have its own administration section as most components do. Modules can, however, be controlled by parameters. Your website's template addresses the various modules directly and integrates them.

Since modules are self-contained programs, they can handle a dedicated task in this template domain, such as displaying a banner. A template does nothing but group several different modules in a visually appealing manner. The module structure allows you to conveniently extend your website in a simple way.

Since you can use templates both for your website and for the Joomla! administration, various modules are also available for these templates. You administer modules in the central module section in the **Extensions | Module Manager** menu.

The different sections that you see here are:

Module Name: Name of the module and header on the website.

Enabled: Displays whether the module is enabled or not.

Order: You can change the order by means of the green arrows. That way you can, for example, control whether the **Joomla! 1.5 Book** menu is positioned above or below the main menu. Sorting directly by entering the position in the input box can be done by clicking once on the **Order** icon; this circumvents the tedious clicking on the green arrows.

Access Level: Access rights for this module (**Public**, **Registered**, or **Special**).

Position: Position tells the template where you want the module displayed. There are default positions defined in the template, such as:

- **banner** (advertising section)
- **left** (left side)
- **right** (right side)
- **top** (top)
- **user1** (user defined 1)
- **user2** (user defined 2)
- **user3** (user defined 3)
- **user4** (user defined 4)

In addition to these positions, you can filter the display with the options list in the top area for an even better general view. You will learn more about positioning in your template later in the chapter.

Pages: The module can be displayed on all pages or only particular ones.

Type: There are various types of modules. The `mod_mainmenu` type, for instance, shows up often since every menu is assigned to that type. The individual menus are only differentiated by their parameters. With the help of the option list on the top, you can filter the display according to these types for a better overview.

ID: The dataset number from the database.

Module Filters

The template has numerous filter options with which you can individualize the display. These filter mechanisms are incredibly useful and Joomla! already includes more than 20 of these by default.

Most of these modules are handled the same way. Besides entering the name, access information, etc., you also have to decide on which pages and at what position in the template the module is to be displayed.

The parameter list is especially important with modules. We will emphasize each of them as they come into use. You can copy modules at will and display them on your website with modified parameters and titles and in different positions.

Site Module

Breadcrumbs

Breadcrumbs are hierarchical indicators in articles.

The individual superordinate elements of the article, the **News** section, and the **Latest** category are linked and thereby give the visitor orientation and navigation options. You can define whether home/front page should be displayed as a parameter. If you deactivate this module, the breadcrumbs are no longer displayed.

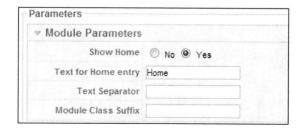

Footer

This module displays Joomla! license information in the footer. You can deactivate it and suppress this information on the front page.

Banner

This module controls the display of the banners. Besides the familiar settings for details and page allocation, you can also configure the following parameters:

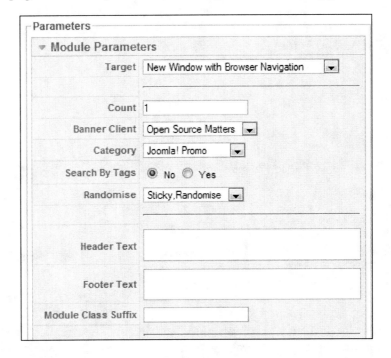

Target: Where should the target URL be displayed—the same window or a new window, with or without navigation?

Count: Number of impressions.

Banner Client: Select the client here if this module is to display the banners of only one client.

Category: If only banners of one particular category are to be displayed (for example only text links), select the appropriate category here.

Search By Tags: Tags can be assigned to individual banners. You can decide here whether you only want to display banners with, for example, the Joomla! tag.

Randomise: You can control the rotation of the banners with this. **Sticky, Ordering** means that those banners that are marked **sticky** are displayed first and then in the order of the sorting as is defined in the banner. **Sticky, Randomize** means that those banners that are marked **sticky** are displayed first and then in randomized order.

Header Text: Text before the banner.

Footer Text: Text after the banner.

Module Class Suffix: You can enter a suffix that is appended to the name of the CSS class with this. Let's assume that you only store `table` in the field. This is transformed to class `module_table`, which is then activated. You then have to implement your class in the respective CSS file of the template.

Main Menus

The internal designation `mod_mainmenu` is used for all menu modules. The **Joomla! 1.5 Book** menu that we set also has the `main_menu` type. There are vertical menus (Main Menu) and horizontal menus (Top Menu). With vertical menus you also have the option of a **flat list**. A flat list is simply a listing of individual items. The module parameters define the most important settings.

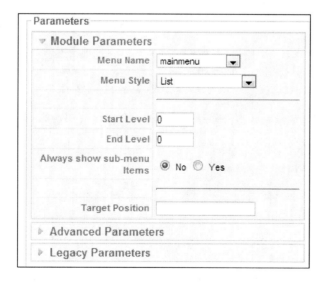

Menu Name: Name of the menu that is assigned to this module.

Menu Style: Vertical, horizontal, or flat list.

Start Level: The nesting level at which this menu should start.

End Level: The nesting level that this menu should include for its last item.

Always show sub-menu items: You can have the menu items always be open, even if another item is clicked. This function only makes sense with nested menu structures.

Target Position: The values that are entered here are used with all menu items that have the setting in a new browser window without menu for the attribute **With a click, Open in**. For example: top=10, left =10, width=200, height=300.

In the compatibility parameters, menu icons can be displayed in the style of Joomla! 1.0.

Show Menu Icons: Should the menu icons be displayed? Display of the icons, in each case, depends on the active template

Full Active Highlighting: This parameter refers to parental elements and whether to also mark them active. Normally this is only done to the individual link.

 Careful: Marking more than one link active is contradictory to the HTML standard.

Menu Icon Alignment: Should the menu icons be on the left or on the right?

Indent Image: You can specify the item to be displayed with the substructures of a menu item. You have the option to use Joomla! default values, to supply a separate image for each hierarchical level, or to display no icons at all.

Indent Image (1-6): You can define six icons for six hierarchical steps.

Spacer: Here you define the separation character that should be displayed between the menu items of a horizontal menu.

End Spacer: If you want to display an end character at the end of the items of a horizontal menu, you can define it here.

Statistics

By default, the **Statistics** module is deactivated. If you activate it, you have to define the pages where it will be displayed. This module displays information about your server.

Server Info: You can set this to display server information.

Site Info: You can set this to display website information.

Hit Counter: Here you can activate or deactivate your visitor counter.

Increase Counter: You can set the starting number of the visitor counter with this.

Login Form

There are two available views for the login module. If the visitors have not logged in yet, they get a login form where they can enter their username and password. Depending on the settings in **Site | Global Configuration | Site** it is also possible to register a new user.

After a successful login, the display changes to give a logout option.

The parameters include the following options:

Caching: You can cache the menu content to save load time.

Module Class Suffix: A special CSS class for the visual configuration of the menu can be entered here.

Pre-text: The text that you enter here is displayed before the form in login mode.

Post-text: The text that you enter here is displayed after the form in login mode.

Login Redirection URL: Here you define the URL that the user is sent to after a successful login.

Logout Redirection URL: Here you define the URL that the user is sent to after a successful logout.

Greeting: After a successful login, the look of the module changes and displays a greeting and a **Logout** button. You decide here whether you want a "**Hi, [Username]**" text to be displayed.

Archive

By default, the **Archive** module is deactivated. If you activate it, you have to define the pages where it will be displayed. This module displays information about the content of your archive. The display of this is grouped by month.

With the parameter **Count** you can define the number of the items to be displayed.

Sections

By default, the **Sections** module is deactivated. This module displays the various sections of the website. If you activate it, you have to define the pages where it will be displayed.

With the parameter **Count** you can define the number of sections to be displayed.

Related Items

The **Related Items** module (similar articles) displays the headers of other articles that are related to this article.

The relationship is based on the keywords that have been entered in the metadata. All of the keywords of the currently displayed article are compared with all of those of all of the other published articles.

If, for instance, you have entered `test` as a keyword in **Joomla! License Guidelines** and also in your newly created news article, the news article and the license conditions are displayed as Related Items when one of them is requested. You can also set a parameter so that the date of creation of the related article will be displayed.

Wrapper

The **Wrapper** module links external, non-Joomla! created content inside a so-called `iframe`. An `iframe` is an HTML tag and produces a scrollable area within a website. You can integrate entire websites that are located online on other servers with this module into Joomla! content. The following figure shows an example using Google's PDA-Portal:

Some of the parameter options are:

URL: Enter the URL of the desired website.

Scroll Bars: If you want scrollbars to be displayed in the `iframe`, you have a choice of **Yes**, **No**, and **Auto** for automatic activation.

Width/Height: Width and height of the `iframe` in percentage or pixels.

Auto Height: Set to **Yes** if you want the height to be automatically adjusted.

Auto Add: An `http://` is inserted before the URL by default if no `http://` or `https://` was found. This switch can be enabled or disabled here.

Feed Display

With this module you can display a news feed in a module on the website.

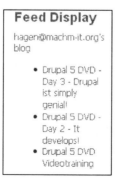

The parameters involved are:

Feed URL: You can enter the URL of the desired news feed here.

RTL Feed: You can set the direction of the scroll to go from right to left.

Feed Title: You can set the title of the feed to be displayed here.

Feed Description: You can set this to display the description of the news feeds.

Feed Image: You can set this to display the logo of the news feeds.

Items: Number of articles that should be displayed.

Item Description: You can have the text of the articles displayed.

Word Count: Here you define how many words of the description of the article are to be displayed.

Who's Online

The **Who's Online** module displays who happens to be on the site at the time. The module also differentiates between guests and registered users.

The **Display** parameter helps you make decisions about the display of the module. You can choose from:

- Number of guests and members
- Usernames of the logged users
- A combination of the above two

Polls

The functionality for the display of polls is fundamentally enabled or disabled with this. The polls themselves are configured in the **Polls** component (see **Components | Polls** menu). You can define the poll that is to be displayed in the module in one of the parameters.

Advertisement

This module is a copy of the banner module. This, by default, has to do with banners that are in the text ads category and that contain text links.

Random Image

This module will display randomly selected images from a folder of your choice. This module is activated by default but not assigned to a page. You have to allocate it to the pages you want before you can see it on your website.

The parameters include:

Image Type: Here you define the type of the image. (jpg/png/gif). You can only select one type at a time.

Image Folder: Here you have to enter the directory where the images are located. For this example we have selected images/stories without a leading slash.

Link: If you enter a URL here, the image is clickable. The target of the link is the URL that you define here.

Width (px)/Height (px): Width and height of the displayed images in pixels. If you don't define these, the images are displayed as well as possible.

Syndication

The website's news feed is delivered by the **Syndication** module. You can define the standards that you are offering in the parameters. The articles on the front page represent the content of the offered news feed:

Newsflash

The **Newsflash** module displays randomized intro texts of your articles:

Joomla! 1.5 - 'Experience the Freedom'!. It has never been easier to create your own dynamic site. Manage all your content from the best CMS admin interface and in virtually any language you speak.

Features   **The Community**

The parameters are as follows:

Category: By selecting from a list of categories, you can define whether the content should come from one particular category or from all categories.

Layout: You decide between a columnated display (**horizontal**) or a presentation (**vertical**).

Show Images: Should the images that are contained in the contents be displayed or not?

Title Linkable: You can decide if the titles should also be links to the entire article.

Read More...Link: Activate **Read More** link or not.

Article Title: You can decide whether to display the title of the article or not.

# of Articles: You define how many articles are to be displayed simultaneously.

Latest News

This module displays the latest (newest) articles. By default it is assigned to the `user1` position. However, you can assign a different position to it, for instance on the right.

```
Latest News

  • Content Layouts
  • The Joomla
    Community
  • Welcome to
    Joomla!
  • Newsflash 4
  • Newsflash 5
```

The parameters include:

Count: The number of elements to be displayed.

Order: Whether the newest or the most recently modified articles should be displayed.

Authors: Lets you limit articles to a particular author.

Front Page Articles: Should articles that are on the front page also be included?

Section ID: If you enter the dataset numbers of the sections to be displayed in a comma separated list, you can force the selection of content to come only from those sections.

Category ID: If you enter the dataset numbers of the categories to be displayed in a comma separated list, you can force the selection of content to come only from those categories.

Popular

This module displays the most popular articles:

Popular

- Extensions
- Joomla! Features
- Joomla! Facts
- Joomla! License Guidelines
- Content Layouts

The parameters are exactly the same as those of the **Latest News** module.

Search

In the default template, the **Search** module is only an input template. This template does not change all of the parameters. The display text is modified in order to demonstrate the configuration options.

Parameters in this module include:

Box Width: Size of the textbox in characters, the example has 30 characters.

Text: Enter the text that will be displayed in the search field.

Search Button: Here you can decide whether you want to have a search button or not.

Button Position: If you have selected a search button, you define its position with this (right, left, top, bottom).

Search Button as Image: You can use a graphic as the search button.

Button Text: This is where you define the description of the search button.

Copying a Module

Image that you would like to display two random images. One module is to display images from directory A and another module should get the images from directory B. In a case like this, select the **Random Images** module by clicking the checkbox in front of the name and then click the **Copy** icon.

A new module with the name of **Copy of Random Image** appears in the list. Change the information the way you want and you have a new module.

If you deactivate the Latest News and Popular modules and switch the two image modules to positions `user1` and `user2`, the new modules are displayed in the content section of the template above the news and/or the front page.

Administrator Module

In the same template, in the **Administrator** tab, you can see a structurally identical section, with modules, however, that are useful for the administration area.

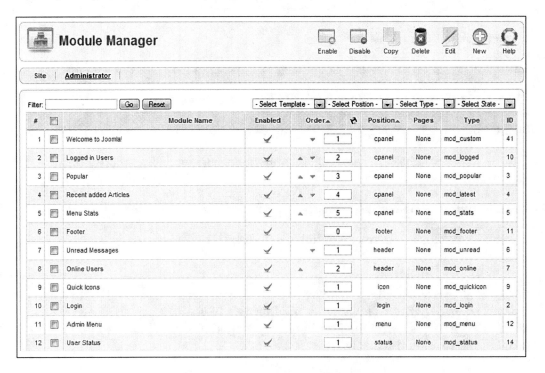

Logged in Users

This module displays a list of the currently logged-in users at position `cpanel`, and also on the tab in the **Control Panel**.

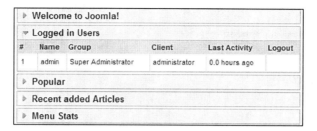

Popular

The **Popular** module presents a list of the most often visited content as a tab in the **Control Panel**.

Recent added Articles

This module displays a list of the most recently published articles as a tab in the **Control Panel**. Articles that were published on the front page are not included in this list.

Menu Stats

The **Menu Stats** module displays statistics about the configuration of the individual menu elements as a tab in the **Control Panel**.

Footer

This module displays Joomla! copyright information in the back end.

Unread Messages

The **Unread Messages** module informs you about the number of unread administrator messages at the `header` position, in other words top right.

Online Users

The **Online Users** module displays the count of logged-in users at the `header` position on the site.

Quick Icons

The **Quick Icons** module offers quick access icons in the **Control Panel**.

Login

This module displays the login form for the administration **area**. Do not deactivate it!

Admin Menu

This module displays the JavaScript navigation in the **back** end. Do not deactivate it!

User Status

The **User Status** module switches the top right information section completely on or off. You shouldn't deactivate this either!

Admin Submenu

The **Admin Submenu** module turns off the section in which the tabs are displayed. Do not deactivate it!

Title

The **Title** module determines the display of the description and the icon on the left of the toolbar. Do not deactivate it!

Toolbar

The **Toolbar** module determines the display of the toolbar. Do not deactivate it!

CSS Admin Menu

The **CSS Admin Menu** module is responsible for the display of the Joomla! administration menu.

Plugins Manager

Plug-ins can absolutely be compared with a Joomla! scripting language. You have already run across an integrated plug-in when you worked with the TinyMCE Editor.

Plug-ins are always assigned to a particular type. At the moment, there are plug-ins from the `authentication`, `content`, `editors`, `editors-xtd`, `search`, `system`, and `xmlrpc` sections.

You can activate and deactivate the individual functions in the **Plugins** section. Except for some isolated exceptions, plug-ins have few or even no changeable settings, since they are mostly programmed and optimized for a very specific purpose.

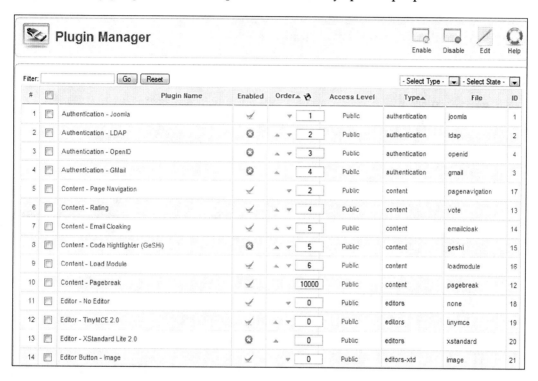

Authentication Plug-ins

In Joomla! 1.5, users can authenticate themselves a number of different ways. This has the advantage that you can do without the cumbersome process of registration on the website and that you don't have to remember another username and another password. In order that these various methods of authentication can be used, you have to publish the plug-in.

Joomla!

The "normal" authentication subsequent to a prior registration on the website.

LDAP

LDAP is a network protocol that is used with so-called directory services. It transmits the communication between the so-called LDAP client (in our case the Joomla! website) and the directory from which person-related data is read. LDAP directories are popular in companies and therefore it stands to reason that one can access this type of person-related data over the company's Intranet.

The LDAP plug-in uses an abundance of parameter settings and therefore is an exception the rule. The parameter settings are self-explanatory.

OpenID

The idea behind OpenID is that the user that has a user account with an OpenID server can log in to your website without having a user account and password. This could be a big advantage, depending on the orientation of your website.

Gmail

With the Gmail service, Google offers the option of authentication by means of the email address. If the users have a Gmail account, they can log in to your website with their Gmail user IDs. Depending on the orientation of your website, this could be a big advantage.

Content Plug-ins

Image

This plug-in has been kept for reasons of compatibility with Joomla! 1.0.x. It interprets the {mosimage} command in the text of an article and then displays the assigned image. The pivotal advantage is that these images can easily be edited with a plug-in. You can define the inside and outside distances from the images in the parameters.

Page Navigation

This plug-in integrates the **Next and Previous** functions under the articles. If you want to use it, it has to be activated.

SEF

SEF is the acronym for **Search Engine Friendly**. This plug-in creates search engine friendly URLs for content elements. If you use that feature, this plug-in has to be activated.

Rating

This is the plug-in that displays the rating bar above the contents. If you want to use it, it has to be activated.

Email Cloaking

This plug-in transforms an e-mail address that you enter into a content element in the form of `name@example.com` into a link and cloaks the email address by means of JavaScript. This has the advantage that email address collection programs cannot read your email address very easily.

GeSHi

The GeSHi plug-in formats exactly like the code-plugin. GeSHi, however, can perform Syntax Highlighting and creates an impressive listing on the website if you embed the code to be formatted within `<pre> </pre>` HTML tags:

```
<pre>
if ($number > 0){
  echo $number;
} else{
  $number++;
}
</pre>
```

Load Module

The **Load Module** plug-in makes it possible to load modules inside of articles. It can be called up, for instance, with `{loadposition user1}`.

Pagebreak

The **Pagebreak** plug-in takes care of Joomla! 1.0.x-pagebreaks in articles. Just like the Image plug-in, it is easy to integrate into the content. Besides a simple page-break, various headers and page titles can also be defined. In Joomla! 1.5, the pagebreak dialog assumes this role (see Chapter 8, section *Images*).

Syntax:

```
hr title="page title" alt=" page title" class="system-pagebreak">
```

Editors Plug-ins

No Editor

This plug-in has to be activated if you want to offer `textarea` fields without an editor.

TinyMCE 2.0

This plug-in has to be activated if you want to offer `textarea` fields with the TinyMCE 2.0 editor.

Editors-xtd Plug-ins

The editors-xtd type contains the **Editor Button-Image, Pagebreak**, and **Read more** plug-ins. These three plug-ins generate the three buttons below the editor window. Clicking on these buttons launches the **Insert Image** dialog, the **Pagebreak** dialog, and the **Read more** dialog.

Search Plug-ins

The Search plug-ins for **Contents, Weblinks, Contacts, Categories, Sections**, and **Newsfeeds** can be activated as you wish. They control the search function of the **Search** module. These plug-ins have to be activated if you want to get search results from the respective sections. If you want to search additional components, the respective plug-ins for them have to available as well.

System Plug-ins

Log

This plug-in makes the system log available. You can determine the location of the log file. An example of such a log file:

```
#Version: 1.0
#Date: 2007-10-29 23:39:56
#Fields: date time level c-ip status comment
#Software: Joomla! 1.5.0 Production/Stable [ Takriban ] 5-October-2007
21:00 GMT
2007-10-29 23:39:56 - 127.0.0.1 - stories/france
2007-10-30 12:00:12 - 127.0.0.1 FAILURE: Invalid password
2007-10-31 13:44:11 - 127.0.0.1 FAILURE: Invalid password
```

Debug

This makes the debug function available. You can configure the parameters to determine what information is displayed.

Legacy

There were and still are lots of discussions going on about this plug-in. This is a linking element to the extensions in the Joomla! 1.0 world. Activating this plug-in makes migration from Joomla! 1.0 to Joomla! 1.5 significantly easier.

Cache

This sets the operation of the cache. You can define the browser cache on the client and you can set the basic caching time in minutes.

Remember Me

This is a method for saving access data locally in a cookie. Once you log in in to that website again, the data are already in the form. This storage is only enabled by explicitly marking a checkbox.

Backlink

This plug-in takes care of the task of correctly transforming "old" Joomla! 1.0 links to Joomla! 1.5 logic.

User Plug-ins

Joomla!

This plug-in creates a user in the database tables after the first successful authentication.

XML-RPC Plug-ins

The XML-RPC interface gives you the ability to operate Joomla! remotely.

XML-RPC-Joomla

This plug-in enables control of Joomla!-specific framework functions from the XML RPC interface.

XML-RPC blogger API

This plug-in enables integration of content from other platforms, for instance Flickr photos. At the moment, the blogger interface is being supported. A lot of the web 2.0 platforms are integrating the MetaWeblog API. This extension will also be available in Joomla! 1.5. You can select the section and category that should be inserted into these articles as parameters.

Template Manager

You are already familiar with the *Template* section from Chapter 4, in which we configured a different template for the website.

Joomla! differentiates **Site** and **Administrator** templates.

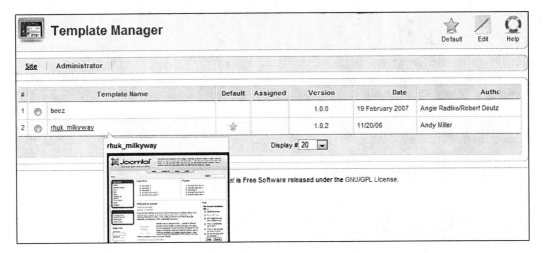

Site

You can see the installed templates here. You can define one template as default and assign other templates for particular menu links. To make a template the default one, mark the checkbox next to the template and click on the **Default** icon. Your website will then change its appearance appropriately.

Editing a Template

After you click on the template, you can modify and configure all the properties of an individual template. The parameter list will, among other things, show you menu links that have been allocated to this template.

Mark the menu links to which you want to assign the template. You can make multiple selections by clicking the desired elements one after the other while holding down the *Ctrl* key. You can also make changes to the colors of the template and to the width of the display.

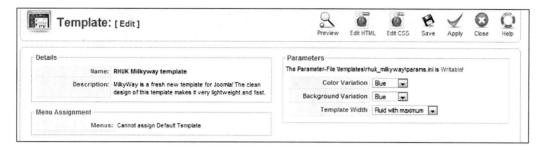

Preview Icon

This will show you a preview of the default template of your website with graphical indication for the module positions. You can position your modules at these spots:

Edit HTML Icon

With this you can edit the HTML source code of the selected template. Templates always consist of an HTML file. There is a box with template snippets in the top section. These template snippets are predefined commands for certain actions within the template.

Edit CSS Icon

Now you can edit the CSS source code of the selected template. Templates can have any number of CSS files. Select the desired file and then click the **Edit** icon again.

 You have to know what you are doing if you try your hand at this. knowledge of HTML and CSS is essential here. It is, nonetheless, interesting for the beginner to see how a template is constructed. More about this topic in Chapter 13.

Administrator

Whatever is valid for your website is, of course, also valid for your administration interface. You can assign other templates to your administration interface just as you were able to assign other site templates. One default template is contained in your Joomla! installation.

Language Manager

We already touched on the **language** section in Chapter 4. Here you have a **Site** and an **Administrator** tab with which you can select the languages for your website and for the back-end section.

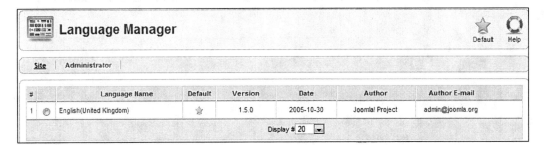

#		Language Name	Default	Version	Date	Author	Author E-mail
1	⊚	English(United Kingdom)	☆	1.5.0	2005-10-30	Joomla! Project	admin@joomla.org

Display # 20 ▾

Summary

In this chapter we learned about the Extensions menu. In the next chapter we will learn about the **Tools** menu, which contains administrator tools: a private messaging system, a mass mailing function, and the global checking in of content elements.

11
Tools

The **Tools** menu contains administrator tools: a private messaging system, a mass-mailing function, and the global checking-in of content elements

Private Messaging System

The **Read Messages** menu, contrary to its title, contains all messages, even those that have not been read. It is basically a mail inbox.

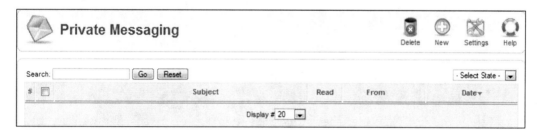

If you click on the subject matter or on the sender of a message, you can read it and the status is automatically set to **Read**. System messages also get delivered, for example if someone has posted a new article. If you click on the **New** icon or the **Tools | Write Messages** menu, you can send a new message to users that have access to the Joomla! administration.

If you click on the **Settings** icon, you can configure the messaging system.

Lock Inbox: You can close your inbox and stop any incoming mail. If you are the only administrator then this is OK, but otherwise you should leave your inbox open.

Mail me on New Message: This feature is really handy. Joomla! sends the messages to the email address that was defined in the user administration.

Auto Purge Messages: You can have the system automatically delete messages when they reach a certain age in days.

Mass Mail

Delight your users with mass mailings!

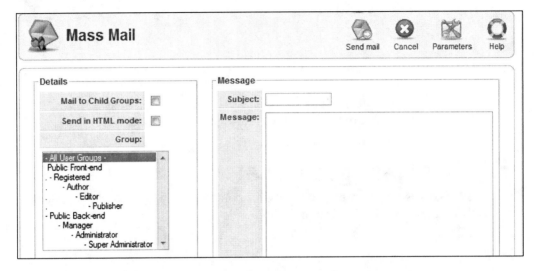

As cynical as this may sound in our age of mass email spamming, it is the best way for contacting registered users. The **Mass Mail** component gives you the tool to do this.

Mail To Child Groups: If you check this, the subgroups of the selected user group also get mail.

Send in HTML mode: Check this if you want the mass mailing to be sent in HTML format. HTML mail is getting more and more popular. Keep in mind, however, that many email clients can deactivate HTML display and that some recipients don't like HTML mail for various reasons.

Group: Here you select which user group you want to target with the mass mailing.

Subject: The subject matter of your email

Message: The actual text

In order to be able to send your mass mailing, the mail settings in **Site | Global Configuration | Server | Mail Settings** have to be set correctly. If you want to send a mass mailing from your local environment, but you don't have a mail server, you can enter the settings of your mail provider's SMTP server.

By clicking the **Parameters** icon you are taken to a screen where you can define Mailbody Suffix and a Subject Prefix for the subject matter line. A prefix is quite useful, allowing email clients to sort emails in a particular order with it.

Global Check-In

If an authorized user requests the edit mode of a content element, this element is *checked out*. This just means that the user who has requested this element is allowed to edit it at that moment. During the edit, the other users will see an icon with a lock symbol in front of the name of the element. Once the document is saved again after the modification, it is automatically *checked in* again and the lock symbol disappears.

But if the user, for example, closes the browser window or if the Internet connection goes down all of a sudden, the element remains checked out and can no longer be modified.

This is where the **Global Check-in** comes into play. If you click on this menu item, all elements that are being edited are checked in and you get a respective listing of the elements.

The disadvantage of this global check-in is the fact that indeed *all* elements get checked in. If someone is just about to make a modification, the element is checked in and somebody else can edit it as well. So be careful with this function and be aware who is online at the time.

Database Table	# of Items	Checked-In
Checking table - jos_banner	Checked-In **0** items	
Checking table - jos_bannerclient	Checked-In **0** items	
Checking table - jos_categories	Checked-In **0** items	
Checking table - jos_contact_details	Checked-In **1** items	✓
Checking table - jos_content	Checked-In **2** items	✓
Checking table - jos_menu	Checked-In **0** items	
Checking table - jos_modules	Checked-In **26** items	✓
Checking table - jos_newsfeeds	Checked-In **1** items	✓
Checking table - jos_plugins	Checked-In **4** items	✓
Checking table - jos_polls	Checked-In **1** items	✓
Checking table - jos_sections	Checked-In **1** items	✓
Checking table - jos_weblinks	Checked-In **1** items	✓

Checked out items have now been all checked in

Summary

In this chapter we learned about a private messaging system, a mass-mailing function, and the global checking-in of content elements in the **Tools** menu.

12
More on Extensions

It is easy to extend Joomla!'s functionality. Due to the popularity of the Joomla! 1.0.x system, numerous customized extensions are available. The Joomla! project team has has opened its own extensions section on its website, which you can access at the URL http://extensions.joomla.org/. Every visitor can download extensions from there, and every registered user can submit his or her extensions to that section.

You will learn how to create your own extensions in Chapter 15. Once you have developed a functional extension, why not offer it on this site? Other users will download it, evaluate, and if what you have developed is also useful to others, you will soon get some feedback and perhaps even offers of help for your continued development.

Extensions can consist of components, modules, plug-ins, or external programs.

It is very easy to install extensions due to Joomla!'s modular structure and the easy-to-use installer. As of November 2007, a total of 2,267 extensions were being offered; 97 of them were components that also work with Joomla! 1.5.

Unfortunately some of the most popular components like Virtuemart (shop system) or the Pony Gallery (image gallery) are not yet available for Joomla! 1.5 at the time of printing. All these popular extensions, however, are being upgraded for Joomla! 1.5 and will hopefully be ready soon. The operation of these extensions will be similar in Joomla! 1.5 to the Joomla! 1.0.x versions. The modifications will mainly show up in the source code and in improved integration.

In this chapter we will install the popular forum software Fireboard, which came from the Joomla!Board project, the DOCman document management system, and a picture gallery called Exposé.

In order for these components to work smoothly, you have to activate the **Legacy Plugin** in the **Plugin Manager** menu. You will know that it is working properly when you see the **Legacy 1.0** display in the menu area of the administration section:

Installation

A component is installed in the **Extensions | Install/Uninstall** menu just like Language packages, Templates, Modules, and Plug-ins.

Every extension package consists of a compressed archive with various files and at least one XML instruction file for the Joomla! installer. The XML file reports the type of extension you are dealing with. Due to this installation method, all types of extensions can be installed from the same installation template in Joomla! 1.5.

You will create some packages like this yourself in Chapters 13 and 15.

Fireboard (Forum)

Fireboard (`http://www.bestofjoomla.com/`) is a terrific forum with numerous features a few of which are:

- User-defined nesting forum categories
- As many forums as you want with access rights
- User profiles and user avatars
- Upload of files and images for a forum entry

Installation

The installation is simple. Download the `Fireboard_Forum_1.0.3_UnzipFirst.zip` program package and unzip it as the filename says. You will find a file called `component_Fireboard_Forum_1.0.3.zip` in the package.

Click on **Extensions | Install/Uninstall** in the menu, select the `component_Fireboard_Forum_1.0.3.zip` file, and click on the **Upload File & Install** button.

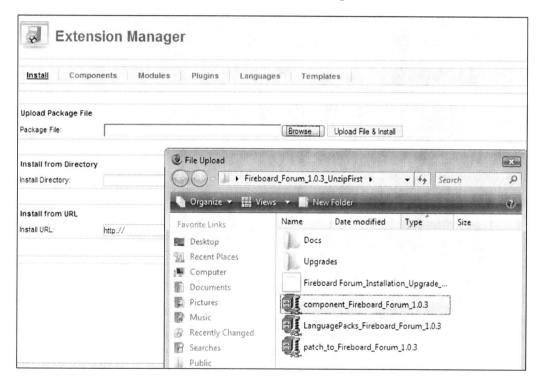

After the upload you will get a screen full of green messages. If you scroll down, you should see the message:

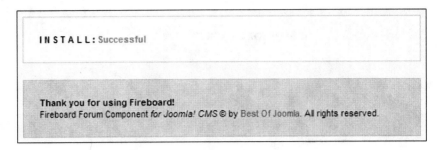

If you check the **Components** menu now, you will see the new item, **Fireboard Forum**. Click on that item and the **Fireboard Control Panel** will appear. But before you can get started, you still have to install the database tables.

Below the **Clean Installation** text, click on the **Apply!** button.

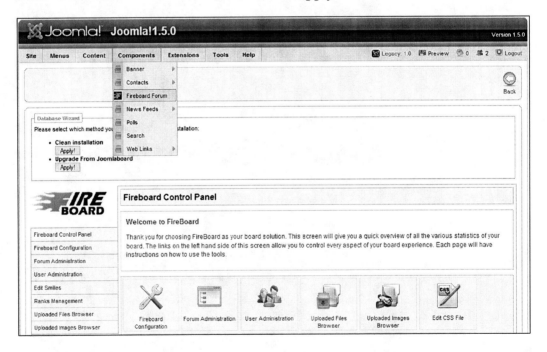

Your forum is now installed.

Configuration

Now that everything has been uploaded, you can define some of the most important parameters. Fireboard has numerous set-up options that could easily fill another five chapters. Hence, only the most important ones are covered here. The configuration section is also well documented; you should have no problems finding what you need.

Enter a name and an email address for your forum under **Fireboard Configuration | Basics**.

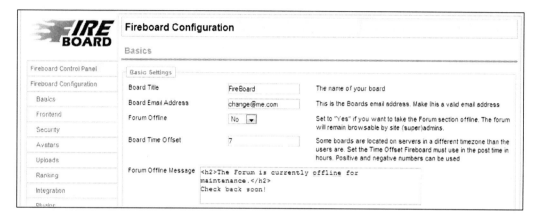

Setting Up a Forum

If you want to work with a forum, you have to, of course, set it up first. It is imperative that you set up a category first, which will act as a container around the forums contained inside.

After you have created the category, you can set up the actual forum, which you can then assign to that category.

Now you can see the category and the forum. The forum is still a little indented to the right in order to symbolize the connection. You still have to explicitly publish the category and the forum.

You have now accomplished the basic tasks for integrating a forum into your website.

Integration into the Website

Let us set up a **Forum** link in the **Joomla! 1.5 Book** menu. To do this, click **Menu | Joomla 1.5 Book | New**. This takes you to the menu item selection. It now has one more item. Click on **Fireboard Forum**.

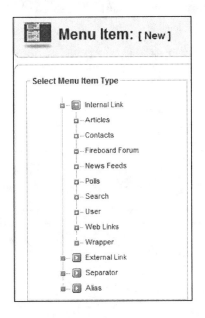

The menu link edit screen opens. Enter a title and an alias name and click on the **Save** icon.

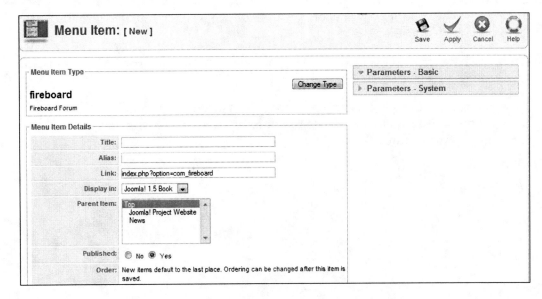

If you reboot and update your website now, you will see the new menu link. If you click on the link, you will see your new forum.

DOCman (Download section, Document Management)

The concept behind DOCman (`http://www.mambodocman.com/`) is to link files with a description and a license, and then offer them to various user groups for download.

DOCman has the following features:

- You can nest your favorite documents in as many categories and subcategories as you want.
- You can store these files on your own server or on a remote server.
- Documents can be protected with access rights.
- You can set up as many user groups as you want in order to control access to the documents.
- You can collect comprehensive download statistics.

DOCman has its own search system. The documents can be searched by file name or their descriptions. There is an additional plug-in, which integrates the search into the Joomla! system.

The actual path to the documents is never revealed. There are various templates for modification of your website. There is growing documentation online in form of a wiki.

Installation

The installation is identical to that for the forum. Download the com_docman_
1.4.0rc1.zip file and install the packages from the menu item **Extensions | Install/
Uninstall**:

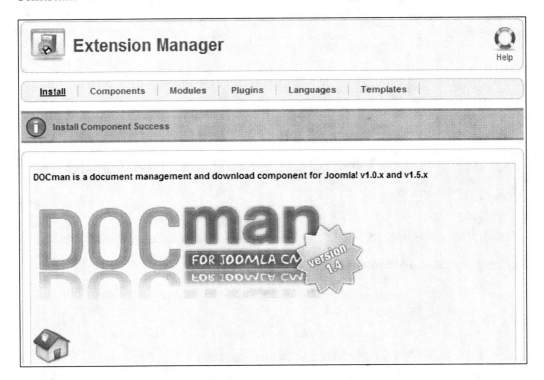

There is a button below the DOCman logo for the installation of example data. Don't
be afraid to click on it. DOCman then installs:

- An example file
- A description for this file
- A category that the description is assigned to
- A user group
- An example license

After the installation of the example data, DOCman is ready to go.

Configuration

DOCman is one of the components that fully support Joomla! 1.5's menu concept.

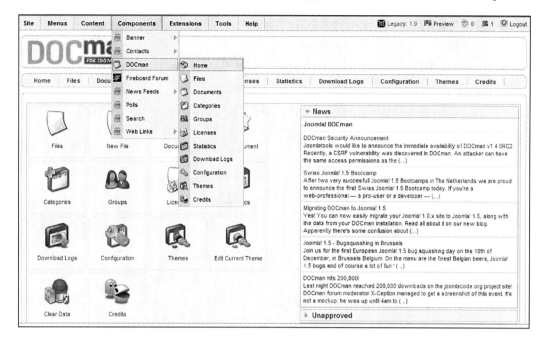

The individual items are found again in the line below the logo. There are also quick access icons in the Docman Control Center and there is an information overview in the right section.

If you click the **Information** link, you will see the extensive DOCman options.

Language

At first you can leave all of the parameters with their default values. You can already see from the numerous set-up options how powerful DOCman has become in the field of document tendering. Take a look at a few individual configuration fields:

- **Home**: This is the Control Panel, the overview page in other words.
- **Files**: This is where you upload the files that you want to offer for download.
- **Documents**: This is where you create a description that you assign to the file. Here you also define who can access the file and what licence is associated with its download.
- **Categories**: This is where you administer the categories that your documents are assigned to.

- **Groups**: This is where you create and administer user groups.

- **Licenses**: Here you define and administer the license terms. You can administer as many licenses as you want.

- **Statistics**: You can see the download statistics here (how often was a file downloaded?).

- **Download Logs**: You can download the log files from here.

- **Configuration**: DOCman's basic configurations.

- **Themes**: DOCman can manage its own themes. You can download additional themes from the project website and then use them for the front end.

- **Credits**: The changelog going back to 2004 is here.

The DOCman Configuration is shown in the following screenshot:

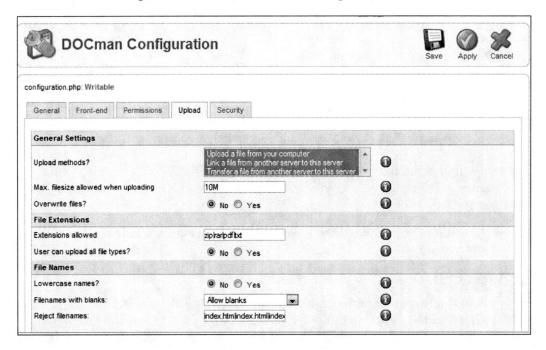

Integration into the Website

This procedure is identical to that for the Fireboard forum. You would like to create a link in the **Joomla! 1.5 Book** to your documents. You have to create a new item in the **Joomla! 1.5 Book** menu. Select **Docman** as menu item type:

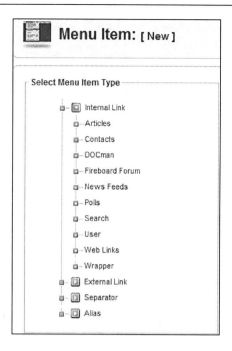

You wind up in the edit screen:

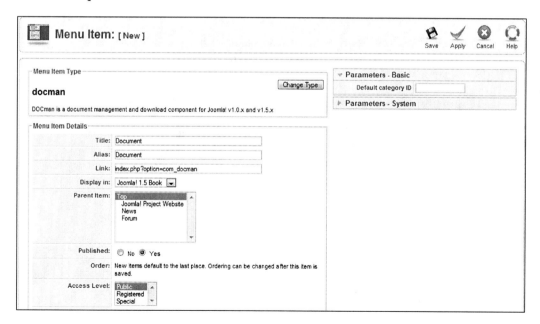

Define the title and the alias for the menu link. You can also activate a particular category of documents directly. Just enter the category ID in the parameters. You will find this ID in the category section of DOCman's administration.

If you click the **Save** icon now and reload your website, you will see a professional-looking download directory:

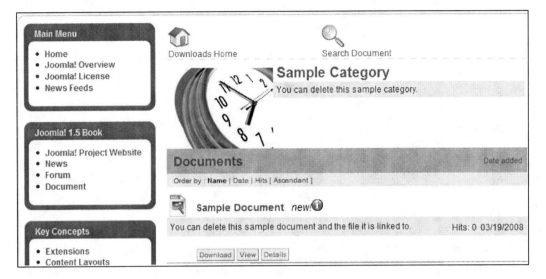

If someone clicks the **Download** button now, the license for this download is displayed. The user has to confirm agreement with it and then the download starts.

Preparing Content

You can set up new files and descriptions for downloading from the administration area or from the front end. For example, if you log in as admin user on your website, you will see an icon and a **Submit File** link in the top area. It takes three steps to upload documents.

In the first step you define where the document is coming from: from your own PC, from another server, or should it "merely" be a link to an existing document?

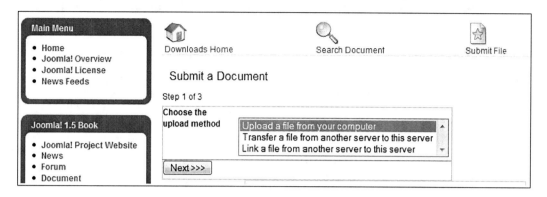

Next **Upload a file your computer** is selected and the zip-file of the component is uploaded.

After the successful upload, we are in Step 3, and we have to select a **Description**, the **Permissions**, the **Category**, and the **License**. By clicking the checkmark in the top area, the new download is saved and immediately published if you are signed in as admin. The admin user also sees a lot more buttons than the normal user.

Normally the document would have to be explicitly approved in the administration area.

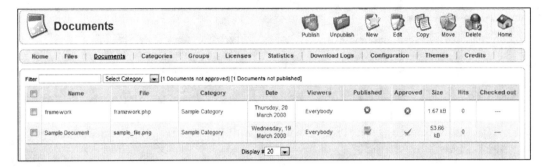

Search Plug-in

You have to install an additional plug-in for the documents to be included in Joomla!'s internal search function. Use the **Extensions | Install/Uninstall** installer again. Download the bot_docman_search_ 1.4.0rc1.zip file and install it with the installer.

You will now find the DOCman search plug-in under **Plugins Manager**, and you still have to activate it.

If you now use the normal website search field to search for the newly added document, it will appear in the hits list with its category.

Supplementary Module

If you are offering a lot of downloads, you may want to display the most often downloaded documents on your website. You need a module for this. Let's install a module that displays the most often downloaded documents. Use the installer to install the mod_docman_mostdown_1.4.0rc1.zip file and activate it under **Extension Modules**.

The module is positioned on the left by default. You can position it wherever you want with the **Edit** function and you can, of course, also change its title. In the parameters you can also define the number of items and whether the icon and the number should be displayed.

Exposé Flash Gallery

Image galleries and video uploads are becoming more and more popular in today's Web 2.0 world. Applications such as Flickr's photo platform (http://www.flickr.com/) and YouTube's video platform (http://www.youtube.com/) make it easier for an individual to publish multimedia content in today's increasingly broad-banded Internet.

The expectations of design are also getting higher and higher. A simple listing of photographs is now considered to be a bit outmoded.

Exposé is one of the Adobe Flash-format-based galleries for pictures, graphics, and videos and it is visually outstanding.

Exposé can:

- Create as many picture albums as you want
- Compress images during the upload to different image sizes
- Create thumbnails for the albums
- Play videos with the Flash Player in a compressed format
- Add audio commentary to the individual images

A version of Exposé that can be installed on your PC allows you to assemble pictures on your own computer. Due to the compact Flash format, the pictures can also be viewed without a broadband connection.

The **Album Manager**, which administers the data in the administration section, makes a few demands on the PHP interpreter; GD, DOMXML, and the iconv extension have to be installed. These preconditions were taken care of by the server in our local XAMPP lite environment.

It is possible that your web space provider doesn't offer these PHP features, but there is a solution for that as well (see *Album Manager in the Administration Section*). When it comes to the front end, the visitor must have at least Flash Player version 8 available in his or her internet browser. This is now installed in 96% of all browsers.

Installation

To install the Exposé gallery, download the `com_expose_4.6.2.zip` package from `http://joomlacode.org/gf/project/expose/frs/ ?action=FrsReleaseBrowse&frs_package_id=2985`. Click on the **Browse** button in the installation template, select the file, and click on **Upload & Install File**. The Joomla! installer uploads the files, deals with the menu items, and displays a success message as shown in the following screenshot. Read this message carefully and remember the password!

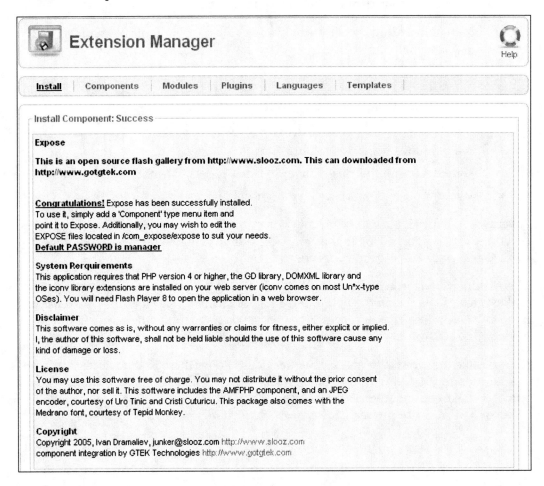

At the time of printing of this book, the gallery had incompatibility problems with Joomla!'s Legacy plug-in. This is peculiar, since Joomla! "merely" uses the gallery as a container and it runs independently. There is a workaround (`http://www.gotgtek.net/forum/index.php?topic=1345.0`) in the gallery's developers' forum. By the time you have this book in your hands there will probably be a customized installation package available for it. If not, you have to insert these SQL commands manually into your database:

```
INSERT INTO 'jos_components' ('id', 'name', 'link',
menuid', 'parent', 'admin_menu_link', admin_menu_
alt', 'option', 'ordering', 'admin_menu_img',
'iscore', 'params') VALUES (51, 'Expose', 'option=com_
expose', 0, 0, '', 'Expose', 'com_expose', 0, '../
administrator/componenets/com_epose/expose_icon.png',
0, ''), (52, 'Manage Albums', '', 0, 51, 'option=com_
expose&task=manage', 'Manage Albums', 'com_expose', 0,
'../administrator/components/com_expose/manage.png',
0, ''), (53, 'Configuration', '', 0, 51, 'option=com_
expose&task=config', 'Configuration', 'com_expose',
1, '../administrator/components/com_expose/config.
png', 0, ''), (54, 'Manual", '', 0, 51, 'option=com_
expose&task=manual', 'Manual', 'com_expose', 2, '../
administrator/components/com_expose/docs.png', 0, '');
```

Subsequently you will have to unzip the file package and copy the files it contains into the appropriate directories as shown in the following figures. You can get the information of what goes where from the `expose.xml` file.

The files in `/components/com_expose` are shown in the following screenshot:

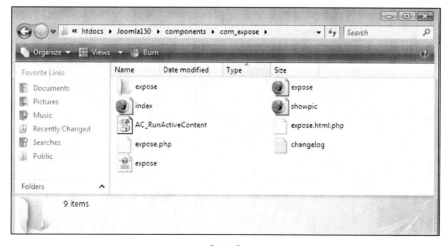

The files in /administrator/com_expose are shown in the following screenshot:

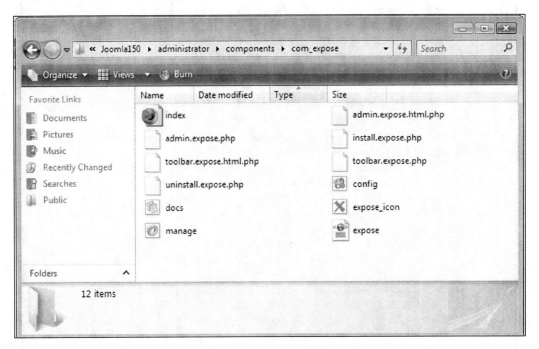

 If the previously described installation of the gallery scares you, keep an eye on the aforementioned forum thread and wait until the developer has a solution.

Integration into the Website

The component is now installed with sample data and still needs to get a menu link in the front end. Let us put it into the **Joomla! 1.5 Book** menu.

Click on **Menus | Joomla! 1.5 Book** and then on the **New** icon. Now create a menu link as described in Chapter 7 in the *Creating a New Menu* section. If you go to your website now, you will see the **Gallery** link in the **Joomla! 1.5 Book** menu. When you click on this link you will see two example folders: one called **Collection**, which contains additional albums, and the other called **Videos**.

If there is an arrow beside the thumbnail picture, it contains additional albums, if there is a number there, the number refers to the number of media files contained in it. If you click on **Sample Collection**, the albums that are contained in it appear.

If you click on **Sample Album,** you are taken to the so-called *Image Strip*.

This strip can be moved manually with the mouse buttons. The image in the middle is magnified. Navigation triangles can be seen on the right and on the left of the Image Strip. You can also move the image strip by clicking on these.

If you click on the picture, you get an individual view:

There you can:

- Scroll forward and backward within the pictures
- Call up an automatic slide show
- Go back to the Image Strip
- Go back to the albums
- Click on the magnifier and see the image in its original size
- Get an indiction which album contains the images
- Call up a help screen that explains the symbols

Videos

Go back to the albums and request the **Video View**. You can see an Image Strip here as well with a preview picture of the video. If you click the picture, you get an individual view of the video.

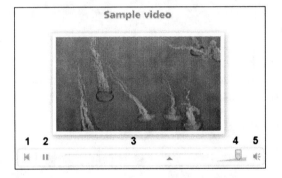

Here you can:

- Navigate through the video
- Turn the sound on and off by clicking on the loudspeaker sumbol and adjust the volume of the sound with the slider

Album Manager in the Administration Section

To load your own pictures and videos into the gallery, go to the Administration section and go to the **Components | Extensions** menu. You will see a login screen asking you for a password. The default password is **manager**. You can (and you should) change the password by clicking on the **Change Password** button. If you make a mark in the checkbox, the password is stored and you won't have to enter it again.

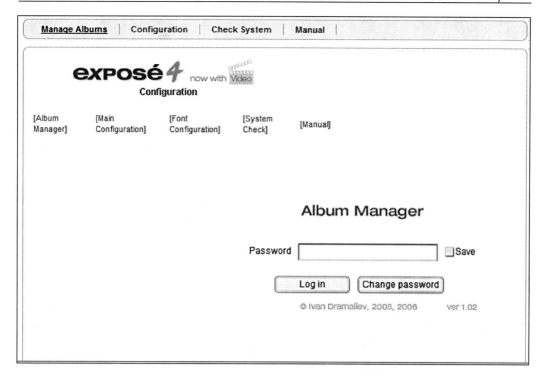

The administration section is divided into several areas.

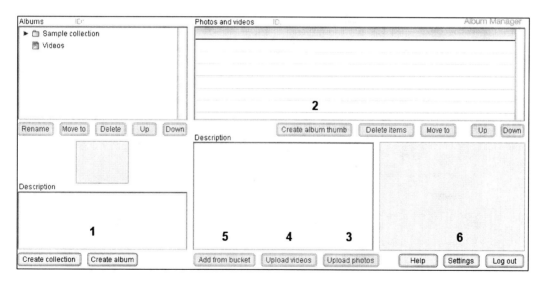

- **(1)** Here you can create a collection and individual albums. In the area above, you can move (**Move To**) the albums, rename them (**Rename**), and delete them (**Delete**).

- **(2)** To create a preview picture for an album, select the picture you want and click on the **Create album thumb** button.

- **(3)** If you click the **Upload photos** button, you can start a dialog with which you can upload a picture from the hard drive to the gallery. The picture is automatically compressed, meaning that you can upload the pictures in the size that they are in the camera.

- **(4)** You can load videos into the gallery in the `flv` format. To convert your videos to that format, you can use the trial version of the Dreamweaver CS3 software, or you can encode the film with the Riva FLV Encoder 2 freeware encoder.

- **(5)** **Add from bucket** is a useful feature. You can use FTP to move files into the `[PathtoJoomla!]components/com_expose/expose/manager/bucket` directory. You can later add these files with the **Add from bucket** function.

- **(6)** In the settings (**Configuration**), you can configure with which parameters pictures and videos are to be uploaded. You can even put a watermark into the pictures.

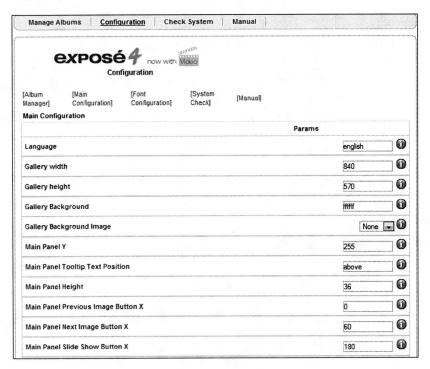

You can finish your management of images by clicking on **Logout** (bottom right).

Uninstallation

If you want to remove this component from your system, go to the **Extensions |
Installation/Uninstallation** menu and remove it in the **Components** tab. Select the
component and click on the **Uninstall** icon.

Album Manager as a Stand-Alone Program

Since working online is sometimes tedious with large files, a *Stand Alone* version of
the **Album Manager** is available for the Windows and Mac OS X operating systems.

You can install the program in Windows by double-clicking the `AlbumManager-2.7-
Setup.msi` file. The **Album Manager** works with the `PathtoJoomla!]components/
com_expose/expose` directory.

If you are working in a local server environment, you can just refer to this directory
when starting the **Album Manager**.

The **Album Manager** will then let you work with the existing structure. The mode of
operation is then identical to the online version.

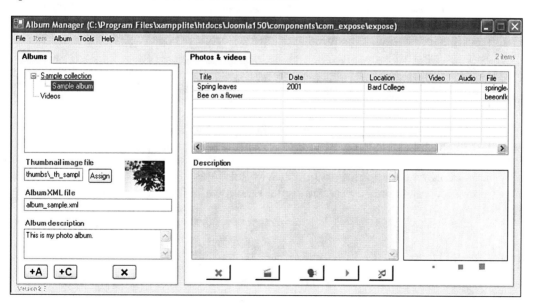

If you want to use the **Album Manager** for a website on the Internet, simply
download the directory before you start working with it and upload it again to the
server when you are finished.

Integration into the Joomla! Framework

Since Joomla! has changed from a pure content management system to a framework, it is now possible to write Joomla! components that no longer look like Joomla! The gallery component, for example, has a very loose connection to Joomla! 1.5. The gallery is displayed in a wrapper component similar to an iFrame. The back-end administration also works with an iFrame; that's why there is a request for a password in the back end. Other components, as for instance the installed forum or the document administration are integrated deeper into the system and in the case of the Community Builder, for instance, swap login procedures.

With Joomla! 1.5, a lot of these features can now be integrated more elegantly and all of the third-party teams have already been working on the integration of their components since the beginning of 2007.

Problems with Third-Party Components

Update problems become more of an issue as the popularity of Joomla! grows.

Updates

This past year, a new improved version of Joomla! was released on the average of once per month and a lot of Joomla!'s previous security problems, among other things, were successfully defeated.

If you are operating a website that consists of only Joomla! core code, you are on the safe side. Download the update package, overwrite the old files, and you have a "fresh" system.

There are rarely any table updates for the database. Even with the upgrade from Joomla! 1.0.x to Joomla! 1.5.x, only two fields have been changed!

But there are often no updates or only cursory updates for additional components. Operators of a website are often afraid of a new installation and therefore stay with the older version.

Security

If you are using a lot of additional components, you will often find yourself in a pickle. For example, the Joomla! development team recommends the use of PHP safe mode, to set register global on OFF, as well as other measures that will make Joomla! very secure.

However, some components don't work with these settings. You now have to make a decision of abstaining from the use of such components or to live with a certain amount of insecurity.

What should you Do?

When you make these decisions, always keep in mind what a broken website (and server) would do to your business. How important and how sensitive is the information on your server?

In some cases it may have been acceptable to have a third party operate a website or email address system for you or to at least have them store all of your information from the user registration; but not anymore. Due to the complexity of the components, there is still an update and security issue and sometimes this is neglected by third-party developers and website operators.

A Google Summer of Code program team this year is tackling the development of an update system for Joomla! that will download updates when needed and perhaps will even install them. An update system of this type would also do a world of good for extensions.

 I am not going to tell you not to use Release Candidates (RC) or even Beta versions online. I live in the real world as well and sometimes clients demand it. Depending on the project, some Beta versions are very stable. MySQL (database) ran for a long time as a Beta version and so did the Apache webserver. Just be aware of the basic risks! If at all possible, try to make do with the standard version of Joomla!. That way you are assured to be on the safe side.

Summary

In this chapter we learned more on extensions. We also learned how to use a customized component available for Joomla!. Finally we discussed the issues concerning the use of third-party components. In the next chapter we will learn about creating our own templates.

13
Writing Your Own Joomla! Templates

In order to customize the appearance of your website to that of your company's image, you have to modify an existing template or create a new one. In this chapter you will learn the basics of building your own Joomla! templates.

Corporate Identity

Corporate Identity (CI) refers to the self-image and the appearance of an enterprise. This appearance, the identity, either arises from the enterprise's tradition or it is completely invented in a newly created establishment. This identity is important to give the customer a feel for the enterprise and to enable recognition.

Corporate Identity includes:

- Corporate Image (price, product, and advertising strategy)
- Corporate Design (visual appearance)
- Corporate Communication
- Corporate Behavior (behavior of employees towards each other and the outside world)

All of the above areas have to be considered when developing a website. In this chapter, we will examine Corporate Design. At a minimum, it consists of a logo, a character font, and the house colors that the enterprise uses.

The visitors to your website should recognize your enterprise on the first visit.

HTML/XHTML, CSS, and XML

The abbreviations HTML/XHTML, CSS, and XML stand for Internet technologies that Joomla! works with. The World Wide Web Consortium standardizes these technologies.

HTML/XHTML

The World Wide Web is based on HTML. HTML is not a programming language, but a text-description language.

Each piece of text consists of structures like headings, lists, bold and italic areas, tables, and much more. HTML works with so-called tags. A tag has an opening portion and a closing portion. For example, a first-level heading looks as follows:

```
<h1>This is a heading</h1>
```

The tags are interpreted in the browser and the text is displayed according to their significance.

HTML is very easy to learn and many online tutorials can be found. HTML is not being developed any further; the successor to HTML is XHTML version 1.0.

CSS

Cascading Style Sheets (CSS) are an extension to HTML. CSS is not a programming language either, but a vocabulary for defining the format properties of individual HTML elements.

With the help of CSS commands, you can, for example, specify that the first-level headings should have a character size of 18 points in the character font Arial, are not bold, and have a spacing of 1.9 cm to the next paragraph. Such options are not possible with pure HTML and were not necessary when HTML was first developed. With the progressive commercialization of the Internet, additional formatting possibilities do, however, become more and more important.

CSS data can be integrated into HTML in the following three ways:

In the Central HTML File

The CSS commands are defined in the head section of the HTML file like this:

```
<head>
<title>title of the file</title>
<style type="text/css">
<!--
```

```
/* ... this is where the CSS commands are defined ... */
-->
</style>
</head>
```

In a Separate CSS File

If the CSS commands apply to several HTML files, they can be stored in a separate file and the path to this file can be specified in the HTML header. This is the version that Joomla! uses.

```
<head>
<title>title of the file</title>
<link rel="stylesheet" type="text/css" href="formats.css">
</head>
```

Within an HTML Tag

CSS commands can also be inserted within an HTML tag:

```
<body>
<h1 style="… CSS commands ...">...</h1>
</body>
```

Combinations

These three methods can be combined without any problem in an HTML file. It is, for instance, possible to subsequently overwrite CSS commands that were defined in a central file in the additional source code of an HTML page. This practice, however, quickly leads to confusing structures; it is better to customize the central file.

XML

The **Extended Markup Language (XML)** is a universe in itself. It represents a meta-language and is derived from the much more complex **SGML (Standardized Generalized Markup Language)** that was developed in the sixties. XML is often used for configuration files and as an interchange format. For our purposes, you need XML as the description language for the metadata of the templates that you want to create. These metadata are primarily relevant for the **Template Installer** and the display in the **Template Manager**.

In principle, these data also consist of opening and closing tags. For example:

```
<name>Joomla! Book</name>
```

The difference between HTML and XML is that no tags are predefined in XML. Because of that, you are completely unrestricted in the organization of the structures and the naming of the tags.

Creating Your Own Templates

Now we want to create our own template. There are several things to consider before we have a finished template packages. Let's take it one step at a time.

Concept

Before you start working, you have to create a concept. The work starts with a sketch or a diagram, especially when producing templates. It is up to you whether you want to create this sketch with an image editing program like Adobe Photoshop, Microsoft Paint that comes with Windows, the open-source program GIMP, or even with a piece of paper and crayons.

Fixed Size or Variable (Fluid) or Both

You can create two kinds of templates. Templates that adapt their structure to the size of the browser window and templates that have a fixed size. An example for the flexible layout: if you have 2048 pixels across your screen and the browser window is maximized, then your page is stretched accordingly. That can look strange if you use graphical, non-scalable elements like logos and signatures in your template. You have no control of what it is going to look like.

Your other choice is to decide on a certain resolution and to position all the elements exactly on the pixels in the template. This has the advantage that your web page always looks the way you want. Unfortunately, you do not know the resolution of the monitor that is viewing your page. If that monitor has a resolution of 800 x 600 pixels, then your page fills the screen. On a large screen with a resolution of 1400 x 1050 pixels, it occupies about a quarter of the screen surface and looks a little lost.

You will have to weigh the pros and cons and make a decision on one or the other, or you can consider barrier freedom (Chapter 14) and offer both versions. You must have seen websites where you can even change the font size. In addition to the font size buttons there is also often a button to select different layouts.

If you prefer the fixed size, you should select a size that looks presentable on most screens, in other words 800 x 600 pixels. Since the browser has a scroll bar on the right side and the browser window is framed, the available width is even smaller, meaning that you have a maximum of 780 pixels to work with.

Structure

You are dealing with structured data and first have to determine a general allocation. Joomla! normally uses a structure as shown in the following figure:

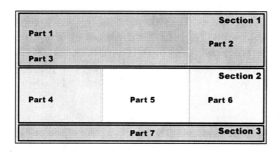

Section 1:

- Part 1: This is where your logo or a picture and the name of the website goes.
- Part 2: This is where the search field is.
- Part 3: This is where the linked navigation path goes (Breadcrumbs).

Section 2:

- Part 4: The most important menus are shown in the left column.
- Part 5: The actual page content goes here.
- Part 6: The right column is a place for additional menus.

Section 3:

- Part 7: The footer.

HTML Conversion

Now you have to convert the concept into HTML and CSS. Depending on the graphics editing program that you have used to create it, there is a possibility that the picture can be automatically exported to HTML code. You can also do the conversion manually in a text editor, in an HTML editor like Dreamweaver (http://www.adobe.com/products/dreamweaver), or in one of the numerous free HTML editors (http://www.thefreecountry.com/webmaster/htmleditors.shtml).

<table> or <div>?

The <div> tag is a replacement and a supplement for the <table> tag in HTML.

You can enclose several HTML elements, such as text and graphics in one common area with it. This general area does nothing for the time being but start in a new line of the continuing text. The <div> tag does not have any other properties. There are big benefits, however, in using a combination of <div> tags with CSS commands. <div> was specifically developed for the purpose of being formatted with CSS commands.

Until 2004, it was common practice to define website structures with generous employment of HTML tables. With CSS and the <div> HTML element becoming more and more popular and with browsers being able to interpret these, more and more templates are being structured without HTML tables. However, rarely do we see websites that contain only semantically correct HTML and that have layouts that are built 100% without tables. The first step in structuring your website in that direction is the use of the <div> tags.

Joomla! 1.5 is also gradually straying from the 'table path' and is starting to deliver semantically correct HTML. Nonetheless, it continues to be possible to structure your site layout with HTML tables.

There are no table tags in the included rhuk_milkyway template; the entire table-like structure is created with <div> tags. Take a look at the original source code of this template to familiarize yourself with this technology. You can get more information about <div> tags at selfhtml (in German). Dreamweaver also supports this technology.

The source code of the HTML conversion looks somewhat like the following listing. The code is kept simple on purpose and is *not* consistent with the XHTML standard in the header. The file name of this layout file has to be index.php since Joomla! searches it for embedded commands per PHP.

HTML file /index.php:

```
<html>
  <head>
    <link href="/joomla150/templates/joomla150buch/css/template.css"
     rel="stylesheet" type="text/css" />
  </head>
    <body>
      <div id="part11">header / header<br /><br />
      <div id="section1">section1</div>
      <div id="section2">section2</div>
      </div>
```

```
        <div id="part2">main display area / main<br /><br />
        <div id="section3">breadcrumbs</div>
        <div id="section6">right side</div>
        <div id="section4">left side</div>
        <div id="section5">content</div>
        </div>
        <div id="part3">footer /footer<br /><br />
        <div id="section7">section7</div>
        </div>
    </body>
</html>
```

The subsequent CSS file from the individual template is integrated into the header area of the code. At the moment this CSS file contains only one command that defines the typeface.

CSS file /css/template.css:

```
body{
font-size: 12px;
font-family: Helvetica,Arial,sans-serif; }
#Part1{ /*header*/
float: left;
border: 2px dotted green; }
#Part2{ /*main*/
float: left;
border: 2px dotted yellow; }
#Part3{ /*footer*/
clear:all;
border: 2px dotted red; }
#Section1{ /*top right*/
float: left; width: 18em;
margin: 0 0 1.2em;
border: 1px dashed silver; background-color: #eee; }
#Section2{ /*top left*/
float: right; width: 12em;
margin: 0 0 1.1em;
background-color: #eee; border: 1px dashed silver; }
#Section3{ /*breadcrumbs*/
border: 1px dashed silver;
background-color: #eee; }
#Section4{ /*left side*/
float: left; width: 15em;
margin: 0 0 1.2em;
border: 1px dashed silver; }
```

```
#Section5{ /*content*/
margin: 0 12em 1em 16em;
padding: 0 1em;
border: 1px dashed silver; }
#Section6{ /*right side*/
float: right; width: 12em;
margin: 0 0 1.1em;
background-color: #eee; border: 1px dashed silver; }
#Section7{ /*footer*/
margin: 0 0 1.1em;
background-color: #eee; border: 1px dashed silver; }
```

You will create this first template manually in the Joomla! directory. When the template is ready, you can turn it into a compressed installation package that it can then be installed by a third party (or by you yourself) using the Joomla! installer. Save the HTML layout file by the name of `index.php` in the also newly created `[PathtoJoomla]/templates/joomla150book/`directory. Save the `template.css` file in the `[PathtoJoomla]/templates/joomla150book/css/` directory.

The basic structure of your template is done. Now you have to define the template more exactly for Joomla! with the help of an XML file so that it will be displayed in the template administration section.

Directory Structures of the Template

Now it's time to take care of certain conventions. As previously discussed, the template has to be stored in a specific directory structure.

```
[PathtoJoomla]/templates/[name of the template]/
```

```
[PathtoJoomla]/templates/[name of the template]/CSS/
```

```
[PathtoJoomla]/templates/[name of the template]/images/
```

The name of the template cannot contain blanks and other special characters. When this template is later installed as a package, the **Template Installer** has to create a directory from this name. Depending on the operating system, exotic combinations of characters can cause problems. In addition, the name should be meaningful. Here we will use `joomla150book` as the name of the template.

Various files with predefined names have to be present in the template directories.

- **Layout File**: This is the HTML file that we created earlier:`/templates/ joomla150book/index.php`. It should have the `.php` ending, since the dynamic Joomla! module elements that we will insert later have to be interpreted by PHP.

- **Preview Picture**: The `/templates/joomla150book/template_thumbnail. png` file contains a preview image of your template for preview selection in Joomla! administration in the **Extensions | Template Manager** menu. Preview pictures have a format of 200 by approximately 150 pixels. You can create this file later when you can see your template.

- **Metadata of the Template**: The `/templates/joomla150_book/ templateDetails.xml` file represents the construction manual for the template installer and contains the installations for the template selection in the template manager. Here you specify the location where the files are to be copied, who the author is, and additional metadata about the template. During subsequent installation of this file by the Joomla! installer, PHP reads this file and copies the files to the place specified by the XML file. For the example template, you can use the file from the following listing (`templateDetails.xml`) and populate it with your own data. For every file that you use in the template, a respective XML container has to be populated with the file name and the correct path.

```
<files>
  <filename> ... enter the filename of a file in the TemplateRoot
                                directory ...
  </filename>
  <filename> ... for every file a filename-Container
   </filename>
</files>
```

The other containers of the XML file are there for the description of the template. Here is the complete functional listing of the XML file:

`templateDetails.xml`:

```
<install version="1.5" type="template">
<name>joomla150book</name>
<version>1.0</version>
<creationDate>11.11.2007</creationDate>
<author>Hagen Graf</author>
<copyright>GNU/GPL</copyright>
<authorEmail>hagen@cocoate.com</authorEmail>
<authorUrl>http://www.cocoate.com</authorUrl>
<version>0.1</version>
```

```
<description>... description</description>
<files>
<filename>index.php</filename>
<filename>templateDetails.xml</filename>
<filename>template_thumbnail.png</filename>
<filename>css/template.css</filename>
</files>
</install>
```

Create the `templateDetails.xml` file in the `[PathtoJoomla]/templates/joomla150book/` directory as well.

- **CSS File**: You can use several CSS files for your template. What name you give the CSS file and how you create it is up to you. There are, however, standard descriptions for various CSS elements. For your first attempt, you need a CSS file with the name `/templates/joomla150_book/css/template.css`.

- **Graphics, Images**: Here you can enter user-defined image files that you need in your template. The installer then copies the files into the `images` folder. The file name appears as `/templates/joomla150_book/images/[user-defined image files]`.

First Trial Run

Once you have reproduced all the structures in the `[pathtoJoomla!]/templates/` subdirectory, you can already see your new template in the **Extensions | Template Manager** menu of your Joomla! administration and you can make it default:

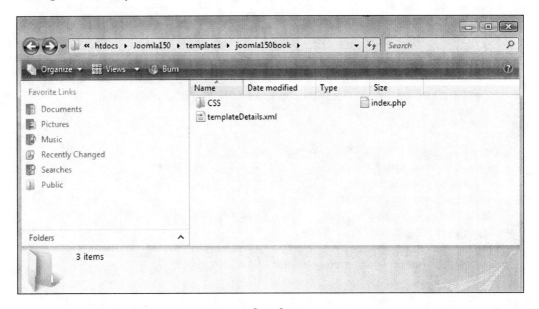

When you call up your website, you will see your new template. Unfortunately, there is no content shown yet. Since this content is produced dynamically, you have to integrate it piece by piece into your new template.

Integration of the Joomla! Module

The integration of the Joomla! module takes place by means of commands embedded into the HTML code. Joomla! uses the namespace `jdoc` to integrate various elements into the template. If you insert the following highlighted line into the header of the layout file:

```
<head>
<jdoc:include type="head" />
</head>
```

the title of the site and the news feed symbol are already correctly displayed.

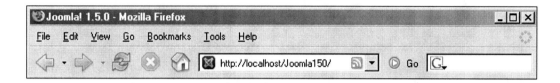

If you call up the source code of this site, you will notice that Joomla! has copied the entire metadata that you had entered in administration into the HTML code. In addition, the RSS feeds have been integrated by means of link tags and these will be displayed as feed symbols in browsers like Firefox that support this technology.

Joomla! Metadata:

```
...
<head>
  <base href="http://localhost/joomla150/" />
  <meta http-equiv="Content-Type" content="text/html;
            charset=utf-8" />
  <meta name="robots" content="index, follow" />
  <meta name="keywords" content="joomla, joomla!, Joomla,
            Joomla!, J!" />
  <meta name="description" content="Joomla! - dynamic portal-engine
            and Content-Management-System" />
  <meta name="generator" content="Joomla! 1.5 - Open Source Content
            Management" />
  <title>Welcome to the Frontpage</title>
  <link href="/joomla150/index.php?format=feed&amp;type=rss"
            rel="alternate"
type="application/rss+xml" title="RSS 2.0" />
```

```
<link href="/joomla150/index.php?format=feed&amp;type=atom"
            rel="alternate"
type="application/atom+xml" title="Atom 1.0" />
<script type="text/javascript"
            src="/joomla150/media/system/js/mootools.js"></script>
<script type="text/javascript"
            src="/joomla150/media/system/js/caption.js"></script>
...
```

Since this has worked so well, we will waste no time and get to the other relevant `jdoc` tag insertions.The command: `<jdoc:include type="modules" name="top" style="none" />` for example, expects the type of insertion as `type` parameter, in our case `modules`. The `name` parameter marks the position of the module (`top`, `right`, `left`, `user1`, ...) on the website. You can assign this position to your module from the **Extensions | Module** menu in the **Module Section**. The `style` parameter, finally, contains a value that pertains to the type of HTML code that is being delivered by the module. For example, `none` delivers pure HTML output without the surrounding `<div>` tags. The following table describes the module parameters:

Parameter	Output
table	The module is displayed in a table.
horz	The module is displayed horizontally in a cell of a surrounding table.
xhtml	The module is output in an XTML-compliant div element.
rounded	The output is in a format in which round corners can be displayed. The class of the element is changed from `moduletable` to `module`.
beezDivision	Special switch for the *Beez* template. The size of the header can be changed with this. This switch is not available outside of the *Beez*-template.
none	The module is output without any formatting.

You can get a description of the `jdoc` insertions in the `index.php` file in the following listing.

`index.php` with `jdoc` insertions:

```
<html><head>
<jdoc:include type="head" />
<link href="/joomla150/templates/joomla150book/css/template.css"
                                rel="stylesheet"
type="text/css" />
</head>
<body>
<div id="Part1">header / header
<div id="Section1">Section1 <jdoc:include type="modules"
                            name="user3" style="xhtml" />
```

```
    </div>
    <div id="Section2">Section2 <jdoc:include type="modules"
                                    name="top" style="xhtml" />
    </div>
    </div>
    <div id="Part2">main display area / main
    <div id="Section3">breadcrumbs <jdoc:include type="modules"
                                    name="breadcrumb"
    style="xhtml" /></div>
    <div id="Section6">right side <jdoc:include type="modules"
                                    name="right"
    style="xhtml" /></div>
    <div id="Section4">left side <jdoc:include type="modules" name="left"
    style="xhtml" /></div>
    <div id="section5">content <jdoc:include type="component"
    style="xhtml" /></div>
    </div>
    <div id="Part3">footer /footer
    <div id="Section7">Section7<jdoc:include type="modules" name="footer"
    style="xhtml" />
    </div>
    </div>
    </body></html>
```

If you call up the website with the modified HTML code on the local server, you can already see the dynamic content. Your new template has already been filled with all of the data. The visual aspect of the result could still use some improvements, but nonetheless the concept works.

Now we still have to pack the template into an installation package.

Creating a Template Package

To give your template to others, you have to compress it into a ZIP archive. Before you do that, create a current preview image of your template (template_thumbnail.png) with a size of 227 x 162 pixels. This thumbnail should now be displayed if you pass your mouse pointer across the name link in the template section.

Now pack all of the joomla150book files and all of its subdirectories into a ZIP archive. In addition, select of all of the files and folders in the [PathtoJoomla]/ templates/joomla150book/ folder and pack them all into the joomla150book.zip file. Make a backup of this file and the ZIP file.

Uninstallation of the Template

You can now pass this package to others or you can install it yourself. If you want to try the installation, you have to remove the newly created template again from your Joomla! system.

To remove it, you first have to designate a different template as the default template. Click on the **Extensions | Template Manager** menu, select the desired template, and click on the **Default** icon.

Now you can uninstall your template. Go to the **Extensions | Install/Uninstall** menu and click on the **Templates** tab. Select the newly created `joomla150book` template and click on the **Uninstall** icon.

Installation with the Joomla! Template Installer

After you have eliminated all traces of your development and have backed up your work, go to the **Extensions | Install/Uninstall** menu.

You can install your ZIP package from here. Select the `joomla150book.zip` file and install it by clicking on the **Upload File & Install** button. The installer will report that the installation was successful and this success message will also display the description from the XML file.

What Source Code Comes from Joomla?

After we have jumped the most difficult hurdles by creating the template, let's take a look into the HTML code that Joomla! delivers to us.

Joomla!, naturally, creates code that is inserted into the container we have created. This code consists of HTML with sprinkled in CSS classes and CSS IDs. Among other things, Joomla! incorporates two CSS files that describe particular classes and IDs and that are inserted into each and every template.

These are the `/templates/system/css/system.css` and the `/templates/system/css/general.css` files.

These are inserted in the `<head>` area with the following commands:

```
<link rel="stylesheet" href="<?php echo $this->baseurl ?>
/templates/system/css/system.css" type="text/css" />
<link rel="stylesheet" href="<?php echo $this->baseurl ?>
/templates/system/css/general.css" type="text/css" />
```

Both these files contain the classes and the IDs that will pop up during the further course of this chapter.

The Left Module Position in Detail

Let's take a closer look at the left module bar.

This is the HTML code in the index.php layout file:

```
<div id="Section4">left side <jdoc:include type="modules" name="left"
                                style="xhtml" />
```

The `<div>` tag for this section is formatted by a CSS ID with the name of Section4.

If you take a look at the delivered HTML code in a browser (right-click on **Website, Display Source Code**), you will, of course, see a lot more code that was created by the jdocs request.

Excerpt from the delivered HTML source code:

```
... additional HTML commands
<div id="Section4">left side
<div class="moduletable_menu">
<h3>main menu</h3>
<ul class="menu">
```

```
<li id="current" class="active item1">
<a href="http://localhost/joomla150/">front page</a>
</li>
<li class="item2">
<a href="/joomla150/joomla-license">Joomla! License</a>
</li>
</ul>
</div>
... additional HTML commands
```

The CSS classes `menu`, `active item1`, and `active item2` are noticeable in this code. You will find additional CSS suffixes right away in one of the CSS files of the default rhuk_milkyway template:

```
div.module_menu h3 {
font-family: Helvetica, Arial, sans-serif;
font-size: 12px;
font-weight: bold;
color: #eee;
margin: -23px -4px 5px -5px;
padding-left: 10px;
padding-bottom: 2px;
}
div.module_menu {
margin: 0;
padding: 0;
margin-bottom: 15px;
}
div.module_menu div div div {
padding: 10px;
padding-top: 30px;
padding-bottom: 15px;
width: auto;
}
div.module_menu div div div div {
background: none;
padding: 0;
}
div.module_menu ul {
margin: 10px 0;
padding-left: 20px;
}
div.module_menu ul li a:link, div.module_menu ul li a:visited {
font-weight: bold;
}
```

In this case the CSS blocks take care of the rounded corners in the menu. There are additional items in the CSS file that format the third-order heading (`<h3><h3>`) and a non-sorted list (the menu links) for this case.

So far, so good. This type of formatting is deliberate and the output of the necessary `<div>` tags can also be changed with the `style` attribute. We used the `style xhtml` parameter in our example template; in this template, the `style rounded` parameter is used. It delivers the respective four-part `<div>` tag.

This type of code creation is really suitable for CSS formatting. If you continue reading through the source code, you will also run across tables again. The **Content Component** still works with tables! This is where the problems start if you want to format the content (the part in the middle) separately without tables. However, Joomla! has a solution for this as well.

Template Overrides (Customize HTML Output without Changing the Core Files)

In order to get grip on the problem of table display, you would normally have to change the Joomla! core files. Your content would then be free of tables, but the file could possibly be overwritten with the next update.

From Joomla! 1.5.0 on there are now the so-called `views` that present a solution for this problem; you will find a number of different views for the display of logic components. With the `com_content` component, these are, for example, `archive`, `article`, `category`, `frontpage`, and `section`. These five folders contain files that make different content views available. I hope you remember the table and the blog view. Each of these five folders also contains a `tmpl` folder, which in turn contains various files that are responsible for the display.

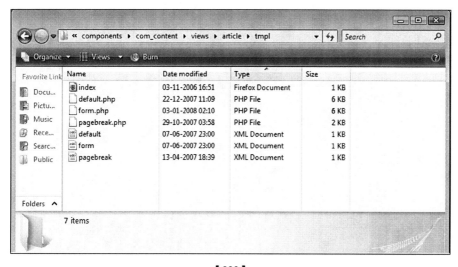

In order to travel down that route you need an additional directory in your template directory. If we are staying with this example, this directory must be called `com_content/article`, since you want to change the layout of the `content` component in display type `article`.

In other words, you have to copy the files from:

> `[PathtoJoomla}/components/com_content/view/article/tmpl/*.*`

into your new template directory and then you can do the customizations that you need.

> `[PathtoJoomla}/templates/[yourtemplate]/html/com_content/article`

This can easily be duplicated in the `Beez` template. The aforementioned files are here in:

> `[PathtoJoomla}/templates/beez/html/com_content/article`

and thus overwrite (override) the core files without changing them.

Joomla! looks for these files in the template directory. If they are there, they are used. If they are not there, the core files from the components are used.

Summary

This chapter has helped you create your own first template. In the next chapter we will learn about barrier freedom and Joomla!.

14

Barrier Freedom and Joomla!

by Angie Radtke

When Hagen asked me whether I would like to take over this chapter of his book, my stomach turned a little; there was only one week left before the deadline. Phew!

But all right, I'm not exactly unprepared. A lot of this chapter is in detailed form in the book *Barrier-free Web Design* that I wrote with Michael Charlier.

I only have one chapter in Hagen's book, so I will have to limit myself to the most important things. I will address the basics of barrier-free web design and describe the concept behind the `Beez` default template with which you can create barrier-free websites under Joomla!.

The question about whether barrier freedom and Joomla! could be combined was a hot potato until version 1.0.3. It was possible, but the amount of work you had to put in to get it done was great. I want to assure you that nothing stands in the way anymore of making your content barrier free.

Barrier Freedom—What is it Anyway?

The Internet has become a matter of course for most people. Information from all over the world is ready for access. And what is perhaps even more relevant: Special offers from the local home improvement store, opening times of the government offices, and the entire telephone book can be called up on your home monitor. It is no longer necessary to spend hours at the library or on the telephone to find information, just check the Web.

However, not everyone can take advantage of this technology. In particular, people that have a physical or mental disability who have difficulties participating in life to the fullest, could benefit tremendously from this communications technology. However, they are often stopped by barriers that it make it difficult or even completely impossible for them to get at the information or to take advantage of the offers. Most of these barriers can be overcome if the technology is designed properly.

Operators of online shops or banks that offer Internet banking should be totally familiar with this not-so-small target group.

The goal for barrier-free web design is to make content and interaction in the World Wide Web accessible for as many user groups and terminals as possible.

There are people who have a physical disability that makes it difficult for them to access information on the Internet. Barrier-free web design is commonly referred to as *Internet for the blind*. However, I want to emphasize that that is not everything; as a matter of fact it is only the smallest part of barrier freedom. I have asked myself many times why this has become the common belief. The cause, more than likely, is that the monitor has become the classic symbol for the computer and if you cannot see, then you cannot use a monitor. I have, however, noticed in my daily routines that visually-impaired people have an easier time with difficult-to-access sites than people with all kinds of other disabilities.

Visually-impaired people are individuals whose remaining sight is only a small percentage of the average person's sight. Some of them can still decipher text and recognize color settings by increasing the font size, while others have to have the information output via acoustic means or they have to touch the text by using a Braille output device.

The percentage of people with less severe visual impairment is significantly higher.

Approximately one quarter of all people in the working age-group complain about various degrees of ametropia (eye abnormalities such as nearsightedness, farsightedness, astigmatisms, and the like). The percentage increases significantly as people get older. Some of these conditions can be compensated for quite effectively with eye glasses, others only in a limited way. Some eye diseases, such as cataracts and glaucoma can be either fixed or at least improved surgically. Others, such as pigmentary retinitis or diabetic retinitis, result in gradual deterioration of vision and finally in a total loss of sight. With a condition called 'tunnel vision', the visual field of the affected person is extremely reduced, sometimes to the size of a silver dollar or a two-Euro coin held in front of the face at arm's length.

About 10% of the male population is affected by a mild case of color blindness. This usually affects them in a way where they cannot differentiate between certain shades of red and green. Color blindness for other colors, total color blindness, or red-green color blindness in women are very rare.

Another potential group of users have problems with the common input technologies. Not everyone can operate a mouse or use a keyboard.

There are a number of reasons for this: arms and fingers are immobilized or only move spontaneously and are difficult to control. Others have no hands and arms or are paralyzed from the neck down or on one side after a stroke. As longs as a person is able to even just enter a binary signal, the well-known 0 or 1, he or she can learn how to operate all of a computer's functions as long as he or she has the energy, puts in the effort to learn, and has the appropriate software.

In the world there are many that suffer from a severe hearing disability. Thousands of these were so severely affected when learning language skills that they only have a limited command of language (as in the fourth to sixth grade of school). This makes it necessary to offer understandable text.

When these people communicate with each other, these people prefer sign language. They also use sign language to understand foreign or more difficult content. Sign language is a system of signs and gestures that is independent from spoken language.

Careful

It is not just people with hearing disabilities that surf the Web without sound or with speakers turned off! It is therefore not sufficient to, for example, to output only acoustic warning signals; they have to always be accompanied by a clearly understandable visual signal.

The more the Internet captures all areas of life, the more apparent are situational disabilities: slow connections in a hotel, uncontrollable lighting conditions in a moving train, having to work without sound at one's place of work.

Everybody profits from accessible websites. And these don't always have to abide by all of the rules that government websites are committed to. Even just small steps in the direction of site accessibility can help to make sites significantly more user-friendly.

Due to its popularity, Joomla! can be at the forefront of this movement. With the default `Beez` template, it is now relatively easy to create accessible websites that can be used by many.

The Legal Backround

The efforts to make computers accessible for disabled people predate the Internet. The United Nations passed the *World Programme of Action (WPA)* in December of 1982, emphasizing access to modern technologies for people with disabilities. Large IT enterprises like IBM, Microsoft, and Sun contributed greatly in the effort to improve access in the following years. In 1993, when the HTTP protocol was barely two years old, the General Assembly of the United Nations passed a resolution, asking for equal rights to information and communication for people with physical disabilities. The first countries soon developed regulations or laws to implement these specifications.

With the founding of the W3C in 1994, there was now expert body that also took it on itself to develop guidelines for barrier-free access to websites in addition to other standardization measures. This work was largely finished when the United Sates passed *Section 508 of the Rehabilitation Act Amendment* in 1998, based on the guidelines. With this, compliance with certain access requirements became a legal responsibility for the US government and its suppliers. The Web Accessibility Initiative WAI of the W3C finally passed these guidelines itself in May of 1999 as *Web Content Accessibility Guidelines 1.0 (WCAG1.0)*. These guidelines, in largely unchanged form, became the foundation for the *BITV (Regulation for Barrier Free Information Technology)* of the German Law for Equal Opportunity for Disabled People of 2002 and for numerous other legal regulations in many countries around the world. In the years after the turn of the millennium, the WAI then developed additional guidelines that apply to, for example, development of browsers that support accessibility and to other User-Agents (UAAG) in regards to authoring tools (ATAG).

Some of the points of the guidelines of the WCAG1 from 1998 are a little outdated today and no longer suitable as the foundation of our work.

The work of the WCAG2, which was to be completed by 2001, has still not been passed. A first draft of the WCAG2 was published middle of January 2007 and is being hotly debated right now.

The Canadian accessibility expert Joe Clark published the WCAG Samurai Errata in June 2007 with relevant and heavily contested recommendations for corrections to the effective WCAG1.0.

Thus the WCAG1/BITV, despite their weaknesses, are the only binding foundations today for development of accessible websites. We therefore recommend that everybody working in this area abide by their guidelines, except for a few causal exceptions, but also follow the partially open discussions of version 2.

The WCAG1 contains fourteen guidelines, each comprising several items. These checkpoints are divided into three priority levels, corresponding to the categories of *must satisfy, should satisfy,* and *may satisfy.* Depending on whether the first, the first and the second, or all three categories have been satisfied, the website may decorate itself with A, AA, or AAA.

Criteria for Accessible Sites at a Glance

Let's take a look at them:

Separation of Content and Layout

The first and most important rule for the developer is separating the content and layout:

- Clean and pure HTML code for content
- No unnecessary data tables
- Formatting to be done exclusively with CSS
- A logical semantic structure
- Jump labels

One of the most important requirements for practical accessibility is content that can be output in a linear format and that is formatted exclusively with CSS.

Only by abiding by this, can Assistive Technology prepare the content as it needs to while ignoring the visual presentation. The removal of the presentation into style sheets allows, for example, the visually-impaired users to define their own style sheets in their browser, and thus customize the pages exactly to their needs. For a screen-reader user linear display of content and appropriate semantic structures are particularly important.

Screen readers capture the content of a website from top to bottom, in other words linearly. If complicated data tables are used, this linearization is no longer there.

The term *semantic web* is hard to grasp at first, but it is important when writing web content. For example, screen readers allow the user to jump from header to header or from list to list, giving them as quickly as possible an overview of the entire document. If a website does not have any headers, this function cannot be used. The formal structure of a web document should predominantly follow the structure of the content. Depending on the web project, selecting the appropriate headers can definitely be a challenge.

Jump Marks

There is, however, a big disadvantage in linear display of content. In certain instances, a lot of territory has to be covered in order to get to the content areas 'out back'. With a triple-column layout, more sections can at least be started at the 'top' and the eye, aided by visual cues, can quickly jump to the area that promises relevant information. The concept of jump marks can be the remedy for this. It provides a virtual, non-visual counterpart to the graphic layout and lets the user using linear output devices identify relevant content areas at the start of a page and then immediately jump to where he or she suspects the relevant information is positioned.

The insertion of virtual jump marks basically involves the positioning of an additional menu at the beginning of every page for internal page navigation. In most cases it would make sense to hide this menu in the graphical layout; it is sometimes highly irritating to users that have full vision to click on a link that seems (apparently) to do nothing, since the target of the link can be seen in the viewport. This jump menu should never be too long and its structure must be deliberated carefully; after all, it itself contributes to lengthening and complicating the path to perception under the constraints of linearization. In general, it is recommended to have the main content as the first jump target; regular visitors that are familiar with a site and that can manipulate the navigation can then take the shortest path to where they want to go.

It is now becoming obvious that sites with more complex content not only require a graphic layout, but also content design that has the goal of structuring the site content in such a way that it presents no unnecessary barriers for users of linear output devices.

Demands on Design and Content

The presentation of a website is more than a nice design; it supports the visitor in getting the information offered. It displays interactive options and at the same time expresses the corporate identity of the site operator. It leads the observers through the most relevant content in a logical order and helps them to grasp the total concept.

In terms of barrier-free presentation, the following points deserve special attention:

- Logical configuration of content
- Well thought out color selections
- Sufficient contrasts
- Changeable font sizes
- Scalable layouts
- No graphic fonts
- No transparent backgrounds for graphics
- Meaningful alternative texts for graphics
- Sufficiently large navigational elements
- Caution with mouse-controlled events

Visual and Content-Wise Arrangement of Content

The visual arrangement of the individual page sections is a central element for presenting content and leading the users through your web offering in a structured way. The more structured and the more logical the presentation is, the easier it is for the users to find their way around your website.

The structure of the content is every bit as important as the creative structure. The concept of content comes with a special responsibility. An important guideline when structuring content is:

Always structure your content the way your users expect to see it.

This isn't always easy because you may have to change your perspective. An operator of a website knows his or her enterprise and the internal workings in such detail that he or she tends to structure things from that viewpoint, a viewpoint that might not make sense to the user.

A few clearly recognizable structural visual conventions have evolved over the years in the Web. The header usually has information about the supplier, the entire purpose of the site, and central navigation elements such as contact information, the masthead, and optional navigation help such as links to a sitemap and a search function. This easy-to-see position is front and center in the user's visual field and can be called upon if there are any problems.

The eye of readers of left-to-right scripts naturally scans pages from left to right and from top to bottom and for that reason the logo is usually top left, in the primary visual section. If a user looks for it, he or she expects to find it there.

Most users expect to see the navigation elements on the left. This concept is often disputed and developers accuse it of being boring and of lacking innovation. However, people move around the Web according to trusted patterns. They have their own experiences and they react accordingly. Familiar positioning shortens the time that the user requires to grasp an overview of the total content and to get to the actual content in which he or she is interested.

Color Selection

Color selection is especially important in connection with barrier freedom. Even people with limited color perception should be able to navigate your website without restrictions.

If you convert a layout into gray scales, you will get an approximate idea of what color-blind people see. Mind you, perception is very individual and depending on the degree of visual problems it can differ greatly. A lot of color-blind people have learned to recognize what the real colors are behind the image that they actually see. For instance, they know that grass is green and by comparing they can even identify various green shades.

Much more common than total color-blindness is the so-called red-green blindness. Those that are afflicted with it cannot differentiate between red and green due to a genetic abnormality. Color combinations that contain these color parts become fuzzy.

 In plain language this means: avoid color combinations of red and green or vice versa.

Contrasts

Colors are also important with all kinds of other visual impairments since not only actual colors, but clear color contrasts can be helpful when using a website.

Colors in the foreground and in the background should form a distinct contrast between text elements, even though it is impossible to select color and contrast settings that are right for everybody. The best possible color contrast is achieved with black text on a white background. In order to avoid a glare effect it may make sense to use a light tinge on the background. A lot of visually-impaired people require very strong contrasts in order to be able to differentiate the content elements of a page. For them, color combinations for instance like white script on a light orange-colored background do not have enough of a contrast. For others, on the other hand, strong contrasts cause blooming, making the content difficult to read.

Variable Font Sizes

Another, also incredibly important, rule is to make the font sizes variable.

Current browsers happily offer an option to zoom in on fonts. However, this only works if we provide relative specifications for font sizes and do not select firm pixel sizes. You have a choice between percent specifications and the `em`-specification. Both these specifications also apply to element-specific font sizes when used with the `font-size` property.

Scalable Layouts

One differentiates between fixed and fluid layouts in web design.

Fluid layouts adapt to the size of the monitor and offer scalable text space. The specifications for widths of the individual design columns are stated in percentages or `em`. This has the advantage of using the maximum display space of the monitor. If the size of the browser window changes, the content is automatically adjusted to fit it.

In general, this is a great way of presenting content. But I believe that you should set a maximum width of about 950 to 980 pixels. This has the advantage that the line length does not get too long with very high monitor resolutions, which would make the content difficult to read.

Graphics

Graphics can be incorporated in various ways on the website. You can insert them into the template or you can insert them in the actual content area.

It is particularly important for the presentation when, for example, inserting a logo, that you avoid transparent backgrounds. Imagine that you have integrated a logo with a black script on a transparent background.

People with certain visual impairments surf in Windows-inversion mode, which as a rule uses a light font on a black background.

The Beez logo has a white background and therefore can still be seen on a black background.

Your logo (black script on transparent background) will not be visible since the script is superimposed on the black background.

You should avoid graphic scripts in general; in most cases you should be able to substitute a text alternative. As a rule, graphic scripts are not scalable and therefore cannot be adjusted by the user.

Sometimes a client may demand a particular script nameplate. If this is the case, make the graphic larger and then use the em size specification to scale it down to the desired size. That way it can, at least, be enlarged somewhat.

Also, remember to provide a meaningful alternative text for the graphic.

You should always keep this in mind. People that cannot see at all and those with restricted vision will not be able to make out the graphics.

With the alt attributes and the em elements you can offer alternative texts.

It is not always easy to decide on such a text. It should be short, meaningful, and concise.

Pictures that don't contain any information don't need any alt text either. Mind you there is a wide range of images from ones with clear, recognizable, and distinct information to those that deliver only a mood or that only serve to shape the space they sit on. Under some circumstances it is really difficult to abide by the regulation to provide a text alternative.

You can use the longdesc attribute to describe images with a lot of information, let's say a graphic presentation of the last presidential primary elections.

This attribute contains a link to an external source, which contains the descriptive text.

```
<img src="electionresults.jpg" width="271" height="265"
alt="Summary
      of the results of the Presidential primary"
        longdesc="electionresults.html">
```

Unfortunately `longdesc` has some weaknesses when it comes to its implementation. Not all screen readers can interpret it.

Sufficiently Large Navigation Elements

People that for various reasons cannot control a mouse have to use alternative technologies. Many of them either use the keyboard or alternative technical aids. Steven Hawking is the classical model for motor function disabilities. The physicist suffers from amyotrophic lateral sclerosis (Lou Gehrig's or Motor Neuron disease) and uses his mouth to control his wheelchair. The aids that are available in many sectors are technical miracles, making things possible that were thought to be impossible.

The guideline to dispense with mouse-driven events has been around for years. The mouse cannot be used by people with motor function disabilities nor by screen reader users, but the technology has in the meantime developed to the point where it itself can deal with it.

However, people that just use a keyboard still cannot deal with mouse-driven events.

In any case, make sure that you provide large buttons. Links that only have a small sensitive area are difficult to click on, and not just for people with disabilities.

Forms

Interactivity on the Web is becoming more and more important for simplifying communication between the user and the site operator. The user enters personal data and a piece of software in the background manipulates it.

In the current state of the art, HTML forms are still the preferred medium to realize this interaction.

This is a good thing for accessibility, since HTML provides essential platform-independent and device-neutral options for interaction. There is no objection as long as these functions are also usable by users of alternative technologies.

Accessible design of HTML forms is first and foremost an issue of linearization and the grouping of content.

The fieldset and label Elements

Web developers tend to design forms as data tables. The design of these forms is indeed significantly simpler that way. Unfortunately, this leads to structures in which the content connection between the description and the form element gets lost.

(X)HTML provides the `label` element for a logical connection between form element and description.

```
<label for="first name" title="first name">firstname:</label>
<input id="first name" type="text" size="20" name="first name"
    value="" />
```

The input field is given a unique name by means of the `ID` universal attribute, which the `for` attribute of the `label` element refers to.

If there are similar input fields in a form, such as separate fields for husband and wife, there is a helpful tool for grouping called `fieldset`, which separates these fields explicitly.

```
<fieldset>
<legend> Wife's information</legend>
<label for="first name of wife">first name</label>
<input id="first name of wife" type="text" size="20" name="first
        name" value="" />
. . .
</fieldset>
<fieldset>
<legend> Husband's information</legend>
<label for="first name of husband">first name</label>
<input id="first name of husband" type="text" size="20"
name="first
        name" value="" />
. . .
```

Caution

Most screen readers will also pre-read the content of `legend` before every label and therefore this has to be kept short and tight.

Using `legend` offers additional navigation help to users of the Jaws screen reader since it can jump from `fieldset` to `fieldset` and thereby gives them a quicker overview of the form elements. Webformator, for instance, cannot do that.

Barrier Freedom in Joomla! 1.5—Possible with Beez

Joomla! is one of the most popular content management systems in the world. The entire Web can make inroads in the direction of accessibility now that Joomla! is shipped with the `Beez` barrier-free template.

`Beez` is the result of a lot of programming work and even more persuasion. `Beez` has a two-pronged goal: For one, to simplify the work of professionals when creating comprehensive barrier-free projects. Development time is significantly shortened. This saves money and barrier freedom will become more economical. This is ideal for local governments and other institutions that value barrier freedom.

At the same time, `Beez` is structured in such a way that even people with limited knowledge can develop moderately complex sites with a high degree of accessibility.

Thus Joomla! with `Beez` is an ideal tool to create web presences for establishments that operate in the disability sector.

The `Beez` barrier-free template is only one way of demonstrating the new path that Joomla! has opened up. It is a foundation that can be modified and expanded at will. With the `Beez` foundation, the design of a website can be modified in an almost unlimited way by modifying the CSS files.

Developers can write their own templates based on `Beez` that literally satisfy all the requirements of high-capacity and at the same time barrier-free websites.

At the moment a Joomla! template is understood to be merely the visual presentation. On first glance, `Beez` does not look that attractive. But keep in mind that the visual design and the associated CSS code are only the surface that can be easily modified with appropriate CSS knowledge.

The structure of the `index.php` file basically differs very little from other templates and for that reason I have not described it in detail.

HTML

Previous versions of Joomla! output content in layout tables by default. Joomla!'s new system uses so-called *template overwrites*.

With Joomla! 1.5 we are therefore in the position of no longer having to use the table-encumbered standard output. This gives us the flexibility that we need to create accessible websites that conform to the standards. It is not that easy to make changes to the HTML code even though the structure of the files is logical and in itself coherent. Basic PHP knowledge, however, is all you need to do your own customizing.

Joomla! uses a system of so-called *template overwrites*. If Joomla! finds an HTML folder with the appropriate content in our template directory, it captures it, otherwise it uses the standard code that still works with tables due to backward compatibility. Beez shows you exactly how to do this.

If you take a look at the Beez structure, you will notice that there is an additional HTML folder when compared to the standard template.

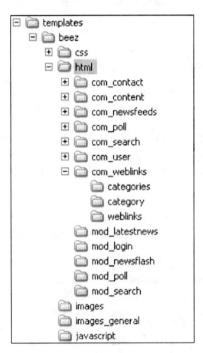

This folder, in turn, contains all the standard modules and components that are integrated into Joomla! The HTML output of all of these files has been customized and reworked. I have developed a markup based on the principle of separation of content and presentation, whose formal structure is largely consistent with the content-wise structure, and which you should be able to use for most applications without having to customize it.

This means:

- That all elements of a document are arranged in the correct and logical order in the source code, independent of the issue whether they will later be displayed next to each other or one on top of the other on the monitor.

- That all elements are displayed in a way that is consistent with their position and meaning in the document (semantically): headers as headers, paragraphs as paragraphs, quotes as quotes, table data as table data, etc. This makes it possible to automatically manipulate the document in various ways, not least as a convenient-as-possible output to a screen reader.

The following figure displays an overview of the Beez visible header structure.

Jump Marks

A linear presentation of content has the big disadvantage that under these circumstances you have to trace your way back for some distance in order to get to the content sections that are at the back.

Beez puts jump marks in two places. The first is in the index.php, where the position is defined and the other is in the components and modules used that contain form elements.

index.php

Here we find the following code:

```
<ul>
<li><a href="#content" class="u2">
<?php echo JText::_('Skip to Content'); ?></a></li>
<li><a href="#mainmenu" class="u2"><?php echo JText::_('Jump to
Main Navigation and Login'); ?></a></li>
<li><a href="#additional" class="u2"><?php echo JText::_(
                   'Jump to additional Information'); ?></a></li>
</ul>
```

These jump marks link to their respective anchors within the documents and are arranged semantically correctly by means of a list. The JText commands are for translation and are automatically translated into the default language that you have chosen based on the language file used. CSS places a header from the viewport in front of every anchor. This header is normally hidden, but is output, for example, to screen readers and greatly facilitates making content structure comprehensible.

```
<h2 class="unseen">
<?php echo JText::_(' View , Navigation and Search'); ?>
</h2>
...
<a name="mainmenu"></a>
```

You could also put the skip links directly on the ID of the surrounding divs, which would serve the concept of a structured document even better, but unfortunately there are a few old screen readers that wouldn't be able to interpret the output.

Skip Links in Forms

When screen reader users send a form that has not been supplied with jump marks, they end up at the start of the site and have to painstakingly navigate their way back to the actual content. To prevent this, the forms in Beez have their own jump marks to the actual site content.

Example: the search form:

```
<form action="<?php echo JRoute::_(
        'index.php?option=com_search#content' ) ?>"
method="post" class="search_result<?php echo $this->params-
        >get('pageclass_sfx') ?>">
```

Beez and Modules

Joomla! comes with various modules with a variety of functionalities. Quite a few things are possible from freely defined HTML code to the output of a list of most-read articles. You can allocate various module positions in the Joomla! back end, which are then placed at the position in the template where they are supposed to be displayed. The names of the module positions are defined in the XML file within the template. This opens lots of possibilities for customizing the site structure to the needs of the particular project.

The following code links the module to the left position:

```
<jdoc:include type="module" name="left" />
```

Beez has its own method of linking modules, which allows you to define the header-level, meaning the semantic specification of the header of the module itself.

If you want, you can mark every module with a header from the hierarchical level. The selection of the type of header is absolutely important when it comes to the global semantic coherence of a website. It has to be integrated logically into the total structure of the site, since different content could under some circumstances have a different content weighting.

```
<jdoc:include type="modules" name="left" style="beezDivision"
        headerLevel="3" />
```

The **most read** module deserves special attention from the viewpoint of designing barrier-free sites:

It displays the articles that were called up the most, and thereby helps your readers to receive the information.

com_content

The `com_content` component controls the output of all content and therefore it is the core of our code.

The corresponding files can be found under `templates/beez/html/com_content`.

In the standard template, Joomla!-specific multicolumn output is realized by means of a table. This is the easiest solution nothing shifts, and everything fits, even without CSS.

If you are using `Beez`, you have to rethink it all. Variously nested `divs` are used, allocated to various CSS classes in order to be as flexible as possible when it comes to the design. There are classes for single rows and columns so that pretty much everything can be changed to what you want your design to look like. If this array of classes is just too extensive for you, you can easily remove it from the code with the 'search and replace' function.

Here is a corresponding excerpt from `beez/html/com_conent/frontpage/default.php`:

```
<div class="article_row<?php echo $this->params>get('pageclass_
sfx'); ?>">
<?php for ($z = 0; $z < $colcount && $ii < $introcount && $i <
$this->total; $z++,
$i++, $ii++) : ?>
<div class="article_column column<?php echo $z + 1; ?> cols<?php
echo $colcount; ?>" >
<?php $this->item =& $this->getItem($i, $this->params);
echo $this->loadTemplate('item'); ?>
</div>
<span class="article_separator"> </span>
<?php endfor; ?>
<span class="row_separator<?php echo $this->params-
>get('pageclass_sfx');
?>"> </span>
</div>
```

Forms

There are no layout tables in `Beez`, not even for formatting forms.

In order to facilitate a logical connection between form elements and description, I have used the `label` element, as the standards demand. The input field receives a unique name by means of the `ID` universal attribute, and the `for` attribute of the `label` element refers to it. All the existing form elements were appropriately redesigned in `Beez`. I have grouped content by means of `fieldset` where it made sense and have provided it with a `legend` (for example in edit forms for content).

Data Tables

Tables aren't always a problem. If you actually want to display data structures, they are the perfect choice.

Joomla! uses non-complex data tables at several places, for instance when displaying web links or in the contact overview.

In principle, data tables are accessible if they have been marked as such and if they have been appropriately programmed.

The `headers` attribute provides a link for every data cell (`td`) between this cell and a header (`th`) by naming the `ID` of the respective associated header or, since there could be several headers, by listing the `ID`s. This design is also used for Joomla! internal data tables.

You can hide the offered tables in the menu configuration of the web links or in the contact overview.

Caution
Please don't do that, since this will affect the accessibility of your data tables.

Design and CSS

When I designed `Beez`, I consciously tried to answer constantly surfacing CSS questions, using content floating just as much as absolute positioning within relative elements.

Web professionals shouldn't have any problems customizing the previously listed code to their needs. It will, however, be definitely more difficult for the layperson.

Beez Internal CSS Files

In the CSS folder are a number of CSS files with various tasks.

Positioning and presentation were intentionally put into separate files. This has the advantage that you only have to modify the `layout.css` file if you want to change colors, with the positioning being left untouched. In other words, there will be fewer errors.

CSS Files in Summary

- `position.css`
- `layout.css`
- `print.css`
- `template.css`
- `ie7only.css`
- `ieonly.css`
- `generell.css`
- `template_rtl.css`

Positioning

Positioning is controlled in the `position.css` file.

You will find all of the CSS commands for the so-called *frame document* here, just as defined in the `index.php` file, as well as the one and two-column structure in the content section and in the leading story. You should only make changes to `position.css` if you know exactly what you are doing and what you would like to accomplish.

The following code puts the background picture of the little bee behind the leading story.

```
.leading
{
background: #EFDEEA url(../images/bee.gif) no-repeat top left;
border: solid 1px #CCC;
color: #000;
margin: 30px 0px 10px 0px;
padding: 20px 20px 40px 120px;
position: relative;
}
```

The Layout

You can rummage around in `layout.css` to your heart's content, because all of the formatting and the coloring scheme have been stored here. You will also find the positioning of certain content elements here.

The following CSS formats the header of the leading story and positions the **Readmore** link in the right lower corner. This happens by means of absolute positioning in the relatively positioned leading story.

```
main .leading h2,#main2 .leading h2 {
background:#EFDEEA;
border-bottom:solid 0 #333;
color:#93246F;
font-family:trebuchet MS, sans-serif;
font-size:1.4em;
font-weight:normal;
margin:0 0 10px;
text-transform:uppercase;
}

#main .leading .readon,#main2 .leading .readon {
background:url(../images/arrow.gif) #93246F no-repeat;
border:solid 0;
bottom:0;
color:#FFF !important;
display:block !important;
margin-top:20px !important;
position:absolute;
right:0;
text-decoration:none;
padding:2px 2px 0 30px;
}
```

Miscellaneous

The `template.css` file is always integrated in Joomla! when popups appear that have no browser navigation, for example in the email to friend pop-up window or if you set up a menu item in this style by means of the navigation. The formatting of this view is created exclusively with this file.

`ie7only.css` and `ieonly.css` take care of browser bugs of various versions of Internet Explorer and are integrated by means of Conditional Comments in the head of the `index.php`.

Conditional Comments are special comments that can only be interpreted from Internet Explorer version 5 on and they exclusively send instructions to only those browsers.

```
<!--[if lte IE 6]>
<link href="<?php echo $this->baseurl ?>/templates/beez/css/
ieonly.css"
rel="stylesheet" type="text/css" />
<![endif]-->
<!--[if IE 7]>
<link href="<?php echo $this->baseurl ?>/templates/beez/css/
ie7only.css"
rel="stylesheet" type="text/css" />
<![endif]-->
```

`print.css` is pretty self-explanatory. It formats the page for printing and is only used for that. You might wonder why the word "content" is in front of the actual content in large font size, even tough it doesn't appear in that form in the source code.

CSS gives you the ability to write content into a document. The following code takes care of that. Not all browsers know what to do with this, but the ones that conform to the standard do.

```
#main2:before
{
content: " content ";
...
}
```

The `generell.css` file is already in the system folder one level higher in the hierarchy. But if you want to customize Joomla! internal error messages to your design, this is the correct place.

Also, last but not least, there is the `template_rtl.css` file. RTL stands for right to left, which refers to the direction that the installed language is read. The direction of reading is specified in the XML file of the selected language and can be used as a variable in the `index.php` file of the template.

```
<?php if($this->direction == 'rtl') : ?>
<link rel="stylesheet" href="<?php echo $this->baseurl
?>/templates/beez/css/template_rtl.css" type="text/css" />
<?php endif; ?>
```

This CSS file changes `Beez`'s display in regards to the direction of reading if you have installed a language like Hebrew or Arabic.

If you want to have some fun, check out what happens if you change the direction of reading in English by setting the respective variable from 0 to 1.

Path: `language/en-GB/en-GB.xml`

```
...
<metadata>
...
<rtl>1</rtl>
...
</metadata>
```

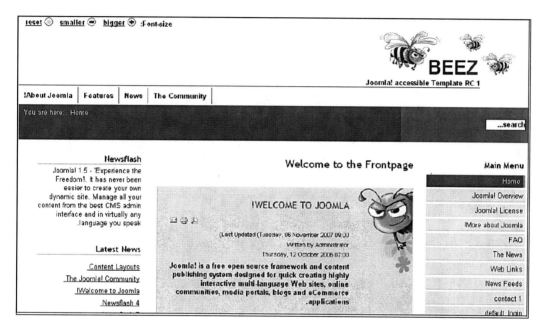

Joomla! Internal Accessibility Features

Joomla! gives you the option of setting up article views that have teasers for individual articles. Older Joomla! versions would have a **Read more** button after each one of these teasers. Up to version 1.5 this link always had the same wording whenever it appeared in the Web: **Read more**.

Since such aids as screen readers only display the links to a page if necessary, link texts have to be formatted in respect of content in order to deliver a recognizable target.

Apart from that, the text content of the **Read more** link semantically belongs to document content and therefore should be freely formattable. If this requirement is not satisfied, your website will fail the very first mechanical test for accessibility.

By default, the article header is positioned in front of the **Read more** link with Joomla! 1.5, since this is redundant information that cannot be edited.

You have already learned about the article parameters, which you can use to individualize the design and/or the layout of the information for each article on every page. There is a new parameter in Joomla! 1.5, the `readmore:text` parameter, which you can find under **Parameters Advanced** in the article overview.

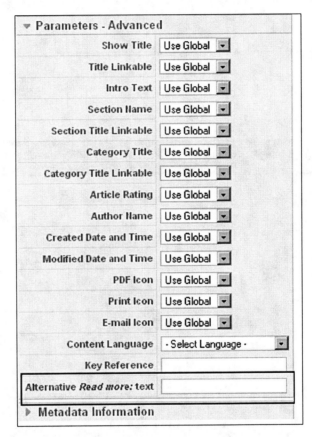

This should be a challenge for the editor. This parameter not only has the task of describing a unique link text, but it should make the visitor curious and incite him or her to read more.

Additional Information about This Topic

Assistive Technologies

Webformator: www.webformator.com/englisch/index.php
Jaws: http://www.freedomscientific.com/fs_downloads/jaws.asp
Windows eyes: http://www.gwmicro.com

CheckerTools

Colour Contrast Analyser: http://www.juicystudio.com/services/
colourcontrast.php
http://www.visionaustralia.org.au/info.aspx?page=628
Vischeck: http://vischeck.com/
Cynthia Says: http://www.contentquality.com
Bobby: http://webxact.watchfire.com
Validator: http://validator.w3.org
Validator: http://www.htmlhelp.com
Wave: http://www.wave.webaim.org/wave/index.jsp

Accessibility Toolbar Moziall/Firefox: http://cita.disability.uiuc.edu/
software/mozilla/

Book Tip

Angie Radtke and Michael Charlier: *Barrier-free Webdesign*

Summary

In this chapter we saw the elements needed for a barrier-free presentation.

15
Your Own Components, Modules, and Plug-ins

Let's say you want to solve a problem with Joomla!, but there are no ready-made components for it yet. For instance, you are a car dealer and you need a listing of your used vehicles on your website that you can administer with the Joomla! administration or you need a list of your branches. Simply extend Joomla!'s functionality with new components, modules, and plug-ins. What looks quite difficult at first can actually be accomplished with a beginner-level knowledge of PHP.

By now, you can figure out what you have to do after your experience building templates. The emphasis this time, however, is not on layout, but on programming.

 As of 01/01/2008 PHP 4 is officially not being developed any further. You should therefore upgrade all new extensions according to the recommendations of PHP version 5. Joomla 1.5 is compatible with both of these versions. To find out more visit: `http://gophp5.org/`.

Model—View—Controller

Joomla 1.5 has introduced a concept (design pattern) for the programming of extensions: the **Model-View-Controller** concept (**MVC**). This approach is being used in modern software development in order to bring a certain order to these things.

Three components are almost always required when it comes to software tasks:

- A Model
- A View
- A Controller

It therefore stands to reason that these three components should be standardized. Since programmers are likely to be allergic to such standards, there must be real advantages to the concept. Let us examine the individual components a little more closely.

Model

The model contains the representation of the information. It is immaterial where the data is coming from. The model knows nothing about the output of the data and has no idea how this data is changed.

View

The view displays the data from the model. There has to be a link between the model and the view so that something can be displayed.

Controller

The controller controls the whole thing—it reacts to user input or other events, administers the models and the views, and hands your information to views.

What is the Advantage with MVC?

As already hinted above, a certain order is forced onto things, in particular with Joomla! If you were used to coding exactly like you wanted to with Joomla! 1.0, this is no longer desirable with Joomla! 1.5. This has nothing to do with patronizing, but with user requirements, in other words you!

You want: barrier-free websites (overrides), search-engine friendly URLs, distributed authentication, internationalization, security and serviceability, reusability, and more, more, more…; and it is exactly the more... that makes it necessary to bring some order into the system. If you have a company with one employee, you can probably handle its administration in your head or with a piece of paper and a pencil. If you have ten employees, this gets a bit difficult. If your company is starting to hum and is growing, you need some sort of system to manage it!

MCV is that type of a system for software. MCV enables programming design that makes subsequent changes easier and that allows you to reuse code. It is not without detractors, but it is definitely not bad. Since everyone is sticking with it, it must be good!

Of course there are concerns:

- Where does my business logic go? Into the controller or into the model?
- How about reusable dialog? In the view?
- How do we control several views (tables, individual view, front end, back end)?

Since there was no comparable structure in Joomla! 1.0, this 'mantra' and its implementation, in my opinion, are the biggest accomplishment that Joomla! 1.5 and its project team have brought to the table. The future will tell if users and developers feel the same way.

So Where is Everybody's Advantage?

It is very simple and you know it yourself. If your kitchen, your cellar, your car, your attic have been straightened up, then it is easy to keep them tidy. This is a prerequisite with software before you can make it grow and be serviceable, and Joomla! is still at the beginning of its potential. This means that if someone (the Joomla! project team) took the time today to tidy up Joomla! 1.0, it will be easier for you to adapt it to your requirements in the future.

The helloworld Sample Component

Components are split into front-end and back-end components. Front-end components are displayed on your website; back-end components are developed for the administration section, mostly to manage front-end components. From the viewpoint of a visitor to your site, you can recognize a component by the way a Joomla! page is requested.

The URL: `http://localhost/Joomla150/index.php?option=com_contact`, for instance, calls up the `com_contact` front-end component.

If you take a look in your database system, there is a whole bunch of components in the `[PathtoJoomla]/components` subdirectory and one of them is the `com_contact` component.

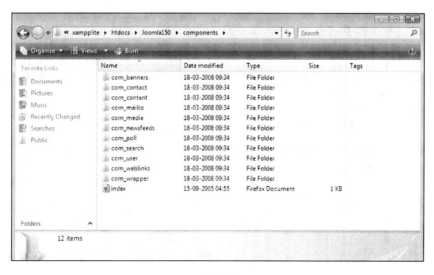

Depending on the complexity of the components, there are additional directories with files for Model, View, and Controller contained in this directory.

A Home for helloworld

Every component inhabits its directory. Joomla! suggests the following sequence:

1. Joomla! interprets the rendered values in the URL: /index. php?option=com_helloworld.

2. It searches the component table for the com_helloworld component.

3. It looks for a com_helloworld directory.

4. In that directory it looks for a helloworld.php file.

5. It interprets this file.

You need several files for the interpretation to be correct:

- helloworld.php — the point of entry into your component.

- controller.php—the controller.

- views/helloworld/view.html.php — the view, which passes the data on to the template.

- views/helloworld/tmpl/default.php — a standard template that will be overwritten by the correct template or that will be used as is.

- helloworld.xml — the familiar XML file, which explains the content of the package to the controller, tells the controller where to install it and who is responsible for it.

If you are totally stressed out now, yearning for Joomla! 1.0 (I used to do this with one file!) — give it a chance!

It is best to let the Joomla! installer install the com-hello.zip component package and set up a menu item. That way you immediately have all of the files in the correct folder and can easily follow the source code.

The Entry Point (/componenet.com_hello/hello.php)

This is the first file to be called when you click on the http://localhost/ joomla150/index.php?option=com_hello&view=hello URL or on the respective menu item. The result is decidedly unspectacular. You will see the text 'Hello World' in the content window.

The source code of the file looks as follows.

`/component/com_hello/hello.php`:

```php
<?php
// restricted access
defined('_JEXEC') or die('Restricted access');
// importing the basic controller
require_once (JPATH_COMPONENT.DS.'controller.php');
// creating our own controller
$classname = 'HelloController'.$controller;
$controller = new $classname( );
// checking to see whether the parameters have arrived (Requests)
$controller->execute( JRequest::getVar('task'));
// redirection inside of the controller
$controller->redirect();
?>
defined('_JEXEC') or die('Restricted access');
```

The first line is a security check to see whether the file was called by Joomla! or directly. Directly called scripts are stopped immediately with the `die()` function.

```php
require_once (JPATH_COMPONENT.DS.'controller.php');
```

After this, the first controller is imported. The absolute path to the current component (`components/com_hello`) is `JPATH_COMPONENT`. `DS` is the `directory separator` of the operating system. Windows would like to have it different from Unix-like systems, thus it is either / or \. Joomla! sets this value automatically.

```php
$classname = 'HelloController'.$controller;
$controller = new $classname();
```

Now you can instantiate the read-in controller and thereby create a controller that we can use. If you 'only' require one controller, as is often the case in the front end, you can also use the following statement:

```php
$controller=newHelloController();
$controller->execute( JRequest::getVar('task'));
```

Statements for the components are stated in the form of `index.php?option=com_hello&task=task` (`save`, `edit`, `new`, ...) in the URL. This line is used to see whether there is anything to read.

```php
$controller->redirect();
```

Under these circumstances the controller redirects the request to another site, as for instance if something is being saved.

The Controller (/component/com_hello/controller.php)

Since the component is really simple, the controller now has the task of displaying something. We do not need a data model and only one `display` method.

`/component/com_hello/controller.php`:

```php
<?php
jimport('joomla.application.component.controller');
class HelloController extends JController
{
function display()
{
parent::display();
}
}
?>
```

The call of the `display` method determines the name and layout of the view. You will see the result of this display version if you are setting up a new menu item, for instance. Our component only recognizes the standard layout.

The View (/component/com_hello/views/hello/views.html.php)

Here it is already, the default view.

`/component/com_hello/views/hello/views.html.php`:

```php
<?php
jimport( 'joomla.application.component.view');
class HelloViewHello extends JView
{
function display($tpl = null)
{
$greeting = "Hello World!";
$this->assignRef( 'greeting', $greeting );
parent::display($tpl);
}
}
?>
```

The view normally contains data (from the model), prepares the data, and sends it to the template.

```php
$greeting = "Hello World!";
$this->assignRef( 'greeting', $greeting );
parent::display($tpl);
```

Due to the assignment of variables, the model is redundant here. The variable $greeting, however, could also contain the result of a database query. The variable is passed to the template with the `assignRef` method.

```
parent::display($tpl);
```

This calls up the template.

The Template (/component/com_hello/views/hello/tmpl/default.php)

And here is the default template. It is always called `default.php` and it looks like the following listing in its simplest form.

/component/com_hello/views/hello/tmpl/default.php:

```
defined('_JEXEC') or die('Restricted access'); ?>
<h1><?php echo $this->greeting; ?></h1>
```

The Result

All in all it looks very unspectacular on the website.

The Installation

All of the files now have to be packed into a ZIP package and then can be installed with the Joomla! installer. The front-end files from /component/com_hello are saved in a `site` directory. The administration area files from /com_hello/administrator/ components are saved in an `admin` directory. All of the files are described with additional information in an XML file and have to be called by the same name as their components, in other words `hello.xml`.

hello.xml:

```
<?xml version="1.0" encoding="utf-8"?>
<!DOCTYPE install SYSTEM "http://dev.joomla.org/xml/1.5/component-
install.dtd">
<install type="component" version="1.5.0">
<name>Hello</name>
<creationDate>November</creationDate>
<author>Nobody</author>
<authorEmail>nobody@example.org</authorEmail>
<authorUrl>http://www.example.org</authorUrl>
<copyright>Copyright Info</copyright>
<license>License Info</license>
<version>Component Version String</version>
<description>description of the component ...</description>
<!-- Site Main File Copy Section -->
<files folder="site">
<filename>index.html</filename>
```

```
<filename>hello.php</filename>
<filename>controller.php</filename>
<filename>views/index.html</filename>
<filename>views/hello/index.html</filename>
<filename>views/hello/view.html.php</filename>
<filename>views/hello/tmpl/index.html</filename>
<filename>views/hello/tmpl/default.php</filename>
</files>
<administration>
<!-- Administration Menu Section -->
<menu>Hello World!</menu>
<!-- Administration Main File Copy Section -->
<files folder="admin">
<!-- Site Main File Copy Section -->
<filename>index.html</filename>
<filename>admin.hello.php</filename>
</files>
</administration>
</install>
```

In order to be able to to pack everything into a ZIP package, you have to abide by the structure. Here is the appropriate structure for the com_hello component:

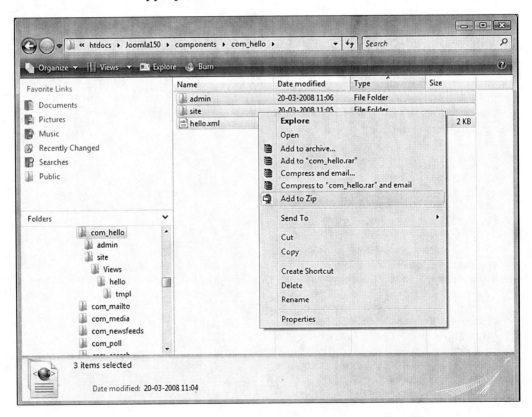

Now you can let the Joomla! installer upload and install the package the normal way.

Conclusion

What you have just created is indeed easily serviceable, expandable, and to be honest, also very clear. At first sight, all of these files seem a little confusing, but look again and you will quickly get over your fear. The fact is that there is very little source code in each file, and because of that you get a much better overview. This is what the MCV concept is trying to accomplish. And if you want to have a special complex template, simply overwrite the view in your self-constructed template.

An Example Component

Now a big leap in direction of complexity. We want to set up a very simple used car list that can be maintained from the administration area.

For this you will need:

- A new front-end component
- A back-end component
- A special table in the database
- (Optional) an additional module to display the items on the website
- (Optional) a search plug-in, so that you can search your new content

So that you get an idea of what I am talking about and what the list should look like on the website, here is the finished example. Simply install the `com_auto.zip` component and follow it yourself.

A list of the cars should be displayed on the website with a small photograph for each. If you click on the photo, a window with a larger photo will open. There is also another module with a listing of the cars.

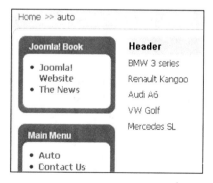

In our case, this list contains automobile types. If you want to, you can fill the example with other types of data (branches, offers, etc.). It is usually sufficient for a visitor to be able to view the list. He or she doesn't have to be able to edit the items.

The administrator, on the other hand, has to manage the list.

Management in this connection means being able to:

- Enter new items
- Modify existing items
- Delete existing items

So that we don't make this example too complicated, let's just display and edit four fields: two fields for the text (type and manufacturer) and two fields for the photographs (URLs to the small and large photos). The principle of programming a component in Joomla! will become clear in this way and you can easily extend this example by a few more fields. The component should be integrated into the existing administration structure.

It should be possible to execute the functions mentioned earlier. In addition, you will of course need a toolbar for the display of the list and another one for the edit mode. You need to have options to publish the items and to hide them and of course you want the **Publish** and **Delete** functions to be able to affect several items at once by marking the checkboxes in front of the items. In this way, for example, you can publish several items at the same time.

Besides the list, you will of course also need a form for modifying and adding an item.

Let's start with the component; here it is called `com_auto`. If you want to duplicate this demonstration, you can download the finished example and install it like any component. You can then modify the component manually. Modification and conversion has the advantage that you will take a good look at the structures and also that you may want to do more.

The MySQL Table

This component uses a MySQL table in which it stores the cars. This table is set up automatically during the installation. You can see the SQL commands after the installation in the `/administrator/com_auto/install.sql` file. There is also an `uninstall.sql` file that deletes the table when you uninstall the component.

If you call up http://localhost/phpmyadmin, you can take a look at the jos_auto table.

The jos_ prefix is assigned by the installer and is based on the information in your Joomla! configuration. The published field either has a value of **1** (published) or **0** (not published). The two fields for the photos contain a path that you will probably have to change. You can do that in the administration.

The Front End

Now we start programming the list in the front end. As with the hello component, you need the following files:

- /components/com_auto/auto.php
- /components/com_auto/controller.php
- /components/com_auto/views/auto/view.html.php
- /components/com_auto/views/auto/tmpl/default.php
- /components/com_auto/models/auto.php

As you can see, we have a model this time and therefore we need data from a database.

The Entry Point (/components/com_auto/auto.php)

There is an entry point here as well. The /components/com_auto/auto.php file collects everything and delegates the tasks.

/components/com_auto/auto.php:

```php
<?php
// restricted access
defined('_JEXEC') or die('Restricted access');
// loading of the Joomla! basic controller
require_once (JPATH_COMPONENT.DS.'controller.php');
// creation of a controller
$controller = new AutoController();
// reading the request task
$controller->execute(JRequest::getCmd('task'));
// redirection from the controller
$controller->redirect();
?>
```

The code is almost identical to that in the com_hello component.

The Controller (/components/com_auto/controller.php)

Here as well, there are all kinds of familiar things from the `com_hello` component.

`/components/com_auto/controller.php`:

```php
<?php
defined('_JEXEC') or die();
jimport('joomla.application.component.controller');
class AutoController extends JController
{
function display()
{
parent::display();
}
}
```

The View (/components/com_auto/views/auto/view.html.php)

You will find the first difference here. Of course we need data for the list.

`/components/com_auto/views/auto/view.html.php`:

```php
<?php
jimport( 'joomla.application.component.view');
class AutoViewAuto extends JView
{
function display($tpl = null)
{
$model = &$this->getModel();
$rows = $model->getAutoList();
$this->assignRef('rows' , $rows);
parent::display($tpl);
}
}
?>
$model = &$this->getModel();
```

The model is instantiated and is available as an object in the `$model` variable.

```php
$rows = $model->getAutoList();
```

The `getAutoList` method is called in the object and returns the `$rows` array.

```php
$this->assignRef('rows', $rows);
parent::display($tpl);
```

The resulting rows are allocated and passed on to the template.

The Template
(/components/com_auto/views/auto/tmpl/default.php)

The rows in the $rows variable are sent through a for loop, transformed into a single $row, and then output separately.

/components/com_auto/views/auto/tmpl/default.php:

```php
<?php
defined('_JEXEC') or die('Restricted access');
?>
<script type="text/javascript">
function OpenWindow (Adresse) {
MyWindow = window.open(Adress, "Auto",
"width=400,height=300,left=100,top=200");
MyWindow.focus();
}
</script>
<h1><?php echo "&Uuml;berschrift"; ?></h1>
<ul>
<?
// Reading of the data sets in the array
foreach ($this->rows as $row) { ?>
<li><?php echo $row->text; ?> <small><em>(<?php echo
                                $row->manufacturer; ?>)
</em></small><br>
<a href="<?php echo $row->photo_large; ?>"
                        onclick="OpeWindow(this.href);
return false"><img src=<?php echo $row->photo_small; ?>></a>
</li>
<?php
}
?>
</ul>
foreach ($this->rows as $row) { ?>
<li>
<?php echo $row->text; ?>
<?php echo $row->manufacturer; ?>
<?php echo $row->photo_small; ?>
</li>
<?php } ?>
```

This loop is the most important thing in this template. You can make whatever changes you want to the rest of the HTML formatting or to the JavaScript for opening the pop-up window, as in the example code; you can add lightbox effects and you can add whatever Dreamweaver, MooTools, and your own creativity can provide. This part of the formatting is now stand-alone with Joomla! 1.5, but not the $rows variable.

Model (/components/com_auto/models/auto.php)

Oh yes the model! How do we get the data?

/components/com_auto/models/auto.php:

```php
<?php
defined('_JEXEC') or die();
jimport('joomla.application.component.model');
class AutoModelAuto extends JModel
{
function _getAutoQuery( &$options )
{
$db = JFactory::getDBO();
$id = @$options['id'];
$select = 'a.*';
$from = '#__auto AS a';
$wheres[] = 'a.published = 1';
$query = "SELECT " . $select .
"\n FROM " . $from .
"\n WHERE " . implode( "\n AND ", $wheres );
return $query;
}
function getAutoList( $options=array() )
{
$query = $this->_getAutoQuery( $options );
$result = $this->_getList( $query );
return @$result;
}
}
?>
```

There are two important methods in the model. One is the `_getAutoQuery` method, which actualizes the access to the data and contains the SQL command, and the other one is the `getAutolist` method, which controls this access and returns the result. I am sure that you can remember the `views.html.php` file. The following line is in that file:

```php
$rows = $model->getAutoList();
```

It accesses the object of the model and saves the result in `$rows`. This result is actualized by means of the `getAutoList` method within the `AutoModelAuto` class.

Conclusion

This is a good time for you to get familiar with PHP and object-oriented programming. You are not necessarily lost without knowledge about classes, methods, inheritance, and similar things, but will be confused for sure.

However, once you get involved in Joomla!'s MCV path you will soon see the connections. If you, for example, compare the com_hello component with this part of the com_auto component, 80% of the code for all intents and purposes is identical (all but the model).

The com_auto Administration

The pure display of data on the website was relatively simple; administration of the data, by its nature, is a little more complicated. As administrator, you have to be able to display, modify, insert, delete, and publish data. This involves significantly more interactivity than there was in the simple listing on the website.

The Component Table

Joomla!, by the way, administers all menu items of the component in the [prefix]components table. The menu items of all of the components in the administration area have to be recorded here as well. The com_auto component was also entered there:

A graphic that is to be displayed next to the menu is also recorded there ('js/ThemeOffice/component.png'). You will find the graphics in the [pathto-Joomla]/includes/js/ThemeOffice folder.

You need several files to be able to create the administration component. You will find the following files in the [pathtoJoomla]/administration/components/ com_auto/ folder:

- /administration/components/admin.auto.php
- /administration/components/controller.php
- /administration/components/controllers/auto.php
- /administration/components/views/autos/view.html.php
- /administration/components/views/autos/tmpl/default.php
- /administration/components/views/auto/view.html.php
- /administration/components/views/auto/tmpl/form.php
- /administration/components/tables/auto.php
- /administration/components/install.sql
- /administration/components/uninstall.sql

The Entry Point (/administration/components/admin.auto.php)

Of course there is an entry point in the administration area as well.

/administration/components/admin.auto.php:

```php
<?php
defined('_JEXEC') or die('Restricted access');
$controller = JRequest::getVar('controller', 'auto');
require_once(JPATH_ADMINISTRATOR.DS.'controllers'.
DS.$controller.'.php';
$classname = 'AutosController'.$controller;
$controller = new $classname( );
$controller->execute( JRequest::getVar('task'));
$controller->redirect();
?>
```

Experts on entry points will notice that this looks very familiar. Everything is familiar except for the if query, which searches for additional controllers.

Controller (/administration/components/controller.php)

The basic controller looks familiar to us as well:

/administration/components/controller.php:

```php
<?php
jimport('joomla.application.component.controller');
class AutosController extends JController
{
function display()
{
parent::display();
}
}?>
```

Another Controller (/administration/components/controllers/auto.php)

Now we see some differences. We have an additional controller and it has quite a bit of code.

/administration/components/controllers/auto.php:

```php
<?php
defined('_JEXEC') or die();
class AutosControllerAuto extends AutosController
{
function __construct(){
parent::__construct();
```

```
$this->registerTask( 'add', 'edit' );
$this->registerTask( 'unpublish', 'publish');
}
function edit() {
JRequest::setVar( 'view', 'auto' );
JRequest::setVar( 'layout', 'form' );
JRequest::setVar('hidemainmenu', 1);
parent::display();
}
function save() {
$model = $this->getModel('auto');
if ($model->store($post)) {
$msg = JText::_( 'Auto Saved!' );
} else {
$msg = JText::_( 'Error Saving Auto' );
}

$link = 'index.php?option=com_auto';

$this->setRedirect($link, $msg);
}
function remove(){
$model = $this->getModel('auto');
if(!$model->delete()) {
$msg = JText::_( 'Error: One or more Autos could not be Deleted' );
} else {
$msg = JText::_( 'Auto(s) Deleted' );
}
$this->setRedirect( 'index.php?option=com_auto', $msg );
}
function publish(){
$this->setRedirect( 'index.php?option=com_auto' );
$db =& JFactory::getDBO();
$user =& JFactory::getUser();
$cid = JRequest::getVar( 'cid', array(), 'post', 'array' );
$task = JRequest::getCmd( 'task' );
$publish = ($task == 'publish');
$n = count( $cid );
if (empty( $cid )) {
return JError::raiseWarning( 500, JText::_( 'No items selected' ) );
}
JArrayHelper::toInteger( $cid );
$cids = implode( ',', $cid );
$query = 'UPDATE #__auto'
. ' SET published = ' . (int) $publish
```

```
. ' WHERE id IN ( '. $cids .' )'
;
$db->setQuery( $query );
if (!$db->query()) {
return JError::raiseWarning( 500, $row->getError() );
}
$this->setMessage( JText::sprintf( $publish ? 'Items published' :
'Items
unpublished', $n ) );
}
function cancel(){
$msg = JText::_( 'Operation Cancelled' );
$this->setRedirect( 'index.php?option=com_auto', $msg );
}
}
?>
```

This controller implements the `edit`, `save`, `remove`, `publish`, and `cancel` methods.
The model is instantiated within these methods and when required, the `store`
method, for example, is called in the model. Messages about success or failure are
output by means of the `JText` and `JError` static classes:

View for the List
(/administration/components/views/autos/view.html.php)

This time the view is a bit larger since the toolbar has to be added.

`/administration/components/views/autos/view.html.php`:

```
<?php
defined('_JEXEC') or die();
jimport( 'joomla.application.component.view' );
class AutosViewAutos extends JView
{
function display($tpl = null)
{
JToolBarHelper::title( JText::_( 'Auto Manager' ), 'generic.png' );
JToolBarHelper::publishList();
JToolBarHelper::unpublishList();
```

```
JToolBarHelper::deleteList();
JToolBarHelper::editListX();
JToolBarHelper::addNewX();
$items = & $this->get( 'Data');
$this->assignRef('items', $items);
parent::display($tpl);
}
}
```

The JToolbarHelper class takes care of the display.

Template List (/administration/components/views/autos/tmpl/default.php)

The list does, of course, also have to be formatted, and therefore the appropriate default template is readied.

/administration/components/views/autos/tmpl/default.php:

```
<?php defined('_JEXEC') or die('Restricted access'); ?>
<form action="index.php" method="post" name="adminForm">
<div id="editcell">
<table class="adminlist"><thead><tr>
<th width="5"><?php echo JText::_( 'NUM' ); ?></th>
<th width="20"> <input type="checkbox" name="toggle" value=""
onclick="checkAll(<?php echo count( $this->items ); ?>);" /></th>
<th class="title"><?php echo JHTML::_('grid.sort', 'Auto', 'a.text',
@$lists['order_Dir'], @$this->lists['order'] ); ?></th>
<th width="5%" align="center"><?php echo JHTML::_('grid.sort',
                                'Published',
'a.published', @$this->lists['order_Dir'], @$this->lists['order'] );
?></th>
<th width="1%" nowrap="nowrap"><?php echo JHTML::_('grid.sort', 'ID',
                                'a.id',
@$this->lists['order_Dir'], @$this->lists['order'] ); ?></th>
</tr></thead>
<?php
$k = 0;
for ($i=0, $n=count( $this->items ); $i < $n; $i++)
{
$row = &$this->items[$i];
$published = JHTML::_('grid.published', $row, $i );
$link = JRoute::_(
    'index.php?option=com_auto&controller=auto&task=edit&cid[]='.
$row->id );
```

```
?>
<tr class="<?php echo "row$k"; ?>">
<td></td>
<td></td>
<td><a href="<?php echo $link; ?>"><?php echo $row->text; ?></a></td>
<td align="center"><?php echo $published;?></td>
<td align="center"><?php echo $row->id; ?></td>
</tr>
<?php
$k = 1 - $k;
}
?>
</table></div>
<input type="hidden" name="option" value="com_auto" />
<input type="hidden" name="task" value="" />
<input type="hidden" name="boxchecked" value="0" />
<input type="hidden" name="controller" value="auto" />
</form>
```

This template contains fairly simple HTML, packed into a form. It takes care of the display of the table:

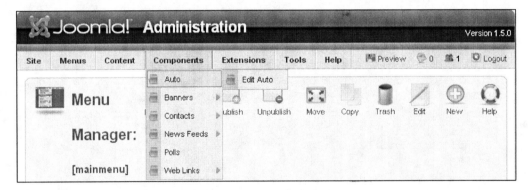

View Form
(/administration/components/views/auto/view.html.php)

The individual view of the automobiles also has to controlled. Pay attention to the name of the subdirectory. We are now in the auto folder; the list is located in the auto folder.

/administration/components/views/auto/view.html.php:

```
<?php
defined('_JEXEC') or die();
jimport( 'joomla.application.component.view' );
```

```
class AutosViewAuto extends JView
{
function display($tpl = null)
{
$auto =& $this->get('Data');
$isNew = ($auto->id < 1);
$text = $isNew ? JText::_( 'New' ) : JText::_( 'Edit' );
JToolBarHelper::title( JText::_( 'Auto' ).': <small>[ ' . $text.' ]</
small>' );
JToolBarHelper::save();
if ($isNew) {
JToolBarHelper::cancel();
} else {
JToolBarHelper::cancel( 'cancel', 'Close' );
}
$this->assignRef('auto', $auto);
parent::display($tpl);
}
}
```

The toolbar for the individual view is constructed in this listing. This view can be used for adding and changing datasets. The variable $isNew differentiates between the two cases.

Template Formular (/administration/components/views/auto/tmpl/form.php)

The form for the individual view is constructed in this standard template.

/administration/components/views/auto/tmpl/form.php:

```
<?php defined('_JEXEC') or die('Restricted access'); ?>
<script language="javascript" type="text/javascript">
... checking the input ...
</script>
<form action="index.php" method="post" name="adminForm"
id="adminForm">
<div>
<fieldset class="adminform">
<legend><?php echo JText::_( 'Details' ); ?></legend>
<table class="admintable">
<tr>
<td width="110" class="key">
<label for="title">
<?php echo JText::_( 'Text' ); ?>:
```

```
</label>
</td>
<td>
<input class="inputbox" type="text" name="text" id="text" size="60"
value="<?php
echo $this->auto->text; ?>" />
</td>
</tr>
<tr>
... additional fields ...
</tr>
<tr>
<td width="120" class="key">
<?php echo JText::_( 'Published' ); ?>:
</td>
</tr>
</table>
</fieldset>
</div>
<div class="clr"></div>
<input type="hidden" name="option" value="com_auto" />
<input type="hidden" name="id" value="<?php echo $this->auto->id; ?>"
/>
<input type="hidden" name="task" value="" />
<input type="hidden" name="controller" value="auto" />
</form>
```

The form is also made up of pure HTML with PHP variables ($this->auto->id) and static class calls (JText).

Automobile table (/administration/components/tables/auto.php)

Last but not least, the table class. Somehow the model has to know what data to work with. The JTable class facilitates access to and editing of data tremendously. It is an abstract class (an interface), which enables derivative classes to use the structure with their methods. The table name and the primary key are listed in the constructor.

/administration/components/tables/auto.php:

```
<?php
defined('_JEXEC') or die('Restricted access');
class TableAuto extends JTable
{
var $id = 0;
var $text = '';
```

```
var $manufacturer = '';
var $photo_small = '';
var $photo_large = '';
var $published = 0;
function TableAuto(& $db) {
parent::__construct('#__auto', 'id', $db);
}
}
?>
```

Installation (/administration/components/install.sql) and Uninstallation (/administration/components/uninstall.sql)

During the installation/uninstallation, the Joomla! installer has to set up or delete the necessary tables. Two files are provided for this:

`/administration/components/install.sql`:

```
DROP TABLE IF EXISTS `#__auto`;
CREATE TABLE `#__auto` (
`id` int(11) NOT NULL auto_increment,
`text` text character set utf8 NOT NULL,
`hersteller` varchar(100) character set utf8 NOT NULL,
`photo_gross` varchar(200) character set utf8 NOT NULL,
`photo_klein` varchar(200) character set utf8 NOT NULL,
`published` tinyint(1) NOT NULL,
PRIMARY KEY (`id`)
) ENGINE=MyISAM AUTO_INCREMENT=5 ;
INSERT INTO `#__auto` (`id`, `text`, `manufacturer`, `photo_large`,
`photo_small`,
`published`) VALUES
(2, 'Smart fortwo', 'Smart',
'http://localhost/joomla150/images/stories/com_auto/smart_large.jpg',
'http://localhost/joomla150/images/stories/com_auto/
                        smart_small.jpg', 1),
(4, 'Roadster', 'Smart',
'http://localhost/joomla150/images/stories/
                        com_auto/roadster_large.jpg',
'http://localhost/joomla150/images/stories/
                        com_auto/roadster_small.jpg', 1);
```

`administration/components/uninstall.sql`:

```
DROP TABLE IF EXISTS `#__auto`;
```

Test

After you have checked all of the files you can test the component and have the Joomla! administration completely manage the datasets. You can enter new text, edit existing text, and publish it. Try to edit and expand a few things. It really is not very difficult.

Creating an Installation Package

In order to wrap up an installation package for your new component, besides the aforementioned tables, you will also need the obligatory XML file with the metadata.

auto.xml

Here you are describing your component for the Joomla! installer. You have to enclose all of the information like metadata and all of the file names in XML tags. The Joomla! installer reads this file, creates new subdirectories, copies the files to the proper place, and sets up the necessary tables.

auto.xml:

```
<?xml version="1.0" encoding="utf-8"?>
<!DOCTYPE install SYSTEM "http://dev.joomla.org/xml/1.5/
                  component-install.dtd">
<install type="component" version="1.5.0">
<name>Auto</name>
<creationDate>November 2007</creationDate>
<author>Hagen Graf</author>
<authorEmail>hagen.graf@gmail.com</authorEmail>
<authorUrl>http://www.cocoate.com</authorUrl>
<copyright>All rights reserved</copyright>
<license>GNU/GPL</license>
<version>Component Version String</version>
<description>description of the component ... </description>
<files folder="site">
<filename>index.html</filename>
<filename>auto.php</filename>
<filename>controller.php</filename>
<filename>views/index.html</filename>
<filename>views/auto/index.html</filename>
<filename>views/auto/view.html.php</filename>
<filename>views/auto/tmpl/index.html</filename>
<filename>views/auto/tmpl/default.php</filename>
<filename>models/auto.php</filename>
</files>
```

```
<install>
<sql>
<file charset="utf8" driver="mysql">install.sql</file>
</sql>
</install>
<uninstall>
<sql>
<file charset="utf8" driver="mysql">uninstall.sql</file>
</sql>
</uninstall>
<administration>
<menu>Joomla! 1.5 Book Auto</menu>
<files folder="admin">
<filename>index.html</filename>
<filename>admin.auto.php</filename>
<filename>controller.php</filename>
<filename>controllers/auto.php</filename>
<filename>controllers/index.html</filename>
<filename>models/auto.php</filename>
<filename>models/autos.php</filename>
<filename>models/index.html</filename>
<filename>views/autos/view.html.php</filename>
<filename>views/autos/index.html</filename>
<filename>views/autos/tmpl/default.php</filename>
<filename>views/autos/tmpl/index.html</filename>
<filename>views/auto/view.html.php</filename>
<filename>views/auto/tmpl/form.php</filename>
<filename>views/auto/index.html</filename>
<filename>views/auto/tmpl/index.html</filename>
<filename>tables/auto.php</filename>
<filename>tables/index.html</filename>
<filename>install.sql</filename>
<filename>uninstall.sql</filename>
</files>
</administration>
</install>
```

To create the installation package, copy all the created files into a directory and pack this directory into a ZIP package by the name of the component, in this case `com_auto.zip`. The files for the front end are put in a `site` folder, while the ones for the administration area are put into an `admin` folder.

Now you can install this ZIP file with the Joomla! installer as usual, and if you want, you can offer it to others for download. Before you do that in your own installation, use the Joomla! installer to uninstall the version that you set up manually. To do that, click on **Extensions | Install/Uninstall**, mark your component and click on the **Uninstall** icon.

Modules

Modules are a lot simpler. Modules don't usually have a real administration interface, but now and then they have parameters. Modules are all about the presentation on your website and the integration into your template. Modules usually attach to existing components. It is therefore assumed that particular tables and content already exist and can be maintained.

You need two files to program your own module. One is for the logic and the presentation and the other one is an XML file for the Joomla! installer. Both file names start with the label mod_.

Source Code

Let's take a look at the source code for these files. Templates are used here as well. They have the files:

- mod_auto.php
- helper.php
- tmpl/default.php
- mod_auto.xml

Let us take a look at these files as well.

Entry Point (mod_auto.php)

The mod_auto.php file is the control file for the module.

mod_auto.php:

```php
<?php
defined('_JEXEC') or die('Restricted access');
require_once (dirname(__FILE__).DS.'helper.php');
$auto = modAutoHelper::getAuto($params);
require(JModuleHelper::getLayoutPath('mod_auto'));
?>
```

At this point a helper class, not a basic controller, is integrated.

Helper class (helper.php)

The helper class combines the controller and the model.

helper.php:

```php
<?php
defined( '_JEXEC' ) or die( 'Restricted access' );
class modAutoHelper
```

```
{
function getAuto(&$params)
{
global $mainframe;
$db =& JFactory::getDBO();
$query = "SELECT *"
. "\n FROM #__auto"
. "\n WHERE published = 1"
. "\n LIMIT 0,5"
;
$db->setQuery( $query );
$rows = $db->loadObjectList();;
$auto = "<ul>\n";
if ($rows) {
foreach ($rows as $row) {
$auto .= " <li>". $row->text . "</li>\n";
}
}
$auto .= "</ul>\n";
return $auto;
}
}
?>
```

In the `helper` class, the query of the data rows takes place one after the other in a `for` loop.

Template (tmpl/default.php)

In this quite simple construct, the variable `$auto` is simply output from the `helper` class. You could just as well execute the `for` loop from the `helper` class here and have more influence on the HTML code that is to be output and thereby enable a template designer to overwrite the source code.

`tmpl/default.php`:

```
defined( '_JEXEC' ) or die( 'Restricted access' ); ?>
<?php echo $auto; ?>
```

mod_auto.xml

To install the module, you will need all of the relevant data for the Joomla! installer in an XML file, just like with the component.

`mod_auto.xml`:

```
<?xml version="1.0" encoding="utf-8"?>
<install type="module" version="1.5.0">
<name>Auto</name>
<author>Hagen Graf</author>
<creationDate>November 2007</creationDate>
```

```
<copyright>(C) 2007 cocoate.com All rights reserved.</copyright>
<license>GNU/GPL</license>
<authorEmail>hagen.graf@gmail.com</authorEmail>
<authorUrl>www.cocoate.com</authorUrl>
<version>0.1</version>
<description>Auto Module</description>
<files>
<filename module="mod_auto">mod_auto.php</filename>
<filename>index.html</filename>
<filename>helper.php</filename>
<filename>tmpl/default.php</filename>
<filename>tmpl/index.html</filename>
</files>
</install>
```

Installation

Copy all of the files into a subdirectory and pack this directory in a ZIP package with the name of mod_auto.zip. As usual, you can now install this package with the Joomla! installer and if you want to, you can let others download it. Before you do that in your own installation, use the Joomla! installer to uninstall the version that you set up manually. To do that, click on **Extensions | Install/Uninstall**, mark your component, and click on the **Uninstall** icon.

After the installation you will still have to activate the module in the **Extensions | Module** menu.

View on the Website

You can now see the items from the jos_auto table at your selected position:

Plug-ins

Last but not least, we want to integrate the component into Joomla!'s general search function. You will need a plug-in of the search type to make your table searchable. In this case not every plug-in has a subdirectory, but every plug-in type does. For that reason we will be working in the [PathtoJoomla]/plugins/search directory.

Source Code

You need at least one PHP file with the logic (see the following listing) and the XML file with the description for the plug-in. The names for these should derive from the component, thus here they are auto.php and auto.xml. If you are writing a user plug-in, for example, you will conform to the function of the plug-in when you are naming it. In this case, there is a concrete relationship with the com_auto component. The plug-ins also have to be announced in a table, in this case, the jos_plugins table. The installer does this for you, of course. The search is very extensive and can be supplied with a number of parameters. The source code will give you an impression of the options. Since our component doesn't track when an item was added or how often an item has been accessed (we don't have an auto detail page yet), a lot of these options will remain unused for now.

auto.php:

```php
<?php
defined( '_JEXEC' ) or die( 'Restricted access' );
$mainframe->registerEvent( 'onSearch', 'plgSearchAuto' );
$mainframe->registerEvent( 'onSearchAreas', 'plgSearchAutoAreas' );
function &plgSearchAutoAreas() {
static $areas = array('auto' => 'Auto');
return $areas;
}
function plgSearchAuto( $text, $phrase='', $ordering='', $areas=null
){
$db =& JFactory::getDBO();
$user =& JFactory::getUser();
if (is_array( $areas )) {
if (!array_intersect( $areas, array_keys( plgSearchAutoAreas() ) )) {
return array();
}
}
$plugin =& JPluginHelper::getPlugin('search', 'auto');
$pluginParams = new JParameter( $plugin->params );
$limit = $pluginParams->def( 'search_limit', 50 );
$text = trim( $text );
if ($text == '') {
return array();
}
$section = JText::_( 'Auto' );
$wheres = array();
switch ($phrase){
case 'exact':
$text = $db->getEscaped($text);
$wheres2 = array();
$wheres2[]= "LOWER(a.text) LIKE '%$text%'";
$wheres2[]= "LOWER(a.manufacturer) LIKE '%$text%'";
$where = '(' . implode( ') OR (', $wheres2 ) . ')';
break;
case 'all':
case 'any':
default:
$words = explode( ' ', $text );
```

```
$wheres = array();
foreach ($words as $word) {
$word = $db->getEscaped($word);
$wheres2 = array();
$wheres2[] = "LOWER(a.text) LIKE '%$word%'";
$wheres2[] = "LOWER(a.hersteller) LIKE '%$word%'";
$wheres[] = implode( ' OR ', $wheres2 );
}
$where= '(' . implode( ($phrase == 'all' ? ') AND (' : ') OR ('),
$wheres ) .
')';
break;
}
switch ( $ordering ) {
default:
$order = 'a.text ASC';
break;
}
$query = "SELECT * FROM #__auto AS a"
. "\n WHERE ( $where )"
. "\n AND published = '1'"
. "\n ORDER BY $order";
$db->setQuery( $query, 0, $limit );
$rows = $db->loadObjectList();
foreach($rows as $key => $row) {
$rows[$key]->href = 'index.php?option=com_auto&view=auto';
}
return $rows;
}
?>
```

The XML file contains the description data about the plug-in for the installer again and looks like the following listing.

auto.xml:

```
<?xml version="1.0" encoding="utf-8"?>
<install version="1.5" type="plugin" group="search">
<name>Search - Auto</name>
<author>Hagen Graf</author>
<creationDate>November 2007</creationDate>
<copyright>(C) 2007 cocoate.com. All rights reserved.</copyright>
<license>GNU/GPL</license>
<authorEmail>hagen.graf@gmail.com</authorEmail>
<authorUrl>www.cocoate.com</authorUrl>
<version>0.1</version>
<description>search plugin for the auto component</description>
<files>
<filename plugin="auto">auto.php</filename>
</files>
</install>
```

After you have installed the plug-in and have activated it in the
Extensions | Plugin Manager menu, your list is searchable by means of the search
field on the website. By entering a search term, the `text` and `manufacturer`
fields in the database are searched and the results are displayed in the general
search template:

The `search` plug-in was kept simple on purpose. A link to an individual view of the
list element should be placed at the positions where the search results are found, so
that the user doing the search can go there. But since we did not build an individual
view into our component, we naturally cannot put a link there.

Summary

This chapter was written to give you an overview of the creation of components,
modules, and plug-ins.

You can easily deduce further developments from comparable components. Our
`auto` component, for example, only has one table view. Look for a component
with an individual view, as for instance `com_contact`, and extend `auto` with its
functionality.

The same is true with parameter assignments in modules. Look for a master and
create your own module.

Things that look complicated at first will reveal themselves as totally transparent
when you look at them again.

Have fun exploring!

16
A Website with Joomla!

You have perhaps read the entire book up to this point. You have seen dozens of administration pages. You have racked your brain about the connection between web technologies and Joomla! structures. You have heard about all kinds of mnemonics like HTTP, HTML, CSS, SQL, PHP, SEO, SEF, DIV, MVC, and others.

But all you wanted was a website! And perhaps you have come to this chapter first because of precisely that reason.

It doesn't matter—welcome to a concrete example. This chapter describes the building of a website from idea to realization.

Idea

The site that will be described here is the website of the vintner family Bertrand. Pascal Bertrand, who manages the winery, is the third generation of his family involved in the business. His product offering includes wines from several types of grapes and vintages.

Until now he has been delivering his wine to a vintners' cooperative and in the summer he sells directly to consumers. Now M. Bertrand would like to sell his wine over the Internet as well and, of course, he wants to do that with the help of Joomla!

The website should:

- Represent the Bertrand family business
- Disseminate information about the vineyard and the wine
- Allow online ordering
- Give M. Bertrand the option to promote new product on the website
- Contain a gallery with pictures and videos of the harvesting of grapes and events

- Contain an internal area where registered users can access special offers and a newsletter
- Offer a way for visitors to contact the vintner
- Allow insertions of news feeds from the wine industry

All of this should be accomplished in two days.

Preparations

Some preparations are necessary to meet all of these demands.

Logo and Appearance

The Bertrand family meets with Ruth Prantz, a friend and designer, to discuss the layout and the content that should be promoted on the website. Ruth asks whether there is an existing logo on printed material. The available printed material means pamphlets, flyers, letterhead, and a store sign. There is a logo that the grandfather had drawn a while ago:

The logo has been used by the family for various reasons over and over again. But there is no consistent image. It has been printed in different colors, with different type faces, and various styles of images and graphics.

Ruth also wants to know what the goals of the website are and what target groups are to be addressed with it.

The Bertrand winery is an ecological company that pays special attention to the quality of the wine it produces and it is quite trendy for the times. They would like to sell 5 % of their product from the website. Their target group is wine lovers and their friends, age 35 and up.

Ruth suggests that the logo, the colors and the type faces should be updated for the current times in order to differentiate it from the competition.

The first draft, which is on her monitor half an hour later, looks like this:

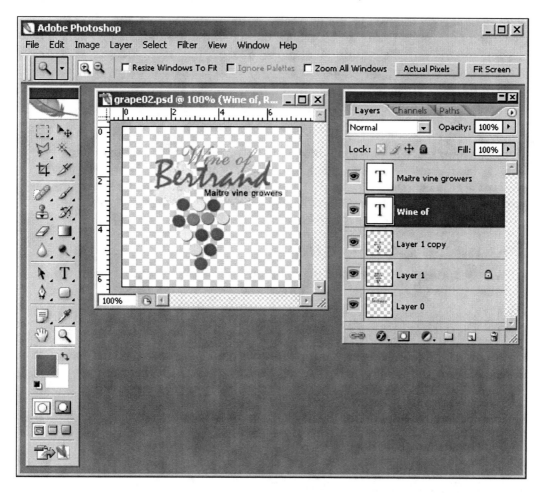

Ruth is using Photoshop Elements to design the logo. A lot of website providers include this program at no charge with a hosting contract. You can, of course, use other graphics programs such as the open-source program GIMP.

The family really likes the draft and Ruth bids her farewell. She will base the development of the Joomla! template on this basic draft and with these colors. The Bertrand family, in the meantime, will collect materials for the website and define the structure of their Joomla! system.

Photographs

Photos are needed to provide an impression of the wine, the area, the vines, the work, and the family. Didier and Marlene, the son and daughter, are given the job of searching through their comprehensive archive of photos and videos for usable material and also taking their cameras to today's wine festival to capture more images and video footage.

Texts

Monsieur Bertrand will personally take care of the text that will appear on the website. He has written the text for countless flyers and also articles for the local press and trade magazines in the past. He also has numerous documents about his land and his wine, which he will scan and offer as PDFs on the site.

Technical Conversion

While the children are busy collecting materials, he is going to start preparing the structure of the website.

Local Installation

He installs a local Joomla! in an Xampp Lite environment as described in Chapter 3. Instead of using the subdirectory `[PathtoJoomla]/Joomla150`, he uses `[PathtoJoomla]/bertrand`.

The connection information for the MySQL server is as follows:

- Hostname: `localhost`
- Username: `root`
- Password: `no password` (he leaves it empty)
- Name of the database: `bertrand`

He runs the installation without loading sample data since he will create his own content. He stores the particulars in the sixth step of the installation procedures by clicking on the appropriate button. The screen cues are a little misleading here. The radio button next to the **Install sample data** is active by default. But if you don't click on it, the data is not installed.

He clicks on the **Next** button. The installer creates an empty Joomla! site. He can already see **Wines of Bertrand** in the title bar window.

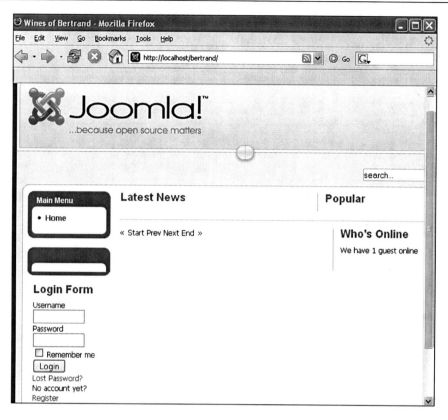

However, the website is not completely empty. M. Bertrand now clicks on the
Extensions | Module Manager menu in the administration area. Here he can see an
activated module by the name of Main menu.

M. Bertrand immediately wonders "*Hmm, where are all of the other system modules, like for instance the login module?*" A quick glance on the **New** icon gives him some comfort. Modules can be created at will with this icon.

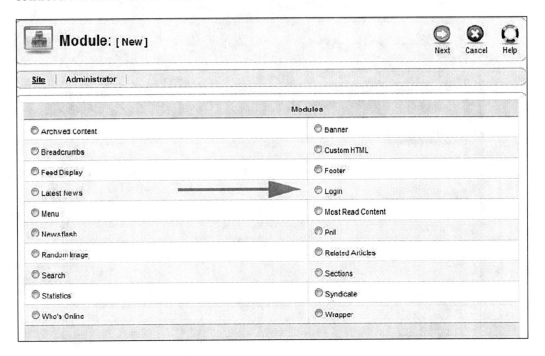

The First Few Articles

Now it is time to work on the structure. M. Bertrand would like to see the news in blog form on the start page of the website. He first wants to set up three pieces of news to see what it looks like. The news doesn't have to be categorized. He goes to the **Content | Article | New** menu and sets up three articles. He positions the cursor at the place where he wants the **Read more** link and clicks on the **Read more** button below the editor; a red line is inserted. **Section** and **Category** are **uncategorized**; he selects the **Yes** button next to **Frontpage**.

The three pieces of news (articles) are displayed on the website and at the menu item **Content Start Page Articles**.

Then M. Bertrand activates the Beez template under **Extension Templates**.

M. Bertrand just wants to see the date of creation under the headline of the piece of news. He wants to hide the name of the author and the update date. Since he will be the only one adding articles to the website for the time being, he changes the settings in the **Author Name** field and in the two date fields below it.

The front page now looks the way he wants. Joomla! automatically creates an RSS news feed for these news items and displays it in Internet Explorer version 7 and up and in the Firefox browser with an orange colored symbol in the URL field.

When clicking this symbol, Firefox adds a dynamic bookmark:

As soon as M. Bertrand writes a new article for the front page, it is immediately displayed in his browser. This, of course, also functions in other feed reader programs. Recently this concept has become popular even with mobile terminals such as telephones and PDAs. M. Bertrand hopes that a lot of customers will subscribe to his news service and will therefore become familiar with his product offerings.

Masthead

A masthead contains various pieces of information: a visitor to a website must be able to see who is responsible for the content of a website.

In M. Bertrand's case, his masthead looks like this:

Responsibility for the content of this site:

Fa. Bertrand

Examplestraße 1

12345 Exampleville

Exampleland

E-Mail: bertrand@cocoate.com

Telephone: 0123 4567-89

Since the site is being used for commerce, he also has to enter the valued added tax identification number.

He sets up another non-categorized content item from the **Content | Articles | New** menu. This time he does not publish it on the front page. The link to the masthead now has to be put into the Main menu. M. Bertrand goes to the **Menus | Main Menu | New** menu. The Menu Item Assistant starts up. He selects **Articles** in the first window and then selects **Standard Article Layout**.

M. Bertrand switches to the edit screen of the new menu item, enters the name of the link (**Masthead**) and now has to select the desired article in **Menu Item Parameters**:

After clicking on the **Select** button, another selection window with all of the articles appears:

M. Bertrand clicks on the **Masthead** article, the selection window closes, and the menu entry is completed. A final click on the **Save** icon makes sure that the link does indeed wind up in the menu.

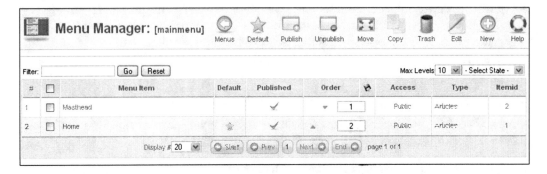

Now M. Bertrand still has to make sure that the link is activated (red cross or green checkmark). Publishing here refers purely to the menu link, not the article. The link can now be positioned with the green arrow buttons.

Now M. Bertrand still wants to hide the creation date and the print, PDF, and email icons. To do that, M. Bertrand calls up the masthead article once more, selecting **Content | Articles | Masthead**, and changes the values for **PDF, email**, and **print icons** in the extended parameters to **Hide**.

The masthead is now complete and M. Bertrand starts working on the structure of the menu links for the rest of the pages.

Menu Structure

M. Bertrand wants to have three menus, a main menu, a horizontal top menu, and a user menu for registered users.

Structure of the Main Menu

The entire structure of the website should be shown in the main menu.

Start Page (News)
The wines (general text)
Wine 1 (Description of the product with purchase option)
Wine 2 (Description of the product with purchase option)
Wine 3 (Description of the product with purchase option)
The vineyard (general text)
Vineyard 1 (Description with link to the wine)
Vineyard 2 (Description with link to the wine)
Vineyard 3 (Description with link to the wine)
Impressions (Gallery Component with pictures of the grape harvest)
Offers (special offers in the user section)
Contacts
Masthead

Structure of the Top Menu

The top menu should provide quick access to four core topics. If someone clicks on a link in the top menu, the links that belong to this link should also open in the Main menu.

The wines (general text)
The vineyard (general text)
Impressions (Gallery Component with pictures of the grape harvest)
Contacts

Structure of the User Menu

After registering and successfully logging on via the login module, registered users should have the option to take advantage of special offers. The goal of registration is to build close long-term relationships with customers. A regularly updated page should be displayed with an attractive wine offer and a way to make the purchase. M. Bertrand will make the scanned documents available to registered users within the **Download** link.

Offers
Download
Log Out

Setting up the Texts and the Menu Links in the Main Menu

All of the texts that M. Bertrand sets up in the **Content | Article Manager** menu, except for the contact form and the gallery, are uncategorized content for the time being. He makes sure that the content is not displayed on the front page. All of the articles should display the three PDF, email, and print icons, but not the creation date.

After he has set up all of the articles, he switches to menu link creation. So that **Wine 1, Wine 2**, and **Wine 3** end up on the second menu level, the parent item **The Wine** must be selected.

There is a tree-like menu in **Menus | Main Menu** that looks like the following screenshot.

Contact Link

M. Bertrand wants to use the integrated contact component that came with Joomla! for his contact form. First he needs a category by the name of *Fa. Bertrand*, which he sets up from the **Components | Contacts | Categories** menu item.

He enters himself as the contact in the **Contact** tab. Over time more contacts will probably be entered here. At the moment, a central form should be sufficient.

Now he adds a contact link into the main menu. To do that he clicks on **Menus | Main Menu | New**. He selects **Contacts | Standard Contact Layout** in the menu item assistant and ends up in the edit screen for the new menu item. The available contacts are now shown in the parameter section. At the moment, of course, he is the only contact. He checks his name and clicks on the **Save** button.

Now he still has to publish the contact link in **Menus | Main Menu** and position it at the right place.

M. Bertrand's information, as well as a form that a user can use to type in a question, are now in the contact link on the website.

Top Menu

Except for the integration of the gallery component, the Main menu is now complete. Now M. Bertrand creates a Top Menu. He selects **Menus** in the menu area and clicks on the **New** icon. He calls the new menu Top menu.

The menu still has to be placed on position user3 under **Extensions Modules** and be activated. M. Bertrand does not have to worry about the title, since the title is not usually displayed with horizontal menus.

He can copy the desired links from the **Main Menu** into the **Top Menu**. For that he goes to **Menus | Main Menu**, marks the links **The Wines**, **The Vineyards**, and **Contact**, and clicks on the **Copy** icon.

The links were copied. He quickly checks the website to see whether the results are there. The links have indeed arrived on the website and are displayed in the Top menu and when he clicks on them, the correct article is shown. However, the proper submenu did not open in the Main menu. When he tries it out he notices different values for the ItemID in the URL. When he takes the value for the ItemID out of the main menu and changes it manually in the URL in the browser, the link behaves as desired and the subordinated links become visible in the Main menu.

M. Bertrand ponders for a while and decides to actualize the Top Menu links as URLs. He wants to bring the two links, **The Wines** and **The Vineyards**, from the Main menu into the Top Menu.

To do that, he goes to **Menus | Top Menu | The Wines** and clicks on the **Change Type** button in the edit template and then he clinks on **External Link** in the menu item assistant that pops up.

The **Link** field is no longer highlighted in gray there, but is writable. He inserts the appropriate link. For M. Bertrand these are:

- The `index.php?option=com_content&view=article&id=5&Itemid=4` link for the wines

- The `index.php?option=com_content&view=article&id=9&Itemid=8` link for the vineyards

There should not be a / (slash) in front of `index.php`. In our case, this would address the document directory of the Apache webserver and the XAMPP lite start page would be displayed. A relative link does not contain the entire declaration of the link, and is always regarded to be the completion of the respectively called address. For example, if one switches an Internet presence to a different domain, all relative links will work again immediately. If one had written these as absolute links (with a slash), all of the links would have to be changed first. Your **ItemIDs**, of course, can have different values than M. Bertrand's.

Shop

A shopping cart system has to be installed on the website so that the customers have a way to pay online. There is no shop component yet that currently works with Joomla! and M. Bertrand would like to install as few additional components as possible in order to avoid maintenance complications and to minimize the necessary updates.

His son Didier suggests integrating a PayPal shopping basket. PayPal is the world's biggest online payment system and is owned by eBay. It offers numerous merchant tools, among them a shopping basket system. M. Bertrand signs up for a PayPal user account. Other systems such as WorldPay and others offer similar features.

At the moment he is offering three products:

- A white wine at 10 Euro per bottle
- A rosé wine at 10 Euro per bottle
- A red wine at 12 Euro per bottle

PayPal has an option of creating buttons that go with the specific products. When you click on these buttons, the respective item is put into the PayPal shopping basket. Shipping costs and taxes can also be added.

M. Bertrand builds these buttons into the **Wine 1**, **Wine 2**, and **Wine 3** articles. He decides to set up his own module. He clicks on the **New** icon under **Extensions | Module Manager** and selects an HTML module. He inserts the PayPal code into the HTML view of the editor (HTML button). To make this job a little bit easier, he can disable the editor in the **Site | Global Configuration** menu. He places the module on the left side below the main menu and selects the pages that he wants to have it displayed on.

In the case of PayPal, M. Bertrand's email address must be put into the source code. The default Email Cloaking plugin that Joomla! installs disguises this email address and therefore PayPal cannot find the correct shopping basket. He disables the plugin in the **Extensions | Plugin Manager** menu.

If a user clicks on one of the buttons now, a PayPal shopping basket pops up. The user can put several items into the basket and change the quantities.

If the customer has a PayPal account, he or she can use it to pay for the purchase immediately. There is a good chance of people that buy wine online having a PayPal account and this trend is increasing rapidly.

The Impressions

M. Bertrand would like to integrate pictures and videos into the website to give his visitors a feeling for the countryside. He installs the Exposé gallery as described in Chapter 12. He sets up a **Grape Harvest** album with a 2007 sub-album, a **Wine Festival** album with a 2007 sub-album, and a **Production** album with a few pictures. His son Didier will add pictures bit by bit.

From **Menus | Main Menu | New** he inserts the link to the Exposé component into the menu. Then he gives the link the title **Impressions**, in the menu link edit screen. After saving it for the first time, he can then place it at the right position. The impressions appear on the website in the following form:

The User Section

A page with special offers and a download area with PDF articles, certificates, ground surveys and the like is to be set up in the section for registered users.

The User Menu

M. Bertrand sets up an uncategorized article with the heading of **Offers**. The article is published, not displayed on the front page, and is only accessible by registered users.

He sets up a user menu in the **New Menus** menu.

He positions the user menu on the left side under **Extensions | Modules Manager**, activates it, and sets up the rights for registered users.

He adds the article to the new user menu and sets the access rights to **registered**.

M. Bertrand can now log on to the website, He uses his admin user account and is delighted to see that in addition to the newly created user menu, there is a pencil icon next to every heading.

By clicking on one of the pencil icons, he winds up in the edit template of one of the articles. Here he can change the text of the article, the parameters, and even the metadata. While working on an article he notices that the **Logout** button from the login module is only displayed on the front page. He goes to the **Extensions | Modules** menu and changes the view to **All** in the **Pages/Articles** section of the login module.

The Download Section

Finally he would also like to have a download section for his scanned documents. He would like to display small graphics of the certificates in the vineyard descriptions and the comprehensive documents in the registered users section. For that he uses Joomla!'s weblinks component.

He switches over to the **Extensions | Web Links | Categories** section and sets up three categories:

- Announcements
- Certificates
- Ground surveys

He adds a small description for each category and later he will also insert a picture. These categories will only be visible to registered users.

The PDFs are to be stored in a special directory in the media section (**Site | Media Manager**). He types the name of the directory pdf into the field next to the path and clicks on the **Create Folder** button.

Now he can upload all of the PDFs to Joomla!. He could also have copied the files into the local C:/xampplite/htdocs/bertrand/images/pdf xampplite directory with a file manager or upload them later via FTP to the server.

The URLs of the PDFs still have to be entered as links in the **Components | Web Links | New** menu. Complete URLs that are valid on the Internet have to be entered in this template.

He also selects the category and with one click defines the target for the PDF to be a **New Window Without Browser Navigation**. Since M. Bertrand is working locally at this time, the URLs refer to http://localhost/bertrand/. When M. Bertrand moves this website to his server, he will have to modify this to his future domain name; or he can enter the correct domain name at this time.

After a bit of typing, M. Bertrand has added a few links to various PDFs.

This collection of links still has to be put into the user menu. M. Bertrand calls up **Menus | User Menu | New**, selects the **Web Links** component in the menu item assistant and once there, selects the **Layout category list**.

He still enters a heading for the section (**Download Section**) in the subsequent editing template. Only registered users are to have access. He saves the link and places it below the **Offers** link. The link appears on the website as planned. The three categories are displayed.

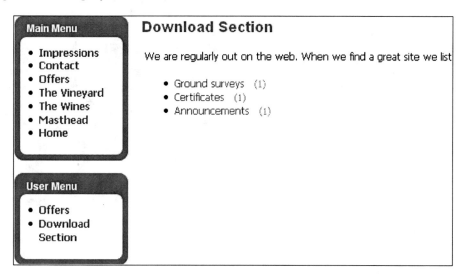

After clicking on one of the categories, a table with the PDFs is displayed.

M. Bertrand is satisfied. Even though it isn't a real document administration, it is totally sufficient for his purposes. Even the frequency of the clicks on the individual documents is displayed in the table. The display of the descriptions and the look of the table can also be defined in **Menus | User Menu | Download | Parameters**.

User Details

M. Bertrand remembers that he saw a link in the user menu in Joomla!'s sample data with which the user could edit his or her information (email address, password, etc.). He also wants that type of link in the User menu of his website. He selects **Users | User Details | View** in the menu item assistant. The user section now has the appropriate link and every user can change his or her information.

First Results

M. Bertrand is pleasantly surprised as to how quickly it all went. He calls Ruth and tells her about the progress of his work. Ruth sounds a little distraught since the templates she had built until now were all for Joomla! 1.0.x and a lot has probably changed. But she is confident that she can show them the template the next day.

She quickly sends two screenshots of her work via email.

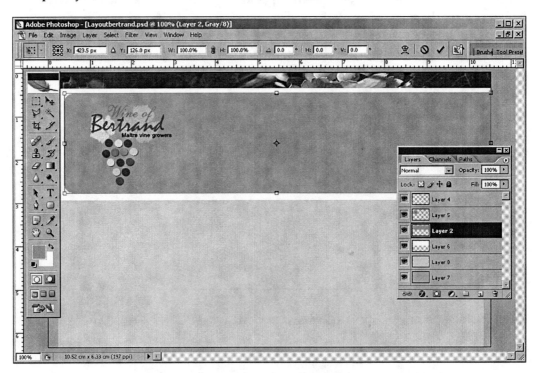

When she integrates Joomla! 1.5., Ruth quickly discovers that a lot of the CSS classes have changed in name from Joomla! 1.0.

To get a good overview of the CSS classes and the rest of the parameters, Ruth uses the Firefox Web Developer (the `web_developer-1.0.2-fx+fl.xpi` file).

 If you already have the Firefox browser installed on your system, just double-click on the file name to install it.

Ruth and M. Bertrand agree that M. Bertrand can already install the website on his server. She will add the template later.

M Bertrand Learns CSS

M. Bertrand is already pretty good at HTML and would love to know how his template works.

An extended conversation ...

Ruth explains to him that the look of the template is determined by two CSS files, which tell the browser how to display the website. For instance, whether the background is to be red or brown, whether an image element is to be inserted and many other things.

These instructions are written with cascading stylesheet commands and deposited into the two CSS files, `template.css` and `joomlastuff.css`.

Ruth has optimized these files for the most common browsers Internet Explorer 6.0 and Firefox 1.5 for Windows as well as Firefox 1.06 and Safari 2.03 for Mac OS X 10.4.

M. Bertrand wants to learn to understand CSS so that he can change or create a template himself.

Ruth explains the principle of the Cascading Stylesheets (CSS): The term Cascading means that the CSS formatting instructions are read by the browsers from top to bottom, just like a cascade. If one instruction is written twice, the lower one overwrites the one above, in other words the latest one overwrites the earlier ones. CSS instructions can be inserted at the following places:

- In an external CSS file
- In the head of an HTML file
- Directly in the respective HTML tag

CSS instructions that are issued directly in the respective HTML tag overwrite the formatting from the external CSS files. It is important to know that, since Joomla!'s elements are sometimes issued with CSS formatting and are integrated directly into the respective HTML tags.

To keep the stylesheet of M. Bertrand's template simple, Ruth has used the CSS hierarchy. For instance, she has defined the font information in the general HTML tags: `body`, `table`, `div`, `p`, and `form`. With this, she has defined that all of the content of these elements is to be displayed in the *Verdana* typeface, in a certain font size and in gray.

If this is to be changed at a particular position on the website, then these HTML tags have to be assigned to a class; the `greytable` class for instance, with the properties:

```
{ background-color: #333; }
```

This is integrated into the HTML framework with:

```
<table class="greytable">
```

That way, individual elements can be controlled differently with CSS classes.

There are numerous such predefined classes in Joomla!, by means of which someone can easily program their own template. Let us, for example, take a look at the site navigation.

The site navigation consists of three Joomla! modules:

- Main Menu
- User Menu
- User Login

Ruth defines the layout of the site navigation with these classes:

HTML Code of the Page Navigation:

```
...
<div class="moduletable_menu">
<h3>main menu</h3>
<ul class="menu">
<li id="current" class="active item1">
<a href="http://localhost/bertrand/">front page</a> </li>
<li class="parent item4">
<a href=»index.php?option=com_content...>The Wines</a>
</li>
<li class="parent item8">
<a href="index.php?option=com_content...">Wineyard </a> </li>
...
</ul>
</div>
<div class="moduletable">
<h3>Announcement</h3>
<form action="index.php" method="post" name="login" id="form-
login">
<fieldset class="input">
<p id="form-login-username">
<label for="modlgn_username">user name</label><br>
<input id="modlgn_username" name="username" class="inputbox"
alt="username" size="18"
type="text">
</p>
...
</fieldset>
<ul>
<li>
<a href="index.php?option=com_user...">Forgot your password?</a>
</li>
...
</ul>
<input name="option" value="com_user" type="hidden">
...
</form>
</div>
<div class="clear"></div>
...
```

Formatting Step by Step

Pattern

By looking at the HTML code, a pattern can easily be recognized:

Ruth has defined the output of the module with `style="xhtml"` in `index.php`.

With this setting and with the parameter setting of the module (Module manager), all of the modules used here are output to `"list"` in `<div>` tags. These `<div>` containers contain a header and lists that are defined with the `<h3>` HTML tag. The links are in the lists. A lot of design options are available with this, since all of the HTML tags can be programmed either directly or with Joomla!'s classes.

The modules have an easy-to-see image background, which is put there with all of the modules and which was therefore defined in the encompassing HTML tag. All of the tags that Ruth has invented herself for her HTML structure are in the `template.css` file. This is also true for the ubiquitous page navigation.

`.naviside` CSS code:

```
.naviside {
background: url(../images/naviside_top.jpg) top left; /*image
background*/
width: 210px; /*width*/
vertical-align: top; /*top alignment of the content*/
border: 0px; /*border*/
padding: 0px; /*padding*/
margin: 0px; /*margins*/
background-color: #fff; /*background color*/
text-align: left; /*alignment at the left border*/
float: left; /*total alignment inside of the HTML structure*/
}
```

In the next step, Ruth assigns properties to the `<div>` tags that are here activated with the `moduletable_menu` and `moduletable` (login form) classes, which are to be valid for all menus: width, distance from each other, and a color. She only needs to know the two classes, `moduletable` and `moduletable_menu`, for this.

The `moduletable` and `moduletable_menu` classes are Joomla! default classes. For purposes of overview, Ruth has saved the classes she has defined herself separated from the default Joomla! classes in the `joomla_stuff.css` and `template.css` CSS files.

CSS code:

```
.naviside .moduletable, .moduletable_menu
{
width: 210px; /*width*/
background: none; /*background*/
margin-top: 18px; /*marin outside of the module, to the top*/
text-align: left; /*left-aligned*/
padding: 0px; /*no padding from the edge of the module to the
                                              content*/

}
```

Title of the Module

It is easy to create a title that looks the same for all modules by addressing the headline of the tables directly with its <h3> tag within the module.

To do this, first state the class again in the CSS, here .navitop. With the .navitop class, all modules are within this <div>. This statement has the effect that only header statements inside the .navitop section are formatted with these CSS commands. And now the crucial <h3> is added. Ruth set up the title with a background image in order to have more variety in the look of the menus.

Module title:

```
/*defining the header of the module on the left */
.navitop h3 {
font: 18px/18px Times New Roman, serif; /*font size/-type*/
font-weight: normal; /*font weight*/
color: #A49A66; /*font color*/
background: url(../images/blatt.gif) top left; /*backround image*/
background-repeat: no-repeat; /*repeat background image*/
padding-left: 25px; /*padding on the left*/
height: 25px; /*div height*/
width: 185px; /*width*/
}
```

Menu Items

After the title is done, the links that are set up in the HTML lists have to be formatted.

Ruth did not want to have any dots before the links and wanted to get rid of the usual indentation of lists. She uses the Joomla! predefined .menu and .moduletable CSS classes to address the list.

Formatting the list in the modules:

```
ul.menu, .naviside .moduletable ul
{
list-style: none; /* list without dot*/
display: block; /* block element, */
/* formatted as boxes */
width: 210px; /* width */
margin: 0px; /* margins */
border: 0px; /* border */
padding: 0px; /* padding */
}
```

Divider Lines

Ruth wanted to show the individual links separated by lines. For this, she addresses the li tags of the lists in a specific way:

```
ul.menu li {
border-bottom: 1px dotted #ccc; /* bottom border */
}
```

The subheadings of the links can be addressed separately; in this example they have an indention on the left border.

Subheadings:

```
/*Formatting the lists of the subheadings*/
ul.menu ul {
/* the margin acts like an indention of the text*/
margin-left: 10px;
background-color: #EEE; /* other background color */
width: 200px; /* smaller width */
}
```

And the subheadings get a differently formatted bottom border that fits with the background color.

```
ul.menu ul li {
border-bottom: 1px solid #fff; /*bottom border*/?
}
```

Each list item could be formatted separately since every `li` tag has its own class.

```
level1 item1, .level1 item2 parent, .level1 item3 parent, .level1
                                                          item4
```

The Actual Links

Now we come to the links themselves. The formatting addresses the a tag that is positioned in the `ul` list with the `.menu` class.

All links should look like this:

```
ul.mainmenu a {?
   text-decoration: none;   /* link without underline */
   color: #6B5E588;          /* color of the font */
   font-size: 11px;          /* font size */
   padding-left: 10px;       /* distance of the text to the border */
}
```

The `hover` effect changes the background or the font color of the link when the mouse rolls over it. Ruth has set it up in the following way:

```
ul.menu a:hover {
   color: #CAC303;
   text-decoration: none;
}
```

And finally, the link of the currently active page is specially highlighted with the help of the following class:

```
.menu li#current a {
   color: #B22819; /* font color */
}
```

... and done!

M. Bertrand is delighted and now finds formatting with CSS a lot easier after this explanation. His head is still spinning a little, but Ruth also gives him the www. w3schools.com/css/ link. That site has a good description of all of the attributes that can be defined with CSS.

Changes for Joomla! Version 1.5

If you have already built templates with Joomla! 1.0.x, here is the good news: Joomla! 1.5 is backward compatible in legacy mode!

There are, however, a few pitfalls that you should be aware of. The previously used mosload() commands in the PHP code and the old CSS classes of the index.php of a template don't work any more at certain places since some formatting has changed.

Changes to the Menus

There are now many options for formatting modules and components compared to Joomla! 1.0. You were able to control the modules in different ways before by assigning them their own CSS class extensions; now their HTML output can also be controlled with the following statements in the template's own index.php.

These are the options that you can select from:

- table (default): The module is displayed in a table column.
- horz: The module is displayed horizontally and output into the cell of a surrounding table.
- xhtml: The module is output in a simple div element.
- rounded: The output is done in a format that enables round corners; with this the name of the <div> changes from moduletable to module.
- none: The module is output witout any formatting.

This is great! This allows you to design a Joomla! site without any tables and to organize the content logically (as needed for barrier freedom).

By using <div> tags you can now design with fewer constraints than with HTML tables, which were never designed for that purpose anyway.

Installation on the Webserver

M. Bertrand's local website is now approximately what he had imagined. He has been looking for a provider for his website in the last few weeks and after a long search has become a customer of a small company in the neighborhood. This company offered M. Bertrand an SSL-protected administration interface by the name of Plesk for the setup of his webserver, the database, the email configurations, etc.

PHP runs in Safe Mode. The database can be administered with an installed phpMyAdmin. M. Bertrand wanted to have web-based administration for his server, because he did not want to have to learn tedious configuration files.

 There are numerous other interfaces, such as Confixx, Visas, and Webmin. Many providers, like 1&1, Strato, Hetzner, and others use their own developments. We will discuss Plesk briefly as an example; other interfaces work similarly.

How to Do the Installation

M. Bertrand used the Joomla! web installer to install the program in his local environment. Subsequently he spent a morning entering data and he does not want to lose these with the live installation. There are at least two options:

- He could load all of the Joomla! files from FTP to the server at his provider, change the configuration file manually, and import the database with phpMyAdmin.
- He could load a Joomla! file to the server at his provider from FTP, install it with the Joomla! installer, and then import the data of the database with phpMyAdmin.

M. Bertrand decides on the first option. In order to be able to start the installation, he needs access data for FTP, MySQL, and the domain name of course.

He finds the following access data in his administration interface.

FTP

Host: `bertrand.cocoate.com`

User: `fusfusfus`

Password: `pwpwpw`

MySQL

Host: localhost

User: dbusdbus

Password: pwpwpwpw

Database: dbdbdb

Installation of Joomla! at the Provider

M. Bertrand starts his FTP program and enters the necessary information. He received the FTP program from his provider free of charge (you can find a free-ware FTP program at www.filezilla.sourceforge.net/).

He transfers his existing installation from the c:\xampplite\htdocs\bertrand subdirectory using FTP into the httpdocs subdirectory on his provider's server.

He backs up the configuration.php file on his own PC and opens it with an editor or with the WordPad program.

A few values have to be changed so that his local version runs on the server as well.

```
/* Database Settings */
...
var $host = 'localhost'; // normally set to localhost
var $user = ''; // MySQL username
var $password = ''; // MySQL password
var $db = ''; // MySQL database name
```

After making the changes, he loads the file using FTP into the httpdocs directory on the server and assigns it chmod 0777 rights. FTP programs can execute this command and with it can assign access rights to a directory. Joomla! requires at least chmod 755; chmod 644 is sufficient for the files.

Importing the Data

In order to be able to import the data to the MySQL database of the provider, they first have to be exported from the local xampplite version. M. Bertrand calls http://localhost/phpmyadmin from the browser, selects the bertrand database and clicks on the **Export** tab.

He clicks on **Select All** to pick all of the tables for export.

- In the **Structure** section he selects **Structure** and **DROP TABLE. DROP TABLE** inserts an additional SQL command into the export file that makes sure that with future imports of data, existing tables that may possibly have the same names are deleted. This is important in M. Bertrand's case, as all of the tables are already there from the web installer's installation.

- In the data section he selects **Data** and **Extended Inserts**.

- In **Compression,** M. Bertrand selects the **Zip-Compressed** radio button, because this will speed the transfer up a little.

- He chooses **Send** to get the downloaded data in file form.

Subsequently he clicks on the **OK** button and a `bertrand.sql` file is being offered for download.

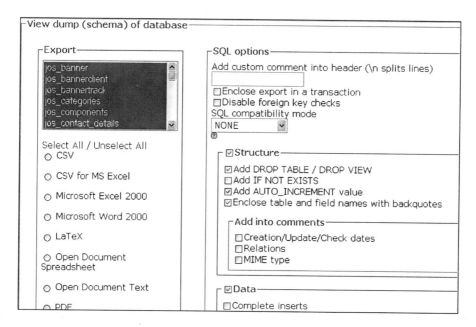

This file contains all of the database content. He saves the file somewhere outside the Joomla! directory and unpacks it, getting the `bertrand.sql` file. The file contains SQL commands that exactly represent the status of the local installation and executed sequentially will recreate this exact status on another MySQL system.

This is exactly what M. Bertrand wants, so he opens phpMyAdmin on his provider's server. There he clicks on the **Import** tab in his database (which is also called `coco_bertrand`). In the template he clicks on the **Search** button and selects the local `bertrand.sql` file. One click on the **OK** button and the file is uploaded, the SQL commands are executed sequentially, and his website on the server is now a copy of the local version.

The website should now be ready on the server, in our case at `http://bertrand.cocoate.com`.

File and Directory Rights

To ensure a normal operation of Joomla!, the directory rights have to be adjusted. M. Bertrand checks the settings in the **Help | System Info** menu:

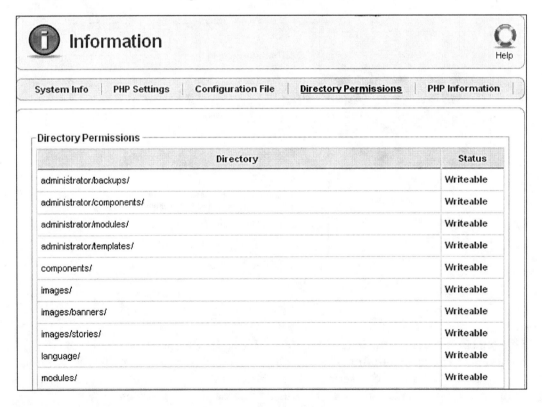

M. Bertrand's provider's server runs under Linux. Linux has users and user groups. M. Bertrand has a user and the Apache webserver also has a user. Depending on configuration, they can both be in one user group or in separate user groups. If they are in different user groups, the directory rights have to be set to `chmod 0777`.

M. Bertrand also changes the password for the Exposé gallery in the administration. It was still set to `manager`.

Search Engines

There are two approaches for M. Bertrand's website to be listed in search engines.

Search Engine Friendly URLs

The option of search engine friendly URLs also depends on the provider. M. Bertrand's provider allows these URLs and M. Bertrand activates this feature in the **Site | Configuration | SEO** menu. Then he renames the `htaccess.txt` file to `.htaccess`. The Exposé gallery, for example, is now accessed via the URL `http://bertrand.cocoate.com/Impressions`

This type of renaming of URLs only works with the Apache webserver.

Metatags

M. Bertrand diligently enters a short description and the keywords into his articles.

Design

The next morning has come, the wine festival is over, Didier and Marlene have taken a lot of photographs. M. Bertrand has created the website to his satisfaction and has even integrated the PDFs.

The PayPal connection works.

They all meet for breakfast and Ruth, in the meantime, has finished the template. She brings the finished components on a USB stick and talks about her experiences with the template for an hour.

Installation of the Template

M. Bertrand copies the template files to the /httpddocs/templates/tmpl_bertrand and /httpddocs/templates/tmpl_bertrand_shop directories using FTP. In the **Extensions | Template** menu he defines the new tmpl_bertrand template as the default:

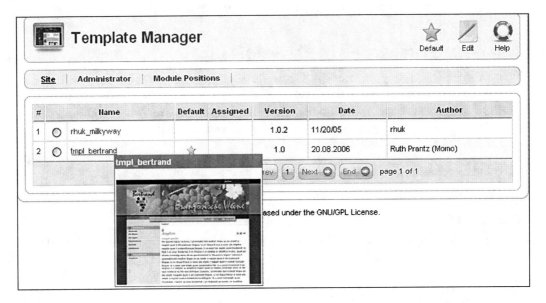

He assigns the tmpl_bertrand_shop template to the wine pages in edit mode. That way the customer will know that he or she is in the shop section.

The Template

Ruth created the template according to the following considerations:

Maintenance

Since M. Bertrand will be maintaining the site himself, she used as simply and clearly arranged a basic grid pattern as possible. M. Bertrand can easily replace the images in the top section with new ones whenever he wants.

Layout

Ruth explains her effort as follows:

There are many ways to creatively implement a website.

M. Bertrand wants to sell wine.

This means that his website needs the visual presentation of a traditional, quality-conscious vintner where the customer would gladly purchase good wine.

A high-tech presentation with a metallic look would be inappropriate even if it were to be modern.

No, the wine, the grapes, and the earth should determine the look and feel of the website and this is interpreted with the color choices and the photographs.

A visual appearance is created from several important elements. These include: logo, colors, the style of the photographs, and the graphics (by graphics she means all image elements that are not photographs, including the buttons and symbols), and the typefaces.

The division of the space and the proportions also have an effect and all of these elements have to work together for the visual impression to be coherent. It is best to use only one typeface. Differences can easily be brought out with bold and italic versions of the same type face.

In the Bertrand template, she did not use a very original, but rather a very classical typeface for the headings, one that leaves an impression of reliability. It is Times Classic, similar to what national newspapers use for headlines. Design does not always have to be particularly original; it is enough if it fits well.

A Portrait

During breakfast and during the telephone conversation when Ruth explained the CSS technology to M. Bertrand, she did a little sketching. She sends these sketches to M. Bertrand via email and he incorporates them into his image gallery.

Happy End

The site is online. It only took two days.

M. Bertrand spends the next two weeks inserting pictures of the grape harvest and polishing the text. He contacts acquaintances and gets them to register as users and he even gets his first order over his new system.

The provider discussed Joomla!'s update problems with M. Bertrand for some time and M. Bertrand took out a service contract. The provider will take care of the update whenever Joomla! releases a new version.

It will be relatively simple to keep this site current, since it uses the standard version of Joomla! and since the Exposé gallery runs in an HTML `iframe`, in other words similar to a wrapper component.

M. Bertrand is glad that he has outsourced the work with updates and the template.

 If you need some design work done, why not contact Ruth: Ruth Prantz, Certified Designer (`http://www.ateliersite.de`).

How Does It Work in Reality?

A lot of small company websites are created just like in this story of M. Bertrand. The bigger websites start like this too most of the time, the companies just don't like to admit it.

With larger projects, the process is in principle the same. A graphic agency handles the design and a technical company does the programming and development. There are often professional departments that take care of the text, the corporate idendity, and the security of the website. Hosting also has to be approved as well.

However, other than that, this is how it is done!

Summary

Finally you are able to make your own website. In the next chapter we will discuss a few bonus templates.

17
Bonus Templates

I bet that after M. Bertrand's experiences and the instructions on how to develop a template in Chapter 16, you are just itching to develop your own template. Thanks to Alex Kempkens, who organized the development of these templates, we can help you with a few ideas and we have two ready-to-use templates to start your adventure.

 Please note that you are allowed to use these templates in your own projects, as a design foundation for customer projects, and for private Joomla! installations free of charge. But there are two qualifications: You are not allowed to sell the templates *as such* (only the authors of these templates have that right), and there are some content-wise restrictions for their use (the details of this are listed in the respective files for each template).

When we chose these templates, we wanted to present you with a variety of websites from different sectors and from different designers.

These are the templates that we have come up with and which you can freely use:

- A template from Tom Bohaček for a non-governmental organization
- A template from Andy Miller for a venture

During the course of writing this book, the chapter about the wine merchant Bertrand and his e-commerce ambitions grew and grew, and there are now two additional templates that were not in the plans in the beginning:

- Two templates from Ruth Prantz for a middle-sized wine merchant in Languedoc, France

The story about how these templates were created and how the website was actualized is in Chapter 16.

NGO

The term *non-governmental organization* principally refers to every organized consortium of people that decide to start activities on a voluntary basis for a certain duration of time without a profit motive and without being organized by or dependent on some governmental body. Employers' associations, trade unions, sports clubs, and animal breeding associations are all examples of non-governmental organizations. Every association that has been founded in respect of the law of its country in the common public interest is potentially a non-governmental organization.

Tom Bohaček

With his agency, designer Tom Bohaček supports other agencies and enterprises with the development of their communication solutions. He works with Joomla! for an easily understandable reason:

> *It allows me the biggest freedom in implementing my ideas.*

Read what Tom has to say about his template!

The World Knowledge Template

The idea was to develop a simple template that could satisfy the changing information status and the multitudinous sources of information of an NGO.

The example of an imaginary NGO **World Knowledge**, which committed itself to the preservation of cultural stores of knowledge and their safekeeping, was devised.

Creative Approach

"Gray, my dear friend, is every theory". With this Goethe quote as support, a friendly color scheme was developed that reminds one of parchment and libraries, associated with knowledge in other words. A light turquoise from the color palette was added for important elements and orientation help. This color that juts from the layout symbolizes knowledge as such and is taken up symbolically in the header.

Since NGOs often operate inter-culturally, the layout is kept neutral and clear. This ensures that people from different countries can quickly orient themselves.

The Helvetica family, which is very popular after the Web 2.0 Hype, was selected as the typeface, not just for its popularity, but also because it represents competence and clarity and because it is installed on just about all systems.

Structural Approach

The layout of the website is divided into four parts—the header section, the navigation bar, and the two-part content section. The content section contains the articles and an additional section that contains pictures and other information such as links that are related to the content.

The navigation on the left does *not* contain a second navigation level. It can, however, be assembled from several navigation sections (for instance *Present* and *Future*). In order to communicate the mission of the organization directly, there is a direct link to a page that delves deeper into the menu item as an article and/or blog. All deeper information is shown either next to the article as a context-dependent link or as a link directly in the article. This ensures that the navigation exhibits a consistent structure, while the individual articles can be exposed to strong dynamics.

Business Establishment

A business establishment is a legal, economic and financially independent unit of an economy with its own business management. The goal of a business establishment, however, is always monetary profit. Therefore, a lot of value is put on respectability in order to gain the customers' trust. Dependent on the product, this respectability has to be reflected when customers view the establishment's website and register in the customers' brains as quickly as possible. The conversion of this respectability to websites keeps countless agencies busy day in, day out, and probably for another hundred years.

You can find one approach to this theme in Andy Miller's template!

Andy Miller

Andy Miller is a programmer and web developer with more than 10 years experience in professional web application development. He is a member of the Joomla! development team and was previously on the Mambo team. In Joomla!'s development, he is primarily responsible for the user interface, design, and barrier freedom.

Andy has extensive experience with Joomla!, in particular in the area of template development. All of the administrator and front-end templates that have been shipped by both Mambo and Joomla! were (and are) designed by him (user name `rhuk`: `http://dev.joomla.org/component/option,com_jd-wp/Itemid,33/cat,8/`).

Andy is also the founder of RocketTheme (`http://www.rockettheme.com/`). RocketTheme offers new monthly templates and a community for the maintenance and continued development of existing templates in a subscription-based business model. The forums can also be read by non-subscribers.

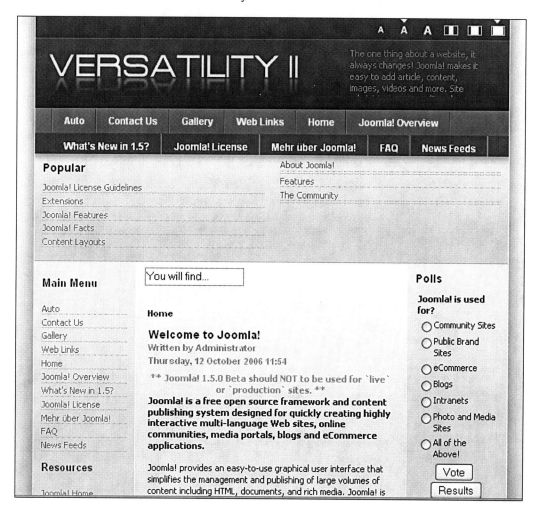

The Versatility II template is a continued development of the Versatility template and is technically very advanced. It, for instance, offers fifteen module positions, each of which is naturally only displayed on the website if the respective module is available. This partitioning makes the template extremely flexible.

The template has four menu options:

- SplitMenu
- SuckerFish
- Drop-down menu
- SuperSucker menu

In addition, your own or third-party menu systems can be integrated with the mechanism. The width and font size of the Versatility II template can be dynamically changed by guests to the website in three steps.

Summary

This final chapter provided you with bonus templates that can help you use templates in a similar way and develop your own website.

Online Resources

Joomla! is an open-source project that collects the ideas and experiences of hundreds of thousands of individuals, merges them, develops them further, and offers them online. You will *always* find the most up-to-date information online.

In the English-speaking world, your best place to start is the joomla.org website at `http://www.joomla.org/`.

It is divided into the following sections:

- `http://help.joomla.org`
- `http://forum.joomla.org`
- `http://dev.joomla.org`
- `http://extensions.joomla.org`

You will really find everything you need to successfully use Joomla!.

There is a well-maintained overview at the moment at: `http://help.joomla.org/ component/option,com_easyfaq/task,view/id,167/Itemid,268/`.

B

Template Modules

The `<jdoc>` element gives you the option to address dynamic sections in your template without using a single PHP command.

Template Code	Effect

`<jdoc:comment>`
`Your comment`
`</jdoc:comment>`
	Comment Line

`<?php echo '<?xml version="1.0"` `encoding="utf-8"?'.'>'; ?>`	Declaration of document type (XHTML header)
`<!DOCTYPE html PUBLIC "-//W3C//` `DTD XHTML 1.0 Transitional//`	
`EN" "http://www.w3.org/TR/xhtml1/` `DTD/xhtml1-transitional.dtd">`	

`<html xmlns="http://www.`
`w3.org/1999/xhtml" xml:`
`lang="<?php echo $this->language;`
`?>" lang="<?php echo $this-`
`>language; ?>" dir="<?php echo`
`$this->direction; ?>" >`	

`HEAD`
`<meta http-equiv="Content-Type"`
`content="text/html; <?php echo`
`_ISO; ?>" />`
	Declaration of the correct content type

Template Code	Effect
```<link rel="stylesheet" href="<?php echo $this->baseurl ?>/templates/system/css/system. css" type="text/css" /> <link rel="stylesheet" href="<?php echo $this->baseurl ?>/templates/system/css/general. css" type="text/css" /> <link rel="stylesheet" href="<?php echo $this->baseurl ?>/templates/<DIRECTORY_OF_THE_ TEMPLATE_/css/template.css" type="text/css" />```	Setting up the CSS file
```<?php if($this->direction == 'rtl') : ?> <link href="<?php echo $this- >baseurl ?>/templates/rhuk_ milkyway/css/template_rtl.css" rel="stylesheet" type="text/css" /> <?php endif; ?>```	Setting CSS support for right-to-left languages
```BODY <jdoc:include type="message" />```	Joomla! system messages display
```<jdoc:include type="modules" name="[position]" style="[style]" />```	Loading of the module [position].[style]: see Chapter 13.
```<jdoc:include type=component />```	Display of the component. The name of the component is derived from the URL.

C

How Do I switch an Image (Logo) in the Template?

To switch a logo, you first have to examine the source code of the respective template. Graphics and images can be defined in the HTML and in the CSS structure. The size of the graphic is usually harmonized to the template.

If you want to exchange one of the images, you can do so by means of various methods.

Method 1

1. Create a graphic in a resolution and file size that fits the space.
2. Load the graphic into Joomla!'s Media Manager.
3. Click on the graphic to get a link to it.
4. Change the respective `<img src="">` tag in the source code of your template to the new image.

Method 2

- Create the new graphic and give it the same name as the graphic in your template.
- Simply overwrite the old graphic with the new one.

Joomla! API

The **API** (**Application Program Interface**) defines what functions/methods are at what places in the source code and what they do. It consists of statements that are produced automatically from the source code, each with an example. The Joomla! team makes this information available to you in English at:

`http://api.joomla.org/li_Joomla-Framework.html`

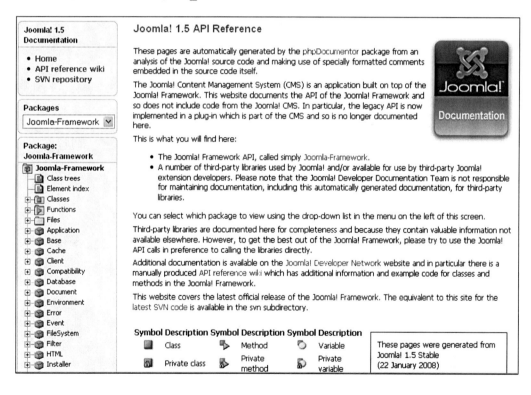

Forgot the Admin Password

If you have forgotten your admin password, you can change it directly in the database. You need a tool like phpMyAdmin to do this. In the xampplite environment, you call this up from your browser at `http://localhost/phpmyadmin`.

Select the database you are using. There is a `jos_users` table in this database. In it search for the user `admin`. The password is encrypted with the MD5 procedure. You can change it by selecting the MD5 entry in the options list on the left next to the field and entering the password in plain text.

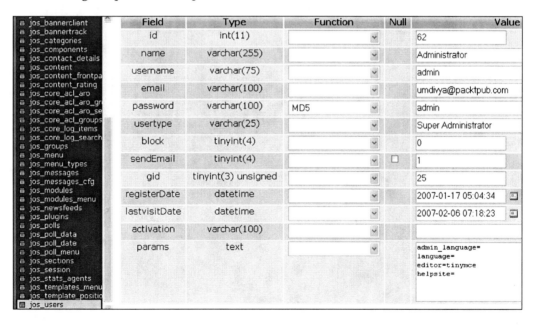

Many providers also supply you with phpMyAdmin to maintain your database.

Migration from Joomla! 1.0.x to Joomla! 1.5

A lot of you are probably already operating a Joomla! 1.0.x or a Mambo 4.5.x website and now want to migrate it to Joomla! 1.5.

You have a number of basic problems:

- You need to back up the entire website.
- The general source-code files need to be updated.
- Additional components, modules, and mambots/plug-ins have to be updated.
- Any changes that you have made to the programs need to be updated.
- Your contents have to survive this update procedure without damage.
- Contents with special characters have to be converted to UTF-8.

You can see from this list that an update can become quite complicated. The more you have worked with standard components, the easier it is; and the more individualized your website is, the more difficult it becomes. There are no general valid rules for updates at this time. This means that you have to first collect information to be able to establish an individual update plan for your site.

Backing Up Your Data

Before you make any plans and try out any migration components, back up your database and your files. Effect a MySQL dump with your provider's appropriate tool. In most cases this will be the phpMyAdmin program, which is also used in the xampplite environment. Click on the **Export** tab, mark all of the tables, and check all of the fields in the **Structure** checkbox. In the **Data** checkbox, select **Complete**

inserts. You have to mark the **Send** checkbox in the lower section and also check the desired format. If the provider permits, use the zipped version. Compressed database files can be up to 95% smaller than normal database files! Confirm your selections by clicking the **Go** button.

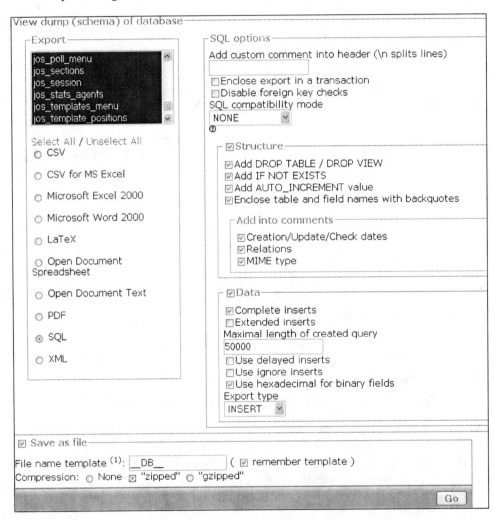

The content of the database is now extracted and made ready for download. The file contains all of the SQL commands needed to create the tables in another database with your content. This is the optimal way of backing up your files.

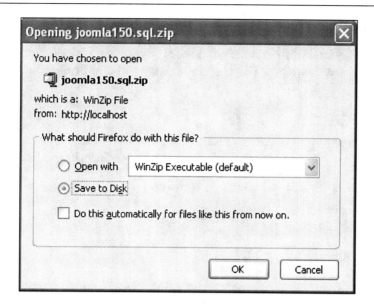

Now you can use phpMyAdmin to restore the data. Click on the **SQL** link, select the file with the backed up data and click on the **OK** button. All of the SQL commands in the file are now executed and your data is restored.

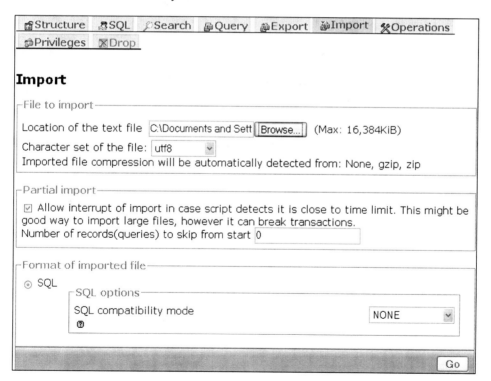

Backing Up the Files

In addition to the data in the database, the source code should, of course, also be backed up. Use your favorite FTP program and copy the entire Joomla! folder.

The Migration Script

There is a migration component that has to be installed into the old Joomla! version 1.0.x. This component creates three ZIP files when you click on the **Dump It** icon:

- A complete backup of the entire website
- A backup of the core components
- A backup of the third-party components

Save these files in a safe place.

These files contain the original, unchanged data of your Joomla! 1.0.x website. This applies in particular to your character set!

New Installation of Joomla! 1.5.0

Set up a new folder and copy all of the Joomla! 1.5.0 files into this folder.

Install Joomla! 1.5.0 with the web installer up to step 6 (as discussed in Chapter 2).

Now select the **Load Migration Script** radio button. Enter the old prefix (usually `mos_` or `jos_`) and select the old encoding. If you are not certain, take a look in the old language files and search for the `_ISO` variable.

Now load the Core export file of the migration component and click on the **Upload and Execute** button.

What happens next depends on your data. Normally you would get a success message and your data are transformed. But if you get database errors, this doesn't have to be a big problem either. Try to figure out what the error messages say and fix the errors manually in phpMyAdmin.

I know that this may not sound terribly helpful, but maybe it will set your mind at ease that the update of our website went flawlessly on the first try. I am going to spare you the story of the other website with all of the additional components and put my trust into the continued development of the installer.

What Happens Now?

All of the core components, like com_content, com_weblinks, com_banner, com_contact, com_newsfeed, com_poll, and com_users have been updated.

The menu links of the core components have been updated. The modules are all set to **Unpublished**. The display positions of the modules and their parameters have to be reworked.

No third-party components have been transferred, nor the files (banners, images, PDF files, etc.).

Manual Method

First the bad news. Changing the tables does not work properly with phpMyAdmin because the extended characters are not interpreted correctly! The data are all imported, but the extended ASCII characters (like Ä, Ö, Ü, ß, ä, ö, ü, ..., and many others) are not displayed correctly.

First you have to export all of the data and bring them into the UTF-8 format, and then you have to make a few changes to the table structures. The export with phpMyAdmin works without problem.

Check the **Complete inserts** checkbox. Now you have to save the exported data with an appropriate editor in UTF-8 format. (This even works with Windows Notepad, as long as the dump is not too large.)

 Careful
Make sure that only the data and not the table structures are exported.

Modifying the Joomla! 1.5 Database Scheme

There are really only two fields that have to be renamed!

- In the jos_core_acl_aro table, the aro_id field is renamed to id.
- In the jos_core_acl_aro_groups table, the group_id field is renamed to id.

Importing the Tables

These tables can be imported:

- jos_banner
- jos_bannerclient

- jos_bannerfinish
- jos_categories
- jos_contact_details
- jos_content
- jos_content_frontpage
- jos_content_rating
- jos_core_acl_aro
- jos_core_acl_groups_aro_map
- jos_core_log_items
- jos_core_log_searches
- jos_messages
- jos_messages_cfg
- jos_newsfeeds
- jos_poll_data
- jos_poll_date
- jos_poll_menu
- jos_polls
- jos_sections
- jos_users
- jos_weblinks

The jos_usertypes table is no longer used in Joomla! 1.5.

Menus and modules can be newly configured either with phpMyAdmin or with the admin interface. And you are done.

If you have some experience with phpMyAdmin and MySQL and/or the SQL language, you will be able to upgrade the core components with no problem.

The migration of third-party components can be more problematic. I am positive that migration scripts will be made available soon.

Last but not least, not a lot has changed with tables other than the character set. The bulk of the component developers' work has been done in the source code, which has to be updated to the new version.

A migration guide is being maintained at joomla.org. Make sure you read it.

G
Security Without Global Variables

Older versions of Mambo and Joomla! demand a default PHP setting with the name of `register_globals = on`. This switch handles visibility of global variables that can, among other ways, wind up in external programs by the use of forms or `get` strings.

This setting is fraught with basic security problems and it is better to use the `register_globals = off` setting. Even though this switch does not protect you from all security problems, it is a tremendous help in raising security.

It was and still is possible to also use this setting in older versions of Mambo and Joomla!. Starting with Joomla! 1.0.11, there is actually an explicit warning message about the `on` setting in the administrator interface with the recommendation to use the `off` setting.

Joomla! 1.5 also has `register_globals = off` as default, just as Joomla! 1.0.11 did. Joomla!'s core will work securely and stably with this setting.

You can find other security tips at the joomla.org website. There is an Administrator's Security Checklist for Joomla! 1.0 and it is also totally valid for Joomla! 1.5.

 When it comes to your extensions, you have to find out whether they work with this setting. At this time some extensions still use global variables. However, since Joomla! 1.0.11, a lot of customers have also been made aware of the problem with the clear warning message and the extensions that were affected are probably being modified.

Index

parameters, graphic banners 156
text links 153

barrier freedom
about 241-243
accessible sites, criteria 245
assistive technologies 265
book tip 265
checkertools 265

Beez
about 253, 257
header structure 255

BITV. *See* **WCAG1**

C

Cascading Style Sheets. *See* **CSS**
changes, in Joomla! 1.5
barrier freedom 21
database support 20
framework 20
FTP system 20
Google projects 21
internationalization 19
search engine friendliness 21
user plug-ins 20
web accessibility 21
XML-RPC support 20
CMS. *See* **Content Management System**
client-server system 29
com_content 258
component, creating
about 275, 276
another controller (auto.php), com_auto
administration 282-284
auto.php, front end 277
auto.xml 290, 291
automobile table (auto.php), com_auto
administration 288, 289
com_auto administration 281
component table, com_auto administration
281
controller (controller.php), com_auto
administration 282
controller (controller.php), front end 278
entry point (admin.auto.php), com_auto
administration 282
front end 277

installation (install.sql), com_auto
administration 289
installation package, creating 290
model (auto.php), front end 280
MySQL table 276, 277
template (default.php), com_auto
administration 285, 286
template (default.php), front end 279
template formular (form.php), com_auto
administration 287, 288
testing 290
uninstallation (uninstall.sql), com_auto
administration 289
view (view.html.php), com_auto administration 284
view (view.html.php), front end 278
view form (view.html.php), com_auto
administration 287
components, Joomla!
creating 275
helloworld 269
contacts, Joomla! components
about 154
category 157-159
details 155
information 156
menu link, creating 156
parameters 156
Content Management System
about 7
CRM 7
definition by Wikipedia 7
DMS 7
ECMS 7
ERP 7
history 8-10
HRM 7
HTML, disadvantage 9
Joomla!, WCMS 8
LAMP 9
PHP, advantage 10
WCMS 8
content menu
about 125
articles 126
article trash 140
categories 144

Packt Open Source Project Royalties

When we sell a book written on an Open Source project, we pay a royalty directly to that project. Therefore by purchasing Building Websites with Joomla! 1.5, Packt will have given some of the money received to the Joomla! Project.

In the long term, we see ourselves and you—customers and readers of our books—as part of the Open Source ecosystem, providing sustainable revenue for the projects we publish on. Our aim at Packt is to establish publishing royalties as an essential part of the service and support a business model that sustains Open Source.

If you're working with an Open Source project that you would like us to publish on, and subsequently pay royalties to, please get in touch with us.

Writing for Packt

We welcome all inquiries from people who are interested in authoring. Book proposals should be sent to authors@packtpub.com. If your book idea is still at an early stage and you would like to discuss it first before writing a formal book proposal, contact us; one of our commissioning editors will get in touch with you.

We're not just looking for published authors; if you have strong technical skills but no writing experience, our experienced editors can help you develop a writing career, or simply get some additional reward for your expertise.

About Packt Publishing

Packt, pronounced 'packed', published its first book "Mastering phpMyAdmin for Effective MySQL Management" in April 2004 and subsequently continued to specialize in publishing highly focused books on specific technologies and solutions.

Our books and publications share the experiences of your fellow IT professionals in adapting and customizing today's systems, applications, and frameworks. Our solution-based books give you the knowledge and power to customize the software and technologies you're using to get the job done. Packt books are more specific and less general than the IT books you have seen in the past. Our unique business model allows us to bring you more focused information, giving you more of what you need to know, and less of what you don't.

Packt is a modern, yet unique publishing company, which focuses on producing quality, cutting-edge books for communities of developers, administrators, and newbies alike. For more information, please visit our website: www.PacktPub.com.

Learning Joomla! 1.5 Extension Development

ISBN: 978-1-847191-30-4   Paperback: 200 pages

A practical tutorial for creating your first Joomla! 1.5 extensions with PHP

1. Program your own extensions to Joomla!

2. Create new, self-contained components with both back-end and front-end functionality

3. Create configurable site modules to show information on every page

4. Distribute your extensions to other Joomla! users

Building powerful and robust websites with Drupal 6

ISBN: 978-1-847192-97-4   Paperback: 330 pages

Build your own professional blog, forum, portal or community website with Drupal 6

1. Set up, configure, and deploy Drupal 6

2. Harness Drupal's world-class Content Management System

3. Design and implement your website's look and feel

4. Easily add exciting and powerful features

5. # Promote, manage, and maintain your live website

Please check **www.PacktPub.com** for information on our titles

Object-Oriented Programming with PHP5

ISBN: 978-1-847192-56-1   Paperback: 250 pages

Learn to leverage PHP5's OOP features to write manageable applications with ease

1. General OOP concepts explained

2. Implement Design Patterns in your applications and solve common OOP Problems

3. Take full advantage of native built-in objects

4. Test your code by writing unit tests with PHPUnit

Mastering Joomla! 1.5 Extension and Framework Development

ISBN: 978-1-847192-82-0   Paperback: 380 pages

The Professional Guide to Programming Joomla!

1. In-depth guide to programming Joomla!

2. Design and build secure and robust components, modules and plugins

3. Includes a comprehensive reference to the major areas of the Joomla! framework

Please check **www.PacktPub.com** for information on our titles

Printed in the United States
110895LV00004B/75-88/P